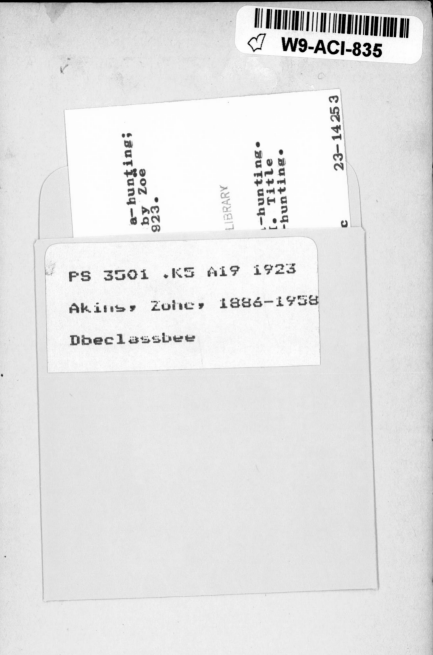

DÉCLASSÉE: DADDY'S GONE A-HUNTING: AND GREATNESS—A COMEDY

DÉCLASSÉE: DADDY'S GONE A-HUNTING: AND GREATNESS—A COMEDY

BY

ZOË AKINS

BONI AND LIVERIGHT

PUBLISHERS :: 1923 :: NEW YORK

23-14253

DÉCLASSÉE: DADDY'S
GONE A-HUNTING: AND
GREATNESS—A COMEDY

Copyright, 1923, by
ZOË AKINS

All rights reserved

PRINTED IN THE UNITED STATES OF AMERICA

Published August, 1923

NOTE

CONTENTS

DECLASSEE

DÉCLASSÉE

Produced at the Empire Theatre, New York, October 6, 1919, with the following cast:

LADY HELEN HADEN	Ethel Barrymore
SIR BRUCE HADEN	Harry Plimmer
RUDOLPH SOLOMON	Claude King
EDWARD THAYER	Vernon Steel
HARRY CHARTERIS	Charles Francis
SIR EMMET WILDERING	Julian Royce
LADY WILDERING	Claire Eames
CHARLOTTE ASHLEY	Beatrice Beckley
MRS. LESLIE	Katherine Harris
ALICE VANCE	Madeline Delmar
ZELLITO	Gabrielle Ravine
COUNT PAOLO DEL MAGIORE	Ralf Belmont
JEAN	Alfred Hesse
THE THREE WONDERFUL WALTONS	Meyer Berenson
	Maurice Somers
	V. Donegin
A SERVANT	Edward le Hay

DÉCLASSÉE

THE FIRST ACT

A drawing-room in the HADENS' *house in London. It opens
to the hall at the back, and to other rooms at either side.
Bridge tables have been arranged and deserted.*

HARRY CHARTERIS, *a distinguished-looking young man, pale,
rather delicate in type, is sitting at the piano, playing
very well—but listlessly, as though not concerned with
the music at all. He watches the central doorway
anxiously.*

LADY WILDERING *enters presently. She is obviously
agitated, although she is doing her best not to appear
so.* HARRY *stops playing instantly and rises. She
comes toward him quickly, leaning over the piano as
they speak.*

HARRY—[*In a low voice.*]   How are things now, Edith?
LADY WILDERING—[*Also in a low voice, hurriedly.*]
Dreadful; I left Charlotte upstairs with Helen—trying to
talk some sense into her. But don't stop playing, Harry,
please. Go on.

[*She indicates the emptiness and silence of the house
about them.*]

It—*it fills in.*

3

HARRY—[*As he continues playing softly, and talking at the same time.*] I know what you mean. . . . Your husband is in there walking Haden up and down—trying to talk some sense into him. But I'm afraid it's no good.

LADY WILDERING—[*With a glance toward the door of the room that he has indicated.*] I'm afraid it's all no good. But where is *he?* He didn't go, I suppose?

HARRY—[*Ironically.*] Our young American friend, Mr. Thayer? Oh, no! I didn't think he would. The beautiful Mrs. Leslie has him in there—trying to talk sense into *him.*

LADY WILDERING—[*With some distaste as her glance goes toward the other door.*] Someone ought to talk some sense into *her.* And I think she's a very mischievous woman, as well as a very silly one.

HARRY—I agree. Personally, I care very little for either of them. But they're really not bad, I suppose.

LADY WILDERING—You mean that Helen, with her gift for the wrong people, has taken up so many who have been so much worse?

[*They agree that she has, by half-grave, half-smiling confidential nods. A very pretty and extravagantly dressed woman enters from the left, smoking a cigarette.*]

HARRY—Here's Mrs. Leslie . . . [*He goes on playing.*]

MRS. LESLIE—[*Uneasily.*] How are things now, Lady Wildering?

LADY WILDERING—Lady Helen is still upstairs.

MRS. LESLIE—[*Impatiently.*] I think I'll go. Lady Helen and Sir Bruce have succeeded in making everybody extremely uncomfortable tonight. I'm not coming again soon.

LADY WILDERING—Of course you know a great many people here now . . . and I suppose you're very busy . . .

[*The music fills in an awkward pause.*]

MRS. LESLIE—[*Apologetically.*] Oh, I realise that you must be thinking that I'm very ungrateful after all that Lady Helen has done for me. Of course, I owe her a great deal. I've met most of the people I know over here through her. But it's particularly embarrassing for me to come here now because *I* introduced Ned Thayer to her. Sir Bruce knows that, and of course he blames me, and——

LADY WILDERING—[*Bluntly.*] Sir Bruce may seem to have very little intelligence, but he has too much to blame anyone for any of Lady Helen's enthusiasms.

HARRY—[*Who has left the piano and comes toward them.*] Besides, no one cares what Haden thinks. It's Lady Helen who happened to be kind to you, isn't it? And just for your own sake, Mrs. Leslie—if serious trouble should come from this, now or presently, don't desert, too frankly, the first friend you had in London.

[CHARLOTTE ASHLEY *enters from the hall, and closes the doors behind her, as if someone might be listening.*]

CHARLOTTE—Edith——

LADY WILDERING—Yes, Charlotte?

CHARLOTTE—[*Quickly, hopefully.*] Go up and talk to Helen. She's begun to laugh now and blame the new cook for Bruce's temper. It seems that he's always expected to get into one whenever the mutton is cooked too long or the fish not long enough, and both happened tonight. Helen admits that under the circumstances Bruce did fairly well, only she's sorry, of course, that she was not— as usual—the sole object of his wrath. [*She drops into a chair half-turned away from one of the card-tables, and relaxes a little.*] I never played a scene on the stage better than I have played the rôle of peace-maker tonight.

My defence of Bruce was a masterpiece—especially so
because I didn't believe a word of what I preached. What
a man! [*Her energy comes back and she straightens up.*]
And here we are—all of us—trying to keep them together
when we ought to beg her, if she has either any pride or
any courage left, to leave him, at once, forever!

LADY WILDERING—But what would she do? What could
she do?

CHARLOTTE—[*Desperately.*] Heavens, she could do
something, *anything!* Anything would be better than—
this—surely!

HARRY—Don't forget that you're talking, and thinking,
as a woman who can make a jolly good living on the stage;
but there is nothing, nothing at all, that Helen *can* do.
And there is nobody—who has the right—to give her anything. And she doesn't know—and will never learn—
the difference between a pound and a shilling!

CHARLOTTE—She knows that a pound is something you
give the maître d'hôtel, and a shilling is something you
give the taxi-driver. Helen thinks that's what actual
money is for,—tips!

MRS. LESLIE—[*Whose presence they've almost forgotten.*] They say she is the most extravagant woman in
London.

CHARLOTTE—In the world, probably!

MRS. LESLIE—But couldn't she marry again? [*There is
a sharp pause.*]

CHARLOTTE—[*Impatiently, rising and walking about.*]
If she were divorced, certainly!

MRS. LESLIE—But isn't that just what you want her to
do—get a divorce?

LADY WILDERING—I haven't heard anyone mention divorce, Mrs. Leslie.

CHARLOTTE—Oh, no! There's no possibility of a divorce!

MRS. LESLIE—But if he treats her so badly—? Surely one can get a divorce from a *brute?*

CHARLOTTE—Not in England. Not even when your husband is a drunken brute of a butcher——

MRS. LESLIE—Sir Bruce wasn't really a butcher?

HARRY—The most successful butcher in the Empire.

MRS. LESLIE—I never knew that. So that is why *he* has a title?

HARRY—You'll find England as quick as America to acknowledge success in business, Mrs. Leslie, even if we're not so quick to acknowledge failure in matrimony.

MRS. LESLIE—[*Defensively.*] Of course, it seems *immoral* to me that a woman has to live with a man who acts as Sir Bruce does.

LADY WILDERING—The law doesn't make her live with him. She can leave him any time she likes.

MRS. LESLIE—[*Not recognising their fine distinction.*] But if she can't divorce him she has no chance of marrying anybody else.

LADY WILDERING—No, she hasn't a chance in the world, as the matter stands now, of marrying anyone else.

MRS. LESLIE—[*Complacently.*] Of course, I'm not defending women who keep on getting divorces and marrying again. My husbands—both of them—died.

HARRY—[*Drily.*] They were more considerate than Haden has ever been willing to be.

MRS. LESLIE—But why did she marry him in the first place?

HARRY—[*More to himself than to her.*] I suppose that he was one of her practical whims.

LADY WILDERING—And he was much more attractive then than he is now, of course.

HARRY—[*With an undertone of bitterness.*] And a hint of the barbaric seems to appeal to most women. [*He rises suddenly.*] I think I'll go up and speak to Helen, Charlotte, unless Edith will go.

LADY WILDERING—No, you go. I've said everything I possibly could.

HARRY—[*To* CHARLOTTE.] Don't you think, by a considerable exertion of your well-known charm, you might woo Haden back to bridge?

CHARLOTTE—[*Drily.*] I'm willing to do my best with the well-known charm, but I won't be his partner again. However, there are two tables and . . . I'll try. [*She smiles, deciding to make the best of it.*]

HARRY—Right-o. [*He goes.*]

CHARLOTTE—[*Sitting down again at the bridge table.*] There's no hurry . . . Helen won't come down immediately.

LADY WILDERING—[*Sitting at the same table.*] I begin to feel hopeful, and a little relaxed. I've been like this—[*she holds out her hand in a gesture of tensity*]—for an hour. I was perfectly certain that the smash had come.

MRS. LESLIE—[*From a chair at the other table, where she sits, gathering up the cards, and shuffling them absently.*] You can imagine how I felt, of course!

CHARLOTTE—[*Not too sympathetically.*] Of course. [*Pause.*]

MRS. LESLIE—[*Suddenly, archly, insinuatingly.*] Did it ever occur to either of you that Mr. Charteris might be in love with Lady Helen?

LADY WILDERING—I suppose that it has occurred to

everybody who has ever known either of them that Harry
Charteris has been in love with Helen Haden all his life.

MRS. LESLIE—[*Amazed   at   their   frankness.*]   Oh!
Has he?

CHARLOTTE—Yes—hopelessly, wonderfully, unselfishly,
beautifully in love—all his life!

MRS. LESLIE—Oh! She's never mentioned it.

CHARLOTTE—She wouldn't.

LADY WILDERING—[*Changing the subject, feeling that
MRS. LESLIE has been sufficiently snubbed.*] Now, about
Mr. Thayer?

MRS. LESLIE—[*Rising.*] I'll go and try again to get him
into a good humour. It may take some time. He's very
difficult. [*She goes. A little silence follows her.*]

CHARLOTTE—I detest that woman!

LADY WILDERING—So do I, and I shouldn't mind her so
much, I think, if I were not an American, too. But she's
a type that particularly annoys me. One is always seeing
them about, and sometimes one meets them like this. They
are always living in hotels, always apparently on the wing;
always good-looking; always beautifully dressed; their
friends are always people they've just met; they're agreeable enough, frequently they're amusing; they never have
such things as husbands or relatives or children; and they
emerge from obscurity, as detached from any background
whatever as silhouettes cut from black paper, and pasted
on a blank page. However, why I'm wasting words on
Mrs. Leslie and her kind I don't know; particularly
when I have Helen so much on my mind.

CHARLOTTE—It's all very well for us to talk of dragging
ourselves back to bridge, and getting through the evening

somehow—and we may manage it this time; but the next, and the next?

LADY WILDERING—I don't know. . . . I don't know. . . . Things seem to go from bad to worse for Helen. They always have.

CHARLOTTE—One feels them piling up. [MRS. LESLIE *returns with* EDWARD THAYER,—*a very attractive young man. She is vivacious; he, a little sullen, but rather boyishly so.*]

MRS. LESLIE—Here he is. He's promised to be a good child.

THAYER—[*Hesitantly.*] I apologize. I'm sorry that I acted badly. I should have gone quietly, and afterward, perhaps—if Sir Bruce— [*He pauses and changes the subject.*] I'm particularly sorry to have caused Lady Helen all this—this trouble; but he— [*He finds it too difficult to continue.*]

LADY WILDERING—[*Gently.*] We understand. Unfortunately, Sir Bruce is quick-tempered, and often unfair.

MRS. LESLIE—But to accuse a man of cheating at cards just because he's jealous——

THAYER—[*Hurrying to interrupt her tactlessness.*] Sir Bruce had a right to his opinion, of course. If he thought I was making a practice of looking over his shoulder—[*He shrugs, and again fails to finish what he is saying.*] But——

CHARLOTTE—[*Interrupting, as again he pauses.*] But he had no right, even if he really believed what he was saying, to speak as he did. We quite appreciate that.

THAYER—I ought to have gone. I would have gone if Lady Helen had not insisted—I've been waiting, only to speak to her, to thank her. . . .

MRS. LESLIE—[*A little impatiently.*]   The thing to do
is to settle ourselves now and start again just as if nothing had happened.   Isn't it, Lady Wildering?

LADY WILDERING—It seems to me the only thing.   I think
people are expected for supper later.   And I hope that
you will help us to make the best of a very awkward situation, Mr. Thayer. . . . Miss Ashley and I are going to
try our wiles on Sir Bruce—Mr. Charteris has gone to
fetch Lady Helen, and—and you won't try to make things
more difficult, will you, Mr. Thayer?

THAYER—But it was so ridiculous of him!   I couldn't
possibly have seen his cards!

CHARLOTTE—We quite agree with you.   But there are
only two things that you can do—overlook the matter, for
this evening, at least,—and smile and do your best, for
all our sakes . . . or go . . . *now.* . . .

LADY WILDERING—[*Quickly.*]   And if you go, you know
what that means.   You will smile and do your best——?

THAYER—[*Suddenly.*]   Yes, I will.   I promise.

LADY WILDERING—That's splendid.   Now we will find
Sir Bruce.   [*She turns to go, but* THAYER'S *voice stops her
as he speaks quickly, with a rather shy, hesitant smile.*]

THAYER—Everyone tells me that your husband is a great
diplomat, Lady Wildering; but I suspect you of being his
unofficial chief. . . . I hope Washington will be your next
stop.

LADY WILDERING—Thanks.   It doesn't seem likely—at
this time.   But . . .

THAYER—[*As she hesitates.*]   But one never knows, you
mean?   Still it's been talked of.

LADY WILDERING—No.   One never knows.   [*She turns
away again, to join* CHARLOTTE, *who is standing near the*

door of the room on the right, when the door from the hall at the back opens and HARRY CHARTERIS *returns.*]

HARRY—[*Quickly.*] Helen's coming down.

[*Before anyone can answer,* SIR EMMETT WILDERING *and* SIR BRUCE HADEN *enter unexpectedly from the room at the right.* SIR EMMETT *looks the successful diplomat,* SIR BRUCE *the successful butcher. Some sort of peace seems to have been decided upon, but* SIR BRUCE *is still in a vicious mood. He and* EDWARD THAYER *avoid looking at each other.*]

LADY WILDERING—Ah! We were just going to find you.

CHARLOTTE—[*To* SIR BRUCE, *charmingly.*] Edith has proposed herself as your partner—against us—[*her quick nod indicates* SIR EMMETT]—quite unscrupulously, without cutting. Isn't the challenge irresistible? You'll have to do your best, you know. Emmett and I are very good. You're not afraid? [*She sits down at the nearest table and picks up a pack of cards, smiling at* SIR BRUCE *gaily.*]

SIR EMMETT—[*Sitting opposite her.*] Of course they're not afraid! Not yet. . . . It ought to be an interesting game, Haden.

SIR BRUCE — [*Ungraciously.*] I'll play. But—[*he looks around, unable to conceal his distaste*]—but not in here.

[*The butler enters, followed by a second man with a tray. They start to set out a small table with whisky and soda, glasses, et cetera; but as they hurry* SIR BRUCE *breaks the pause by turning to them, and as he addresses the butler, secures for himself the first drink, ignoring his guests.*]

SIR BRUCE—[*Sharply.*] Brandon!

BRANDON—Yes, Sir Bruce. Whisky and soda, or brandy, sir?

sir bruce—Brandy. And Brandon—I want my table moved into the other room——

[*He indicates the room at the right, the door of which stands open. Then, as he regards the glass that* brandon *anxiously fills and hands him,* lady helen *appears in the doorway.*]

brandon—Yes, Sir Bruce. Very good, sir.

sir bruce—At once, you understand! [*He drains his glass.*]

[lady helen *enters. She is curiously aflame, but she drives her voice guardedly. It is easy to surmise that she has heard her husband's command, as she checks the butler and his assistant quickly, in their hurried act of carrying out his order.*]

lady helen—And then, Brandon, *after* you have served the others, you may move the *other* table into the *other* room.

brandon—Very good, my lady.

[*The first table is quickly disposed of; nobody wishes to be served with anything, and* brandon *and his assistant move the second bridge-table into the room at the left, and return for the small chairs to put them in place, while* lady helen, *roving the room impatiently, makes her friends smile as she talks a streak of easy hurried nonsense to no one in particular, her eyes alert, watching for the servants to finish and go.*]

lady helen—I was telling Edith a while ago about having my fortune told today. It amused her enormously. Zellito. She's the new Spanish dancer in that review at the Gaiety. She's a real gypsy. She doesn't tell fortunes professionally, you know. Dancing is her real work. Fortune-telling is just a sort of gift. She's the seventh

daughter of a line of seventh daughters, it seems. Edith
thinks it's nonsense—believing her. But she won't tell
you anything unless she takes a special interest in you.
It's immensely flattering to have her take a special interest. It makes you feel so important—psychically, as if
you had a destiny, or something of the sort. Zellito won't
say what she sees in my hand. . . . Some sort of spec-
tacular doom, I suppose—[*she smiles down into the palm
of her open hand*]—I wonder? I never believe doctors,
and I never believe lawyers. But I always believe fortune-tellers.

SIR BRUCE—[*Insolently.*] Yes, you would—being one
of the mad Varicks.

LADY HELEN—[*With a laugh but with a significant
glance, both of pity and contempt, at her husband.*] The
mad Varicks will soon trouble the world no longer. [*Then
she turns with nervous gaiety to* MRS. LESLIE *and* EDWARD
THAYER—*and talks rapidly, lightly to them as she moves
about, smoking and playing with the pearls that hang in
many long strands from her throat—all the time keeping
an eye on her husband, for whose benefit there is something
a little like a theatrical performance in her words and manner.*] I suppose you don't know about the mad Varicks?
There were once quite a lot of us, and now I'm the only one
that's left. We were at our best about five hundred years
ago. But even then we were a little mad, too, I suppose.
And we kept on being gay and mad through some of the
soberest days that England has ever known. Sometimes
we lost our heads; sometimes we went to house parties in
the Tower; sometimes we hunted with the King, and knew
all the secrets of the Queen; but there never was a battle
fought for England, by sea or land, in which some Varick

did not offer his gay, mad life. Perhaps that's how we
got the habit of dying. We've always died . . . I think
we've rather liked dying—just as we've always liked our
ghosts and our debts and our hereditary gout, and our
scandals, and even our white sheep. We do admit an occa-
sional white sheep in the family—one every century or
so— You may go, Brandon— [*The servants obey and
quietly leave the room.*] And now—before we attempt to
play again—[*she grows stern and takes them all by surprise*]—I think that my husband wishes to apologise to
Mr. Thayer, before all of you, for what he said to Mr.
Thayer, before all of you, in this room, a little while ago.

SIR BRUCE—[*Furiously, as he advances.*] By God,—
I——

THAYER—Lady Helen, please——

SIR EMMETT—[*Going to* BRUCE, *quickly.*] Be very careful, Haden—don't lose your head again—or——

LADY WILDERING—[*To* LADY HELEN, *anxiously.*] My
dear—just this once, don't insist——

CHARLOTTE—Helen, Mr. Thayer doesn't insist——

MRS. LESLIE—Oh, is it going to start all over again?

LADY HELEN—[*Unmoved, to her husband.*] You ac-
cused one of my friends, a young man who is a stranger
in this country, and who came to this house on my invi-
tation, of trying to cheat you at cards. You cannot prove
your statement—but on the other hand he cannot disprove
it. There is no way of getting at the truth, apparently.
But, in this case, even if I had never seen Mr. Thayer
before—even if I did not know him incapable of your
charge—I should insist, *as I insist now,* upon giving him
the benefit of the very great doubt that your suspicions
had any justification whatever!

sir bruce—I tell you, my suspicions——

lady helen—[*Stopping him.*] Wait a minute, Bruce! You were very headstrong a moment ago in calling this friend of mine a cheat and a liar, and ordering him from the house; and I know you well enough to know that the story would have got about, even if everyone else in this room had kept decently silent. . . . Oh, I know!

sir bruce—Well, I let him stay, didn't I? There he is! I'm willing to say no more.

lady helen—[*Losing her temper for the first time.*] You—let him stay! Because I would have left this house just as surely as I'm standing here—if you had not re- tracted. And you didn't want that! God knows why you didn't, but you didn't!

sir bruce—I tell you I'm willing to say no more—if you want to let the matter drop now. I know men who *wouldn't* let it drop, but I'm willing.

lady helen—But I'm not! Not until you've said to Mr. Thayer that you apologise!

sir bruce—[*After a slight pause, going toward* thayer, *half-humorously, half-ironically.*] Do you want me to apologise, Mr. Thayer? Will that do any good?

thayer—[*Steadily.*] All things considered, Sir Bruce, I think that it might do some good. [sir bruce *takes the time to light a cigarette. He has had enough to drink to make his movements rather unsteady.*]

sir bruce—[*At last, brutally.*] Considering I'm a little bit drunk, you mean; and maybe a little bit jealous—and can't prove anything——

lady helen—[*Turning about suddenly.*] Good night, all of you! [*She starts a little blindly toward the door at the back.*]

SIR BRUCE—Wait! Helen!

LADY WILDERING—Helen! My dear——

THAYER—Lady Helen——

LADY HELEN—[*Turning at* THAYER's *low cry, and speaking in a low, hopeless voice.*] This—is impossible.

THAYER—But, I beg of you, please—don't make me feel so responsible! I wouldn't for the world have caused you any trouble.

LADY HELEN—I know that. And you must know the very great regret I feel for having exposed you to insults against which you are as defenceless as I. I will let you know, later, where I am.

THAYER—You are going, really—because of what's happened here, tonight?

LADY HELEN—I should have gone sometime. It isn't your fault—so don't worry. For any stranger invited to my house I should have asked the simple justice that I have asked for you. A fantastic love of justice happens to be one of the things for which the mad Varicks have died.

[*This she flings half-humorously, half-disdainfully at* SIR BRUCE, *who is watching closely, sobered and troubled.*]

SIR EMMETT—[*Taking a hand.*] But, my dear, just suppose that your husband *does* believe himself in the right? Are you just to *him*?

LADY HELEN—[*Sternly, but with some hesitation at first, then with reckless anger.*] To accuse is so easy that it is infamous to do so where proof is impossible! And to damn a guest, a stranger, in this particular fashion is a thing so grave that I cannot forgive it—even though my husband happens to be a little drunk—and a little jealous

—and a little more brutal than usual. I'm sorry. Good night.

[*She turns and leaves the room. Perfect silence follows her, but as she is about to pass from sight along the hall at the back,* SIR BRUCE *turns violently to* THAYER, *arresting* LADY HELEN'S *progress by his loud words.*]

SIR BRUCE—By God! I can't have my wife doing a thing like this for you! [*He hurries to the door.*] Helen! Come back! I—I will apologise! [*She stands stone still, hesitating.*] Come back! [*She comes slowly back into the room, closes the door behind her, and stands, waiting and stern. After the slightest pause he speaks in a suddenly matter-of-fact manner, but carefully, heavily.*]

SIR BRUCE—You've all heard. . . . Well, she's right. I was wrong. I'm very sorry. I apologise to Mr. Thayer; I apologise to my wife; and I apologise to you all. I'm not a very pleasant sort, I suppose, but—well, I apologise; and I hope that everyone here realises I spoke hastily and unjustly, and that I'm very sorry.

LADY HELEN—[*Quickly, warmly.*] That's splendid of you, Bruce. That's just what I wanted you to say.

[*She smiles at him radiantly. She is a little touched. He pours himself another drink, however, turning his back, in some embarrassment, to the others.* HARRY CHARTERIS, *who has been standing by the piano, once more begins to play, lightly, nervously, but with great relief.* LADY WILDERING *and* CHARLOTTE ASHLEY *are suddenly laughing about nothing.* MRS. LESLIE *leans toward* THAYER, *speaking under her breath with an easy laugh—managing to seem nonchalant.* SIR EMMETT *goes, smiling, toward* LADY HELEN. BRANDON *enters.*]

BRANDON—Miss Timmins wishes to know if she might have a word with your ladyship?

[*Even* BRANDON *detects the change in the atmosphere and a certain dog-like concern for his mistress is turned into something happier as he scents her more comfortable mood.*]

LADY HELEN—Certainly; ask Miss Timmins to come in here, Brandon.

[BRANDON *goes. A murmur of conversation hums through the room, accompanied by the low, gay music that* HARRY CHARTERIS *continues to play.* MISS TIMMINS *enters, as if she had been waiting just outside the door, with scarcely an instant's delay. She is a middle-aged spinster in black and both affection and concern for* LADY HELEN *are in her hovering manner and plaintive voice.*]

MISS TIMMINS—I'm so sorry to disturb you, Lady Helen; I told Brandon not to speak to you if you were playing again. . . . [LADY HELEN *feels her concern, and smiles.*]

LADY HELEN—[*Significantly.*] It's quite all right, Miss Timmins. . . . [MISS TIMMINS *smiles back, with a sharp sigh of relief.* LADY HELEN *continues.*] What is it?

MISS TIMMINS—A message has just come from Buckingham Palace. Their Majesties will attend the bazaar on Thursday, and the Queen wishes you to know that she was delighted to learn that you suffered no ill effects from your fall, last week.

[SIR BRUCE *has turned, and is listening.*]

LADY HELEN—Thanks, Miss Timmins. [*She includes* SIR EMMETT *in her next remark.*] That's splendid, isn't it—that their Majesties are coming? [*Her nod dismisses* MISS TIMMINS, *who leaves the room;* SIR EMMETT *joins* SIR BRUCE, *as* LADY HELEN *turns to speak very casually to* MRS.

LESLIE, *who has just approached.*] I can't desert my bazaar on Thursday to lunch with you and your Jewish friend. He will have to have me some other time.

MRS. LESLIE—He will be so disappointed, but he will understand, of course. Could you make it Friday, dear?

LADY HELEN—No. . . . Sometime next week. [*She turns abruptly away, finds a cigarette, and goes to the piano, where* HARRY *is still playing.*]

MRS. LESLIE—[*To everyone in general.*] We were speaking of Rudolph Solomon. He's the man who buys Rembrandts. Of course he buys other things, too. He's just bought a Velasquez that the British Museum wanted. I suppose you've heard of him? [*Her question is focussed on* CHARLOTTE ASHLEY, *who is nearest.*]

CHARLOTTE—Oh, yes . . . yes, of course. [CHARLOTTE *joins* LADY WILDERING. *They light cigarettes.* SIR EMMETT *includes them in a question that he puts to* SIR BRUCE.]

SIR EMMET—And now, don't you think we might have our game?

SIR BRUCE—The sooner the better, I say. [*He turns abruptly and goes into the room at the right.*]

SIR EMMETT—[*With a glance back at* CHARLOTTE *and* LADY WILDERING *as he follows.*] Are you coming?

LADY WILDERING—In just a moment, as soon as we've finished our cigarettes.

[SIR EMMETT *goes.* HARRY CHARTERIS *stops playing. Then after one instant he begins again, but he is playing a wistful air now, instead of a gay one.* LADY HELEN *leans against the piano, listening.* MRS. LESLIE *joins* EDWARD THAYER, *who is standing in front of the fire, looking down into it, his back to the room.*]

LADY WILDERING—[*To* CHARLOTTE, *in a low tone.*] I

thought she'd gone too far. . . . What desperate reck-lessness.

CHARLOTTE—It's been a good lesson for Bruce.

LADY WILDERING—Possibly; still— [*She decides to say no more.*]

MRS. LESLIE—[*To* THAYER, *also in a low tone.*] They arranged it. You and I will be partners.

THAYER—I'd rather not play tonight.

MRS. LESLIE—Nonsense! It's been arranged, I tell you; everyone wants to play again. . . . You and I, against Lady Helen and Mr. Charteris.

THAYER—I'm not in the mood. I should think you would understand that.

MRS. LESLIE—[*Drily.*] Give me a cigarette, please. [*He obeys her request. Then he goes to the table and pours a drink for himself.*]

CHARLOTTE—[*To* LADY WILDERING.] Shall we go?

LADY WILDERING—[*Still smoking.*] I'm not in the mood. I shouldn't think anyone would be.

CHARLOTTE—However, it's been arranged.

LADY WILDERING—Oh, I'll go through with it, and as I'm to be Bruce's partner, I won't dare to play badly.

[*She puts her cigarette on an ash-tray, and they move toward the door at the right.* LADY HELEN *joins them, however, detaining them an instant.*]

LADY HELEN—Well—? Bruce was in great form to-night, wasn't he?

CHARLOTTE—So were you, Helen.

LADY HELEN—Yes, I know I was. I was very upset. When I begin invoking the mad Varicks for Bruce's bene-fit you can always know that I'm a bit desperate. It's the one thing he still likes about me—being a mad Varick,

I mean: though, of course, he always pretends to scorn it.

LADY WILDERING—Of course.

LADY HELEN—But I think he thinks I'm the maddest of the lot. We had had a discussion earlier in the day —about a few bills that seemed particularly mad to him. Bruce believes in being extravagant economically. He's made a fine art of it. . . . His apology was very pretty, I thought—prettier than anyone could have hoped for, under the circumstances.

LADY WILDERING—Yes; I think he said just the right thing.

LADY HELEN—[*With sudden gravity.*] Thank God, he did. It's not supremely jolly—being married to Bruce, but I don't know what I'd do if he threw me over, or I had to throw him over. Run a hat-shop or something, I expect—though every time I've run anything—even a booth in a bazaar—I've managed, in some mysterious way, to be in debt to somebody as a result. No, I'd have no luck with hat-shops, and things like that. It would be easier to sell a pearl every day or two—until they were all gone——

CHARLOTTE—Yes? And then?

LADY HELEN—[*With a shudder and a smile.*] Then—? I suppose I'd become déclassée, in time—and the Queen wouldn't care whether I was hurt by a fall or not. . . . I love that Deserted-Fisher-Girl song Harry is playing; only it's like—like rain and ghosts—and the moors in winter—and last year's styles—and photographs of one's self—at seventeen. There's no doubt about it—it's depressing. But don't let me keep you, when my lord and master is waiting! [*She walks with them toward the door at the right.*]

LADY WILDERING—Au 'voir, Helen.

LADY HELEN—Au 'voir, both of you. . . . Bless you. [LADY WILDERING *and* CHARLOTTE *go.* HELEN *looks after them a moment; then, seeing* THAYER *standing alone by the table, she joins him. To* THAYER, *gently.*] Of course, you're in no mood to play again.

THAYER—Not—not exactly. Not tonight. [HARRY CHARTERIS *has stopped playing and is coming toward them.*]

MRS. LESLIE—[*Who has been listening.*] What are you saying? Aren't we going to play? [*She throws a note of childish disappointment into her voice.*] You want to, don't you, Mr. Charteris?

HARRY—I? [*To* LADY HELEN.] What do you think, Helen?

MRS. LESLIE—[*Significantly, looking at* THAYER.] I think we ought. They may think it funny if——

LADY HELEN—[*Quickly.*] I suppose that we might as well as not.

HARRY—[*Going to the door at the left and opening it, and speaking to* MRS. LESLIE, *who follows him.*] Your game is so clever that it's easy to understand your enthusiasm.

THAYER—[*With a wry smile to all of them.*] Somebody will have to be clever for two tonight. I know I shall be no good.

MRS. LESLIE—The thing for you to do, my friend, is to buck up. Come along. . . .

LADY HELEN—In a moment. [*She moves to the table where the drinks are.* THAYER *follows her.* MRS. LESLIE, *after a glance at the backs of the two of them, goes with* CHARTERIS *into the room at the left.*]

THAYER—[*To* LADY HELEN.] What can I get for you?

LADY HELEN—A glass of barley water. It's in that pitcher, I think. [*He pours it for her. She barely touches it and sets the glass back. Their eyes meet. There is a little pause. She speaks slowly, softly.*] I'm so sorry—about tonight.

THAYER—I'm sorry, too. But I couldn't help it.

LADY HELEN—I know you couldn't. There's nothing—nothing at all too dreadful for my husband to say when he's in a bad mood—or jealous.

THAYER—[*Unhappily.*] I suppose—at least, according to the tales one hears—that he's had occasion to be jealous a great many times.

LADY HELEN—[*With a laugh, yet grave.*] He's thought so. But I think he's learned a lesson tonight.

THAYER—You were so wonderful! . . . If I didn't know better I might have thought that you really cared for me.

LADY HELEN—What I said on your behalf tonight, just as I told my husband, I would have said on behalf of any stranger in the same situation.

THAYER—Oh!

LADY HELEN—But it wouldn't have meant so much to me, of course, if it had not been on behalf of a person I cared for.

THAYER—[*Doubtfully.*] Look here. . . . *Do* you care for me?

LADY HELEN—You know.

THAYER—I wish I *did* know.

LADY HELEN—If you don't know—if you *really* don't know, why bother about it? [*She smiles, but a penetrating person would detect the emotion in her voice.*]

THAYER—One shouldn't bother about it. You are right. After all, I'm just an incident in your life—just someone

who happened to interest you for a month or so, one spring
out of all the other springs. Last year it was someone
else, and next year it will be another, and after that another——

LADY HELEN——[*Still smiling, but with a catch in her
breath.*] So, you don't mean to let yourself care for me
one little bit more than you think I care for you, do you,
Ned? [*He does not answer; she continues, lightly.*]
You think you are just one of my caprices, don't you?
[*He nods his head "yes"; again her tone is light but very
tender.*] I suppose, after all, there was someone whom
you thought you cared for last spring . . . and the spring
before? And surely there will be someone this time next
year——? And perhaps she will be the right one, and will
have all the other springtimes, as well. I hope so. And
I hope that she will have a very firm hand——for she will
need it with you, my dear; and a very tender heart, and
a very wise head——you are not very wise, yourself, you
know—— And I hope that she will be young and lovely,
and that you will be always very happy together, and very
sad apart,——as long as you both live.

THAYER——That's a strange way to talk.

LADY HELEN——Poor Ned! Hasn't anyone ever wanted
you to be happy before?

THAYER——Not anyone who pretended to be in love with
me. [*She laughs and then she frowns.*]

LADY HELEN——Love is something that not many of us
know much about——and I've never *pretended* to love you,
Ned—— Love is a word I've never used——to—anyone——

THAYER——But only a week ago——I don't understand
you!

LADY HELEN——My dear, you are stupid.

THAYER—You wrote me such wonderful letters from the country. Is it stupid to think you cared for me when you wrote them?

LADY HELEN—No, I don't believe that the stupidest person could doubt that I cared for you when I wrote them. . . . But let's not talk about what we feel or don't feel, tonight. [*She shows weariness for an instant, but he is impatient and does not heed her appeal.*]

THAYER—[*Arguing his case against her, more to himself than her.*] And then, this last week, since you've come *back,* you've scarcely let me see you at all. Of course, everybody says that you get tired of everybody and everything, that you're always taking people up and then dropping them, so I suppose you're tired of me, now. . . . I was sure of it when I came here tonight. Then, afterward, I thought perhaps you did care—after all; then——

LADY HELEN—Come here a minute. Sit down. [*She sits, and makes him sit beside her.*] Now listen; it isn't really important whether I care for you or not, or whether or not you care for me. If you were Tristan and I were Isolde, and we'd drunk a deathless love potion, there would be nothing that we could do about it—*nothing.* Don't smile. There are some things one can do nothing about. One is being born. One is love. And one is death. Oh, yes— Tristan and Isolde could go into the wilderness for love, perhaps, but not you and I. At least, not together. I don't know about you. You are younger; less sophisticated, not so restless, I hope; but you *are* selfish; and you are comfort-loving, just as I am—and, after all, there are no wildernesses any more, are there? So even if this feeling between us, this—shall I call it, like Juliet, "this bud of love" *should* prove a beauteous flower, it could bloom only to be

trampled in the mire, and I don't want that. I'd rather—
[*She breaks off, the catch in her voice again, but a certain
amusement, more at herself and at Fate than at him, in her
smile.*]

THAYER—[*Soberly.*]   I wish I could believe that, at
least, you'd like for things to be different, and we could
begin all over again together.

LADY HELEN—[*With touching grave earnestness.*]   I
don't know what I wish for myself, Ned. My life is like
water that has gone over the dam and turned no mill wheels.
Here I am, not happy, but not unhappy, as my days run
on to the sea, idly—but too swiftly—for I love living. But
you—oh, I want something very fine for you! I want to be
so proud of you that there will be tears in my eyes when
I think of you. And so I want you to go away, my dear.
London is no place for you. You've told me something of
your life in that small American city—how you hated it—
how you drifted to New York after your father's death—
of your idleness there—of this aimless trip to London—of
your half-formed dream of going to South Africa in search
of a fortune. Last week when I was in the country, I
thought a great deal about all you had told me. Why don't
you go to South Africa, at once?

THAYER—[*Slowly, not quite believing in her sincerity.*]
I haven't much philosophy, I suppose, but I believe in living
and letting live, and if I want to stay in London as long
as I can afford it, I don't see why *you* should object. I'm
finding London a pretty jolly place. Besides, I've had
some good business offers lately——

LADY HELEN—[*Ironically.*]   From Mr. Rudolph Solomon?

THAYER—He was *one*, yes. He's a big man, in America.

LADY HELEN——But rather lonely in London. I know . . .
go on.

THAYER——Yes, I know all that, too. You've taken me
up, as they say, and Rudolph Solomon thinks you might
do the same thing for him if he paid me a salary. But——
even that——wouldn't be so bad as—— I never told you, did I,
that I went to Alaska once? I was educated to be a mining
engineer. I went out there thinking all I had to do was
to remember what I'd read in books. I stood it for two
years; then I came back. Good God! You don't know
what those places are! The loneliness, the dirt, the cold.
You're just an animal living in a world outside the world
——where nothing ever happens, except your own misery.
You read newspapers half a year old, and think it would
be better to be back in civilisation——even behind the bars
of a jail——than to hang on any longer to a life that isn't
a life. . . . The thought of a dinner in a decent restaurant
makes you limp with homesickness. Oh——[*his voice
changes suddenly, and he is apologetic for himself*]——it's
only that I haven't the stamina for that sort of thing, I
suppose. I suppose I'm really no good, maybe, but I've
decided that my future, if I've got one, is going to be spent
in the pleasantest places I can find.

LADY HELEN——[*Rising, with a laugh.*] I've been fantastic again. After all, as you say, why shouldn't you stay
in London?

THAYER——Yes, why shouldn't I stay in London? [*He
rises and stares into her eyes.*]

LADY HELEN——And there will always be Mrs. Leslies
to make even the pleasantest places more pleasant!

THAYER——[*With genuine amazement.*] Mrs. Leslie! I
thought——

LADY HELEN—[*With a smile.*]   Whatever you thought —make no mistake—I'm not jealous, Ned.

THAYER—But don't you like her?

LADY HELEN—She's very pretty; she's amusing some-times; and she plays admirable bridge.   I'm not jealous, but I think I might like her better if I liked you less.

THAYER—But she's nothing to me!   We met on the boat.   She's absolutely nothing to me——

LADY HELEN—I believe that. . . . Well—we mustn't keep her and Harry Charteris waiting any longer, must we? [*She starts toward the door at the left.*]

THAYER—She's a good sort, but you're tired of her, just as you're tired of me, now.   She told me only today that. you'd be throwing us both over, soon.

LADY HELEN—You make me feel a thousand, sometimes, Ned!   Do you really believe that I'm tired of you—when I upset all my lack of principles in order to give you good advice?

THAYER—What else can I believe—when your good advice would send me to South Africa, a million miles away from you?

LADY HELEN—[*Gently, indulgently, but with wistful-ness.*]   Believe it, then, my friend.   Believe anything you want to believe.   That's what most of us do.   But if, in the future, you don't see a great deal of me, and your healthy vanity suggests now and then that you're not a young man whom a woman ought to get tired of, just remember *everything—everything*—that I've said—or not said—to you tonight.   You're very young, my dear; when you're forty, I'll be—oh—never mind!   [*She laughs just wryly enough to make him smile and leads the way into the next room, quickly.   The door closes behind them.*]

[*The stage is dark for an instant to denote the passage of an hour or so. Then the room flashes back, just as it was before. Suddenly* MRS. LESLIE, *abject and trembling, enters from the room at the left. She hesitates in sheer terror, near the door to the hall, as if powerless to go on.* HARRY CHARTERIS, *grave and alarmed, after an instant follows her.*]

MRS. LESLIE—[*In a frightened whisper.*] What—what is she going to do?

HARRY—[*Curtly.*] I don't know.

[LADY HELEN *enters from the same room, in so furious a rage that she wears the superb aspect of a violent goddess walking on wind.* EDWARD THAYER *follows, helpless, humiliated, and in despair.*]

LADY HELEN—[*Looking at him, and shuddering away— intense bitterness in her voice.*] Oh, God!

THAYER—[*As he sees her contemptuous, angry smile.*] Don't—don't—don't—don't!

LADY HELEN—Harry—it was absolutely undeniable, wasn't it!

HARRY—Absolutely!

LADY HELEN—[*Looking from* EDWARD *to* MRS. LESLIE.] You fools! Fools! God knows what you thought! [*To* THAYER.] God knows why you should have done this a second time! You must be insane! Or—did you— Did you think that *I* was insane? Did you think I had such supreme faith in you that I wouldn't believe the evidence of my own eyes? Not when your miserable signals— [*She pauses, growing rigid with the thought.*] Or has dishonesty become such a habit with you that you've got to cheat whenever you get the chance? Is that it? You'd better go, Mrs. Leslie. Don't try to speak to me. Just go!

MRS. LESLIE—Yes, yes, yes, I'll go! I'll . . . You couldn't understand— [*Her words end in a sob.*]

LADY HELEN—[*Interrupting.*] You're quite right! I couldn't possibly understand, thank God!—Let her out, will you, Harry?

[HARRY *leads the way from the room, silently.* MRS. LESLIE'S *sobbing ceases, but as she pauses in the doorway to the hall, she turns a look of envy and hate on* LADY HELEN *and speaks bitterly.*]

MRS. LESLIE—I suppose *you've* never done anything to be ashamed of? [*There is insinuation in her vicious tone, as her glance sweeps both* THAYER *and* HARRY *and she continues.*] Well, if you ever do I hope you'll find people just as merciless as I've found you!

LADY HELEN—I hope that I will find them just as merciful, Mrs. Leslie. I shall never mention your name to anyone again, and I don't believe that Mr. Charteris will, either.

HARRY—Perhaps not, if Mrs. Leslie gives up bridge. [*He turns to her, as he opens the door.*] Are you ready?

MRS. LESLIE—Yes. [*They go.*]

[LADY HELEN *and* EDWARD THAYER *face each other.*]

LADY HELEN—[*Unsteadily.*] This—this is the first time I've ever caught anyone cheating at cards, and it's made me —a little—ill. [*She moves, her eyes closed, toward the table, and manages to pour some water into a glass.* THAYER *starts to help her, but she holds him off by a gesture.*]

THAYER—[*In a low voice.*] You want me to go too, I suppose? Well, good night and good-bye.

LADY HELEN—Not yet.

THAYER—There's nothing I can say now—except that I'm sorry.

LADY HELEN—You must say that to my husband.

THAYER—To your husband!

LADY HELEN—Yes. . . . He said it to you. You must say it to him!

THAYER—You mean—to tell him?

LADY HELEN—Of course.

THAYER—You won't!

LADY HELEN—I will!

THAYER—But why? You'll only be putting yourself into a hole. You'll only be admitting that you were wrong. And I won't ever come here again. I'll keep out of your way—but you can't—you can't tell *him!*

LADY HELEN—He was right. . . . I was wrong. Of course, I'll tell him; and I expect you to apologise to him before everyone who heard him apologise to you.

THAYER—I won't! I tell you, I won't! You know what sort of man he is. He'll tell his story all over London and it won't stop there. They'll know it in New York. It will ruin me for good and all. . . . I am sorry. I'll never do it again. I needed the money. . . . It didn't seem so awfully wrong to fake a bit in the beginning and win off people who didn't need it—and who didn't mind much whether they lost or not. Then it got to be a habit—it got so I couldn't resist a chance—just as you said. But I'll never do it again—only, for God's sake, let me go— without the scandal that your husband will surely make! Charteris will keep quiet if you ask him. . . . [*Turns to her.*] But life won't be worth living if everybody knows!

LADY HELEN—Is that all? Have you never heard of *fair play?* Well, turn about is fair play. It's my husband's turn now!

THAYER—[*After a pause.*] You don't dare.

LADY HELEN—I don't dare? Dare what? Admit that he was right and I was wrong?

THAYER—You said tonight that if he kicked me out of the house, you'd go out of it, too, forever. Very well; I say that if he kicks me out, you *will* go out of it, too, forever. [LADY HELEN's *expression is one of utter bewilderment. He continues, desperately, recklessly.*] You don't get what I'm driving at, do you? I mean that I've got letters of yours——

LADY HELEN—What?

THAYER—I've got letters of yours. I've got them right here. If you tell on me, I'll tell on you. If you're so keen on playing fair with your brute of a husband, I'll play fair with him too! You're willing enough to see me sent to the devil, yes! But how about yourself!

[HARRY CHARTERIS *returns.* LADY HELEN *turns to him, indicating the door at the right.*]

LADY HELEN—Open that door, will you, Harry, and ask Bruce and the others to come here at once!

THAYER—Wait——!

[*But at a gesture from* LADY HELEN, HARRY *goes to do as she has asked. There is a pause while he disappears. Then he returns, followed by the others, their cards still in their hands.*]

LADY HELEN—[*To the amazed group, and particularly to her husband.*] I've something to tell you—all of you—about Mr. Thayer. You were right, Bruce—and I was wrong—quite—quite wrong. He . . .

THE CURTAIN FALLS AS SHE IS SPEAKING

THE SECOND ACT

*Three years later. The lounge of a hotel in New York,
where, at a little after six o'clock on the afternoon
of a winter day, people are still idling over the tea-
tables. There is a wide doorway from the foyer at
one side, and at the back are steps leading up to the
main restaurant; they form a sort of balcony at the
top, to which there is another entrance, to another foyer,
on the opposite side from the one below.*

SIR EMMETT *and* LADY WILDERING *and* CHARLOTTE ASHLEY
*are here, and there are several other groups scattered
about. The orchestra (at the end of the balcony opposite the entrance to the foyer) is playing the last number of its tea-time programme. Presently the musi-
cians put their instruments away and go out. Waiters
move about; a man and a woman rise and depart;
there is a low hum of talk not quite lost in the sound
of the music, and presently the voice of a young woman
is heard addressing her companions, a young man and
an older woman at the same table.*

THE YOUNG WOMAN—[*Suddenly arrested, as she has
turned to glance about curiously.*] Do you know who that
is? It's Charlotte Ashley.

THE YOUNG MAN—The actress, you mean?

THE YOUNG WOMAN—Yes, she's playing the leading part
in the new Shaw play. They say she's very intellectual.

THE OLDER WOMAN—You're wrong, my dear. That's not

34

Charlotte Ashley. She's much darker. I saw her when I
was in California last winter. She was pointed out to me
several times.

THE YOUNG WOMAN—Do tell me about her. They say
that she—of course they talk about everybody, but—
[*She and the young man lean a little closer to listen; their
companion smiles and shrugs, and begins in a voice that
is now only a whisper.*]

SIR EMMETT—[*Quite unconscious of the glances that are
directed by the gossips at his table.*] Just how long have
you been in America, Charlotte?

CHARLOTTE—Eleven weeks. . . . The play has been running seven, now.

SIR EMMETT—It's the first time you've been over for
several years, isn't it?

CHARLOTTE—Four. . . . May I have some more tea, Edith?
[*At a third table a man and a woman, with quiet interested
voices, are speaking of the* WILDERINGS.]

THE MAN—You really think that's our new ambassador
from England?

THE WOMAN—It may not be Sir Emmett Wildering. I
think it is, but I don't know him. However, I'm sure about
its being Lady Wildering. I know her quite well, by sight.
She's an American, you know. Everyone says she's
charming.

THE MAN—He's quite the most famous man they've ever
sent over.

THE WOMAN—I know; I've read his books—not all of
them, of course.

THE MAN—You mean the political and historical ones,
I suppose . . . ? [*She nods, and he continues.*] . . . But
did you know that he's also a great authority on butterflies,

and has written a large volume—which isn't so well known as it ought to be—on the subject? I must send it to you.

THE WOMAN—How interesting. . . . It's almost half-past six. I must be going. [*They glance again at the* WILDERINGS *as they rise, and pass them, on their way out.*]

LADY WILDERING—[*With a far-off look in her eyes.*] I wonder how my dogs are . . . ?

CHARLOTTE—[*With a smile, and also a far-off look.*] I wonder how my children are . . . ?

LADY WILDERING—They both looked jolly well when they came to say good-bye to me two weeks ago.

CHARLOTTE—Oh, they're well cared for—I know that; but when the time comes for me to leave England and leave them at home, I almost wish that there weren't such a thing in the world as a play, or a theatre, or such a place as America.

LADY WILDERING—I know what that feeling is. I used to wish that there weren't such a thing as an education when the time came to send our boys away to get one. [*There is a little pause.*]

SIR EMMETT—[*In a low voice.*] You have noticed, haven't you, that Harry Charteris never mentions Helen Haden?

CHARLOTTE—Oh, yes. [*There is a bare pause.*]

LADY WILDERING—All the same, that's why he is in America.

CHARLOTTE—He's come in for some money since his uncle's death, of course.

LADY WILDERING—Yes, but I'm afraid it's much less than one might have expected. Do you ever see Helen, Charlotte?

CHARLOTTE—[*Haltingly.*] No, I've not been over very

long, and I've not—I—I don't believe I'd know what to say if I should meet her.

LADY WILDERING—I'm afraid it would be awkward—almost painful—meeting her. What could one say? And it would be just as difficult for her. What could she say?

CHARLOTTE—One would be thinking of all the things one knew, or didn't know; and she would be thinking of all that she knew one knew—or didn't know.

SIR EMMETT—[*Very quietly.*] I should be seeing ghosts—ghosts of the mad Varicks racing their phantom horses down the winds of eternity; swift riders with their plumes streaming and their armour flashing, their phantom hounds leaping before them, a great race—warriors, courtiers, sportsmen, riding into oblivion . . . and Helen, the last of their line, following,—a ghost of tomorrow. The Varicks should have made a better ending.

[*At this instant* LADY HELEN HADEN *appears on the balcony at the back. She is radiant and childlike, delightfully dressed, and there is no outward sign, at least, that Fortune has not dealt gently with her. As she enters she is seen by the group at the first table.*]

THE YOUNG WOMAN—There's Lady Helen Haden. [*She bows, but* LADY HELEN *does not see her.*]

THE YOUNG MAN—She doesn't seem to know you.

THE YOUNG WOMAN—Oh, I suppose she is so used to being cut that she never looks at anyone any more, but I met her when she first came over—with some very nice people—and I always speak to her.

THE OLDER WOMAN—What a fool she was to let herself get so completely déclassée! She's really the daughter of an earl, you know. And once they couldn't give a dinner party without her in London.

[LADY HELEN *catches the attention of the maître d'hôtel, who hurries up the steps toward her.*]

LADY HELEN—Has anyone been asking for me, Jean?

JEAN—No, my lady.

LADY HELEN—What time is it? [*She looks at her wrist, but remembers that she has no watch. She laughs at her futile gesture.*] I've no watch!

JEAN—Twenty-two minutes after six, my lady.

LADY HELEN—So late? Order some tea for me, Jean, while I'm telephoning. I'll have that table. There should be five or six of us if the people I'm expecting turn up.

JEAN—Very good, my lady.

[*She goes out and he sets about supervising the arrangement of her table. Another woman, followed by a man, enters, passing* LADY HELEN *going out.* LADY HELEN *recognises her, and gives her a short swift nod as she hurries by, but the woman with great pompousness turns away. The man is amazed, and as they descend the steps speaks in a low, troubled voice.*]

THE MAN—She spoke to you, didn't she?

THE WOMAN—[*With malicious satisfaction.*] Yes—I cut her. You know who she is, don't you?

THE MAN—No. She looked—all right.

THE WOMAN—[*With a shrug.*] She's Lady Helen Haden.

THE MAN—Lady Helen Haden! But—what's she doing over here?

THE WOMAN—Haven't you heard? Just going about with all sorts of queer people and living by her wits, I understand. Oh, here's my cigarette-case! I told you I left it here. . . . [*Having found the object she mentions, on a recently deserted table, she puts it into her bag, and the two go out again, but by the other doorway, at the side.*

There is an instant's quiet. Then CHARLOTTE ASHLEY'S *voice is heard.*]

CHARLOTTE—I shall never forget her rage against that unfortunate young man who *did* cheat at cards, after all.

LADY WILDERING—What a terrible thing it was—his giving Sir Bruce those letters!

SIR EMMETT—Just at a moment when peace might have been made for all time between them. Haden had been very much impressed by Helen's fairness.

LADY WILDERING—But only an hour later, after we'd gone and he had read the letters,—every one,—she walked out of the house, picked up a taxi, and drove to Claridge's, just as she was, without even a shilling for the driver. They paid him for her, of course, at the hotel. She sat up all night, she told me, waiting for her maid to come in the morning to undress her.

SIR EMMETT—And read one of my speeches, I remember.

LADY WILDERING—Yes, one that she found in a newspaper that had been left in the taxi.

SIR EMMETT—And a week later, when I saw her for the first time afterward, she seemed more upset by certain passages in that speech—with which she didn't agree—than by her own grave troubles.

CHARLOTTE—Has anyone ever heard what happened to the young man? His name was Thayer, wasn't it?

SIR EMMETT—He might have died that night for all I've ever heard. Even Haden must have held his tongue about what happened.

LADY WILDERING—[*With a shrug.*] His pride, I suppose. Otherwise he would never have been so delicate.

CHARLOTTE—Whatever Helen had written in the letters, she evidently had written nothing that gave grounds for divorce.   He didn't even mention them in his suit, a year later.

SIR EMMETT—He didn't need to. . . .

LADY WILDERING—Yes; whatever she wrote, there could have been nothing in them to convict her of faithlessness, or her husband would not have waited a year to divorce her.   That was why I was anxious, at one time, to see if things couldn't be patched up between them.   But she wouldn't hear of it.   He wouldn't have her back, she insisted. . . . They were silly letters, she said, almost school-girly, and they had turned up just on top of some sillier bills that had already spoiled Sir Bruce's suavity for one day; and no husband, Helen maintained, could have been expected to forgive both these letters and those bills in the same twenty-four hours.

CHARLOTTE—I suppose it was a case of "Oh, my daughter.   Oh, my ducats!"—Except that it happened to be his wife instead of his daughter.   That was another grievance, of course—that there wasn't even a daughter.

SIR EMMETT—Well, *that's* changed.   The new Lady Haden, it is announced, has just achieved twins; both boys.

CHARLOTTE—And with that dazzling event Sir Bruce passes out of Helen's sorry tale forever, I suppose.

[*Their thoughts silence them for the moment.   There is a chatter in the doorway off the balcony, and* ZELLITO *and* ALICE VANCE *enter.* ZELLITO *is a handsome Spanish woman who has the look of a gypsy in spite of her bizarre Parisian clothes.* ALICE VANCE *is younger, and is wistfully lovely. They enter quickly, feeling that they are late, but hesitate on the balcony as their eyes search for someone whom they do not see.   Presently* JEAN *hurries to them, and leads them*

to the table he has prepared for LADY HELEN HADEN.
*They are instantly under discussion by the group at the
first table.*]

THE YOUNG MAN—There are two celebrities——

THE YOUNG WOMAN—Of a sort.

THE YOUNG MAN—Don't be a cat.

THE OLDER WOMAN—[*Recognising them.*] Oh, Alice
Vance, and Zellito. They say she's a dope fiend—Zellito,
I mean.

THE YOUNG MAN—[*Impatiently.*] How can anyone be
a dope fiend who has to keep herself in condition to dance?

THE OLDER WOMAN—[*Defensively.*] Don't ask me—I
was never either a dope fiend or a dancer.

THE YOUNG WOMAN—As for Alice Vance, she was
chamber-maid in a hotel in Chicago, they say. I believe
she was in the habit of stealing; they say the Chicago
police have her finger-prints.

THE OLDER WOMAN—Yes, I've heard that. They say
she still takes things.

THE YOUNG MAN—Why should anyone "take things"—
as you put it—when Rudolph Solomon takes care of her?

THE YOUNG WOMAN—I don't believe that he takes care
of her. She hasn't any jewelry or furs—and she doesn't
dress particularly well. Besides, she may be just a patho-
logical kleptomaniac.

THE YOUNG MAN—There's nothing under heaven that you
can't hear in New York.

[ZELLITO *and* ALICE VANCE, *in the meantime, have settled
themselves at the table reserved for* LADY HELEN HADEN;
but while ZELLITO, *speaking in French to* JEAN, *is ordering
cigarettes brought immediately,* ALICE VANCE *recovers a
bracelet that falls, unnoticed, from* ZELLITO'S *wrist as she*

jerks off her glove. She stares at it for an instant after the waiter has gone, and then hands it to zellito, *speaking quietly.*]

alice vance—This came off with your glove. If I had not seen it fall to the floor it might have been lost.

zellito—[*Very much excited, and with a very florid Spanish accent in both her French and her English.*] Oh! What good fortune! Merci, chérie! It is of great value. I must see why the catch so easily gives away. [*She holds it up, and then kisses it as she speaks, continuing with shining eyes as* alice vance *laughs at her emotion.*] It is beautiful, is it not? Jewels! Ah, but they are my passion! And you say you care for them nothing! Is it really true? You mean that?

alice vance—It is true, I care nothing for them, Zellito.

zellito—[*Replacing her bracelet on her arm, testing the clasp, and becoming intimate and practical as she leans across the table.*] You are foolish, chérie. You should, at least, pretend a longing for them; you should want this, and want that, and get many fine ones from your friend; for jewels are like money. [*As* alice *is about to protest, she hurries on, cynically.*] Oh, yes, I know that he is generous, but even a rich man finds it pleasanter to give jewels than money. A fortune of jewels you should get from him!

alice vance—[*Dreamily.*] I care nothing for diamonds and pearls and money, Zellito. Rudolph knows that.

zellito—[*With a shrug.*] He would better like you if you did!

alice vance—Thousands of women do. They are not difficult to find.

ZELLITO—[*Half amused, half impatient.*]   Ah, sweet
little fool!   Do you think really lives the man who has
appreciation of the woman who asks nothing but love?
Eh, bien, live he may, but he is not Rudolph Solomon.

ALICE VANCE—[*Quietly.*]   You do not know him.

ZELLITO—I know men.

ALICE VANCE—He is not like other men.

ZELLITO—And when he tires?   You do not dream he
is not to tire?   What then?

ALICE VANCE—It will not matter.   [*Her voice is profoundly sad.*]

ZELLITO—[*With unction.*]   I thank the good God that
a lady he did not make me!   A sweet fool no man has
found Zellito!   In London, in the Bank of England alone
I have a hundred thousand pounds.   And my jewels make
another fortune.   Let us smoke these abominable cigarettes,
chérie, though one would say that they were made for
babies when they tire of milk.   However—   [*She lights
one of the cigarettes that the waiter has just brought.*]

[RUDOLPH SOLOMON, *an important-looing man, middle-
aged, a Jew of great distinction, enters through the doorway on the balcony.   Both* JEAN *and his assistant see him
at once, and hurry to meet him.*]

JEAN—A table, Mr. Solomon?

SOLOMON—Has Lady Helen Haden been here this afternoon?

JEAN—Yes, sir.   This is her table, sir.   She's ordered
tea——

[*He leads the way, and places a chair for* RUDOLPH
SOLOMON *at the table with* ZELLITO *and* ALICE VANCE.   *Their
greetings are a murmur lost, for the moment, in the gossip*

of the group of busy-bodies near by, who of course are watching him with great interest.]

THE YOUNG WOMAN—There's Rudolph Solomon now!

THE YOUNG MAN—Yes, with Alice Vance. What did I tell you? She was here a minute ago.

THE YOUNG WOMAN—That doesn't mean anything. Lady Helen Haden was here a moment ago: probably he's come to meet her. . . . They say his new house cost two million dollars.

[RUDOLPH SOLOMON, *who hasn't yet sat down, is about to do so, when, glancing toward the doorway as if he might go in search of* LADY HELEN HADEN, *he pauses, arrested and amazed at finding himself face to face with* EDWARD THAYER, *who has just entered hurriedly, but who, to the eye at least, is a far more impressive figure of a young man than the* EDWARD THAYER *who cheated at cards, at* LADY HELEN HADEN's *house, three years ago.*]

SOLOMON—Thayer! Edward Thayer!

THAYER—Oh, Mr. Solomon! How do you do? You've not forgotten me?

SOLOMON—Certainly not.

THAYER—I supposed everyone had.

SOLOMON—But where have you been all this time?

THAYER—That's a long story.

SOLOMON—I want to hear it.

THAYER—You're very kind. I don't know that it would interest you. It's a pretty dull story.

SOLOMON—Are you in a hurry? [*He indicates the tea-table.*]

THAYER—[*Reluctantly.*] Yes, I'm sorry; but I must catch a train in fifteen minutes. I'm looking for the man who is going with me. He's not here—so——

SOLOMON—I won't keep you. When will you be back?

THAYER—A week from today.

SOLOMON—Dine with me that night. [*He finds a card which he gives* THAYER.]

THAYER—Thanks—I——

SOLOMON—At my new house. About eight. Here's the address, on this card.

THAYER—Thanks. Eight o'clock. A week from to-night. I'll be there.

SOLOMON—And if you're still looking for something to do——

THAYER—Thanks—that's ever so good of you—but I'll tell you about that later——

[*They touch hands and then* THAYER *is gone through the side door by which he entered.* SOLOMON *sits. The waiter brings the tea.*]

SOLOMON—[*Half to himself, glancing after* THAYER.] Curious, isn't it, how one is always meeting people? That young man, for instance: I was thinking of him this morning for the first time in months. I met him in London several years ago. I liked him, but I wasn't very sure how he'd turn out. I'm glad that he looks as if things had gone well with him. . . . Why did I think of him this morning, Zellito, and see him today? Do your fortune-telling gifts explain coincidences of that sort?

ZELLITO—I will tell you, but— [*She leans toward him, and talks with considerable animation.*]

[HARRY CHARTERIS, *who has entered by the balcony door-way, like a man hurrying in a dream, goes quickly to the* WILDERINGS' *table, leans over a chair, and speaks in a grave, low voice.*]

HARRY—Well—I've seen her.

CHARLOTTE *and* LADY WILDERING—[*Together, as they look up, startled.*] Helen?

HARRY—Yes, Helen. [*It is as though he were still seeing her—not his companions.*]

CHARLOTTE—Really? Where? When?

HARRY—An instant ago—going into a telephone booth. She didn't see me. [*He sits. There is a slight pause, then he continues, half angrily, half bitterly.*] What are we going to do about her?

CHARLOTTE—There's nothing we can do . . . is there?

LADY WILDERING—I'm afraid she wouldn't want us to do anything.

HARRY—You mean she tries to avoid old friends? [*His tone is ironical as he pronounces the last two words, but* CHARLOTTE *hurries to speak, gently, persuasively.*]

CHARLOTTE—I think so, or she would have looked me up at the theatre.

LADY WILDERING—She's never written to any of us since she came to America. Yes, I'm afraid she wouldn't want to see us.

HARRY—If she doesn't, it will be very simple not to intrude, since we don't even know where she lives. . . . But Helen's an Englishwoman and our own kind, and although she's tried—in every possible way—to cut herself adrift from us, there's nothing—nothing in the world—that I wouldn't do for her——

SIR EMMETT—But it's just because she is an English-woman and our own kind that we must be stern with ourselves about her. She had a great name, great traditions, great charm, great gifts, and in God's name what has she done with them? For her personal misfortune one might be sorry—one is sorry, sorry beyond all words; but as an

Englishman, and as the representative of my King, I cannot forgive an Englishwoman for making, in a strange country, a sneer of her class, a joke of her rank, and a miserable adventure of her life.

CHARLOTTE—[*As if she had been listening to her own thoughts instead of to his words.*] I keep thinking of that dreadful night when those people cheated at bridge. We were all there, and now we are all here. How strange!

HARRY—And Helen is out there alone, trying to find someone, I suppose, to have a cup of tea with her. . . . Good God! [*As he has glanced toward the door while speaking,* LADY HELEN HADEN *has appeared on the balcony. But she comes forward, not noticing anyone in the room until his gaze seems to draw hers. Her voice as she recognises him is a cry—but a sudden radiance, more moving than tears, brings the tears with it to her eyes as she looks from one to another.*]

LADY HELEN—Harry! Charlotte! And Edith! And— all of you! It's too wonderful . . . [*There is a bare pause. A sudden panic of shyness sweeps over her as* SIR EMMETT *rises slowly, his face grave. But as he looks at her he indicates his own chair.*]

SIR EMMETT—Sit here, my dear.

LADY HELEN—Oh, may I?—One minute?—Charlotte— Edith—bless you!

LADY WILDERING—Helen, dear——

CHARLOTTE—Oh, Helen!

LADY HELEN—One never knows how much one loves England . . . [*She does not finish, but lays her hand for an instant on* SIR EMMETT'S, *and then turns quickly to the others, talking rapidly.*] This *is* like home, isn't it? How does it happen that we are all really here? Of course—

[*to* CHARLOTTE]—you're easily explained. I'm so glad your play is a success. I've been to see you five times! How are the children? They're at home, I suppose? And so grown up that I wouldn't know them any more—the darlings!

CHARLOTTE—Yes, they're at home and very grown up —the darlings! I must show you their pictures. Will you come and dine with me, soon?

LADY HELEN—Rather!

CHARLOTTE—When?

LADY HELEN—Any time at all, except a week from to-night. [*Her lips twist with sudden amusement at her own thoughts.*] I really have an engagement a week from tonight. . . . [*Then she hurries away from the irony of what she is saying—and turns quickly to* LADY WILDERING.] I read that they were sending Emmett over. It's a good thing, too. Isn't it a pity that England hasn't enough Emmett Wilderings to go round? She can only send him one place at a time. When did you arrive?

LADY WILDERING—Only today at noon.

LADY HELEN—Oh, that accounts for my not knowing! I always read every name on the list of passengers that every ship brings. How are the Lepidoptera, Emmett?

CHARLOTTE—The what?

SIR EMMETT—That's what we scientists call butterflies —among ourselves! I've had to neglect the Lepidoptera these last few years, my dear.

LADY HELEN—I was afraid so. You see, I've read all your books as they've come out, and all your speeches, and I knew you'd had to neglect something in order to do so much real work. But I'm glad it was only the butterflies and not Edith. She doesn't look neglected, does she?

But I think you're wrong about our policy in Egypt. We ought to— [*She laughs and stops.*] No, I haven't the courage to argue with you any more about anything. I haven't even seen England for two years. I don't know what we ought to do; only certain things have looked very mysterious from a distance. Then there's the labor question; and there still is, always was, and always will be, Ireland! I worry a lot about Ireland.

SIR EMMETT—Shall we have a long talk and thrash it all out?

LADY HELEN—Yes, rather.

SIR EMMETT—When are you going to dine with us?

LADY HELEN—Any time—you're probably frightfully busy. I suppose you're going straight through to Washington.

SIR EMMETT—Yes. Our train leaves in less than an hour. But we'll be back before Sunday.

HARRY—[*To the* WILDERINGS.] You're dining with me Sunday. You'll see Helen then.

LADY HELEN—Am I dining with you, Harry, on Sunday?

HARRY—If you will.

LADY HELEN—[*Quietly, as she tears the tea-card and writes on half of it.*] I must give you my address and my telephone number. Then you can let me know if you want to change your plans—or if anything happens.

CHARLOTTE—Nothing is likely to happen before to-morrow, in any event, so shall we say my hotel—the Plaza—at seven? I must be at theatre early, you know.

LADY HELEN—[*Laying the card that she has written on the table before them; and flashing her answer at* CHARLOTTE *swiftly.*] Seven. The Plaza. Thanks. . . . Now I must be going. . . .

LADY WILDERING—But you haven't had your tea. Let us order some for you.

LADY HELEN—No, no! It's been enough for one time—seeing all of you, even for a few minutes. I can't tell you how I—how I've loved it. [*She moves as if to rise, but doesn't; then her impulse of sudden shyness passes, and she hurries on, with a sort of breathless gaiety, turning to* LADY WILDERING.] You haven't told me about the dogs yet, but you must next time. I still have Plato. You gave him to me when he was a pup, remember? He will want to know all about his relatives at home. Plato and I have talked a lot about you—Plato and Blossom and I. You remember Blossom—my maid? She's still with me. . . . Poor Blossom! [*She stops short, then turns to* HARRY, *speaking quietly, gently.*] I haven't tried to tell you and I didn't try to write—how sorry I was to hear of your uncle's death. It was a great pity. He wasn't old, or tired of living, or unhappy. . . .

HARRY—Yes, it was a great pity. He loved life to the very end. He thought it was—on the whole—a very good show.

LADY HELEN—I know. Englishmen are like that. They love life more and value it less than any other people in the world. . . . I won't say even au 'voir. . . . [*Again she moves as if to go, but a great reluctance prevents, as she talks on and on, nervously, gaily, in an exquisitely husky voice that has nothing to do with the words it is saying.*] Zellito's waiting. You remember Zellito? The Spanish dancer at the Gaiety who used to tell fortunes in my booth at every bazaar? What fun they were—those bazaars! And we used to think them bores—at least, I thought I did. . . . She still tells fortunes sometimes, although she will never tell mine. She pretends that she can't make out whether I'm to live on forever, or die eventually as most people do—particularly if they're Varicks. . . . The Three Wonderful Waltons are coming to tea. They're acrobats——

CHARLOTTE—Acrobats!

LADY HELEN—[*Smiling at her amazement.*] Oh, yes. Zellito discovered them in one of her music-halls. They're Croatians and they have splendid characters. They send their money home for their relatives to buy goats with. Their only immorality is cream-puffs. Cream-puffs are not for acrobats, but they admit that they can't resist them. [*She finds* RUDOLPH SOLOMON's *eyes meeting hers and signals a greeting to him with a little wave of her hand, as she hurries on.*] And Rudolph Solomon. . . . You must have heard of Rudolph Solomon—the American rival of the British Museum? He's a wonderful person really, even if he used to seem a bit too keen on knowing us. And, Harry, —you'd really like my friend Alice Vance. She's a Broadway celebrity, but she has a real voice, and she's a great dear. . . . "Oh, to be in England—now that April's there!" . . . Only it isn't April, is it! I suppose it's snowing in the fens. . . . I won't say even au 'voir. . . . [*This time she rises. The others do the same.*]

CHARLOTTE—[*A bit unsteadily.*] I ought to go——

LADY HELEN—There are my acrobats now! [THE WONDERFUL WALTONS *have entered—squat, swarthy men with bullet-shaped heads, dressed to the very tip-top of fashion, with somewhat alarming results. They conduct themselves in their best public manner—a manner which is not without naïveté and charm. They are not exactly disconcerted at seeing their hostess talking to her friends at another table,*

*but when they see her rise they know it is more correct to
stand while she is standing, and they wait in rigid formation for her to join them.* LADY HELEN *continues swiftly.*]
The poor darlings—they've gone and dressed themselves in
their best! Perhaps that's why they're so late. . . . I must
go now and ply them with the iniquitous cream-puffs. . . .
So—[*She hesitates just an instant, her voice again deep
with feeling, her eyes bright.*]   I won't say even au 'voir—
bless you. [*She turns quickly and hurries to greet* THE
WALTONS.]

[CHARLOTTE ASHLEY *and* LADY WILDERING, *followed by*
SIR EMMETT *and* HARRY CHARTERIS, *go up the steps and disappear through the door that leads from the balcony.*]

LADY HELEN—[*To* THE WALTONS.]   How do you do? I'm
very relieved at seeing you.   I was afraid that you had
been tossing one another about too carelessly at the mati-
née.   Do sit down.   [*She sits, nodding to the others.*]
Have I been long?   I'm sorry.   I hope you've had your
tea—and that there's some for me.   Oh, thanks— [ALICE
VANCE *gives her a cup that she has just poured.*]   But you
haven't met, have you?   Mr. Rudolph Solomon—the Three
Wonderful Waltons.   [*The introduction excites* THE WAL-
TONS *enormously.   The tallest of the three hisses to his
brothers.*]

THE FIRST WALTON—Millionaire! [*He rises promptly
and makes his best stage bow with his best stage smile,
addressing* SOLOMON.]   I am delightful.

THE SECOND WALTON—[*Also.*]   I am delightful.

THE THIRD WALTON—[*Also.*]   I am delightful.   [*They
sit.   It is obvious that they do not bore* LADY HELEN.]

LADY HELEN—[*To* SOLOMON.]   And aren't you delightful, too? They've their best English out for your benefit.

SOLOMON—[*Directly to* LADY HELEN *but with a smile for* THE WALTONS *who are beaming at him.*] I am as delighted as *you're* delightful.

LADY HELEN—[*To* THE WALTONS.] Tea?

THE FIRST WALTON—No tea; no coffee. Ver' bad for peoples in our professions.

LADY HELEN—Then what shall I order for you?

THE THREE—[*Together.*] Milk.

LADY HELEN—[*To a waiter hovering for the order.*] Milk for three—and pastries. [THE WALTONS *put their heads together and whisper about something.*]

SOLOMON—[*To* LADY HELEN.] You were with the Wilderings, weren't you?

LADY HELEN—[*Briefly.*] Yes.

SOLOMON—He's a very great man. I'm glad that England has sent him over. [*It is obvious that he is interested in the* WILDERINGS, *but she is not eager to discuss them.*]

LADY HELEN—He's a great dear—they both are. . . . I want you to meet Harry Charteris, Alice. [*She has turned to* ALICE VANCE.] I was just speaking to him about you. He's very musical. I think he knows all the folksongs in the world. I've often heard him play the one you sing about the fisher-girl.

ZELLITO—[*Ironically.*] It is a sad song about love, I suppose. All Alice's songs about love are sad.

LADY HELEN—Sad—but beautiful, too, Zellito. Especially the music. Although I like the words too. [*She recites the words, quickly, carelessly, but with a sudden far-off look of patient pain in her eyes, as if somehow they had a special meaning for herself.*]

"Oh, silver sea-doves from the North,
Why fares my lover never forth
Any more at eventide
To walk the beaches by my side?

"For has he ridden out to sea,
On some sea-wind, forgetting me?
Or has he wandered to the town
To some girl in a silken gown?

THE FIRST WALTON—[*Who has been bursting with importance, breaking the sharp pause that follows by addressing* SOLOMON.] We wish that we place moneys in your hand. We wish that you take money—make more—keep some, and give to us fortune. [*His brothers nod violently in agreement.*]

THE SECOND WALTON—We give ten thousand you.

THE THIRD WALTON—You make fifty maybe, maybe hundred thousand. We go home then like kings.

THE FIRST WALTON—You take money; we trust you; no writing.

LADY HELEN—[*To* SOLOMON.] You probably never received a greater compliment in your life. . . . Ah, here are the cream-puffs and the chocolate éclairs and your milk. . . . [*The waiter serves* THE WALTONS.]

SOLOMON—[*As the three hang on his answer.*] But suppose I lose your money? [*They again put their heads together—this time eating and drinking as they whisper. To* LADY HELEN.] I hope you'll bring your friend—Charteris was his name, wasn't it—to dine next Friday. Alice is coming later, after the theatre and they might try some of their folksongs together.

LADY HELEN—Thanks; I'll ask him.

SOLOMON—[*As if aware that she is careless about dates.*] Friday—a week from tonight—remember!

ZELLITO—[*In a panic.*] Zis is not Friday!

SOLOMON—Yes, it is Friday, Zellito.

ZELLITO—[*Bouncing up from her chair.*] Mon Dieu! And I thought it was Tuesday! I have no head for such things! I cannot remain one moment longer. I have an engagement of great importance.

LADY HELEN—But it's rather late if you're going on for tea somewhere else.

ZELLITO—Tea! It was a dinner, chérie, at seex, wiz a millionaire from Cuba!

ALICE—But you won't be very late. It's only——

ZELLITO—[*Interrupting.*] Do you think it possible to dine—like zis—wiz a millionaire? I am not a fool. I do not neglect opportunities. He has seen me dance in Paris—and I must at least be chic. I will get at once to a telephone and then make quick haste. Be an angel, Alice, and drop me from your motor. I have quite lost my head!

ALICE—Of course. I'll meet you at the door.

ZELLITO—I will be just one instant at the telephone. Au revoir, Lady Helen. [*She turns to* SOLOMON.] Au revoir, mon ami, he is not so rich as you, but it ees my type he happens to admire. . . . Friday—and I thought it was Tuesday! [*With a nod to* THE WALTONS *she hurries away.* ALICE VANCE *rises.*]

LADY HELEN—But must you really go, too?

ALICE—I'm afraid so. [RUDOLPH SOLOMON *has risen.*]

SOLOMON—I'll order your motor.

ALICE—Please, please, don't bother—— [*But he has followed* ZELLITO *through the door to the right.*]

LADY HELEN—[*Holding* ALICE'*s hand an instant as if to detain her.*] Next time we'll begin earlier. . . . And I hope you'll sing for me alone again soon.

ALICE—I will. May I telephone?

LADY HELEN—Yes, rather.

ALICE—Au revoir, then, and thanks so much for asking me today. You—you always seem so—so kind. [*She moves away quickly, but meets* RUDOLPH SOLOMON *returning. They speak for an instant in a low, intimate voice.* LADY HELEN *is aware of them, although she does not turn her head, and there is a look of troubled speculation in her eyes as she thinks of them.* THE WALTONS *have reached some decision and are now energetically finishing the last of their pastries.*]

ALICE—[*To* SOLOMON, *casually, yet with great wistfulness.*] Shall I see you tonight, Rudolph?

SOLOMON—I'll telephone later.

ALICE—If you're busy don't bother. I'll go straight home after the theatre, so come if you like—though I won't let myself really expect you.

SOLOMON—[*With sudden gentleness.*] I think I must make you promise to go straight to bed, and straight to sleep. You're looking tired. I'll telephone in the morning and find out if I've been obeyed. How's that?

ALICE—[*Looking away from him and seeing beyond the doorway.*] There's Zellito. Please go back to Lady Helen. Good-bye.

[*She goes quickly without giving him a chance to answer. He stares after her an instant, then he resumes his seat at* LADY HELEN'*s table.*]

THE FIRST WALTON—[*Instantly to* SOLOMON.] You take

money; make fortune maybe. Maybe lose money; all right!

THE SECOND WALTON—Yes, all right.

THE THIRD WALTON—Yes, all right. We decide it.

THE FIRST WALTON—You think and decide, too. We bring ten thousand to you tomorrow what hour you like.

SOLOMON—Very well, my friend; if you want me to risk it for you come to see me between ten and one. Here's the address. [*The Croatians beam with pleasure as* SOLOMON *gives them a card.* THE FIRST WALTON *rises and makes an elaborate bow.*]

THE FIRST WALTON—Thanking you, Gentleman! [*The others do the same.*]

THE SECOND WALTON—Thanking you, Gentleman!

THE THIRD WALTON—Thanking you, Gentleman! [*Then they turn to* LADY HELEN.]

THE FIRST WALTON—[*Repeating his bow, kissing her hand.*] We go now—thanking you for delicious supper, my lady.

THE SECOND WALTON—[*Doing the same.*] Very much thanking you, my lady.

THE THIRD WALTON—Next time we spik more in new Englees, maybe. Thanking you, my lady.

LADY HELEN—It was charming of you to come. Good-bye. [THE WALTONS *assemble as if for a curtain call, to bow a farewell to* SOLOMON.]

THE FIRST WALTON—At stylish function you give maybe sometime Wonderful Waltons will perform free for you, gentleman, many superb acrobatic acts. Good-bye, one and all. [*Bowing, and blowing one airy kiss from the finger-tips of their hands, they smile once more, and then march with high, elastic steps through the door at the right.*]

LADY HELEN—[*Turning from watching them back to* SOLOMON, *laughter in her eyes.*] You'll feel like Trimalchio—or some other opulent old Roman—when my Croatians do their superb acrobatic acts for your especial benefit. You must promise to let me be there to see them.

SOLOMON—[*Quietly, with a note that is faintly warning in his voice.*] You're very child-like, Lady Helen.

LADY HELEN—Is that why you are looking at me so sternly? Are you thinking that I've got my frock very soiled?

SOLOMON—I'm thinking that you've played very hard, and been very reckless.

LADY HELEN—So I have. It's sometimes very difficult to realise that this is a serious world—and that life is something more than a hilltop in the sun, with an adventure lurking back of every flower. There are so many things to make one smile, and the older one grows, and the more one is alone, the oftener one smiles to one's self. I don't say that they are always happy smiles—but just the fact of being alive is rather gay:

> "For to admire and for to see,
> For to behold this world so wide"—

only an Englishman would have thought of saying that. . . . [*She breaks off sharply and then resumes.*] Thank you for the set of Conrad's books. I love them. Do you know the South Sea Islands? We cruised among them all one winter. The stars are very wonderful. We lived on the yacht, and put in at every port that took our fancy. You should do that sometime—if only for the stars and the big strange nights. Where are the cigarettes? [*She pauses.*

*He lights a match for the cigarette that he gives her. She
draws at it, thoughtfully, suddenly silent.*]

SOLOMON—Go on.

LADY HELEN—There's nothing more. . . . I was just
rambling. Have I bored you? [*He looks at her without
answering. She smiles at his intentness.*] Now, what are
you thinking of, my friend?

SOLOMON—[*Slowly, quietly, almost coldly.*] I was
thinking of a shooting star, Lady Helen—a star that I
once saw fall from the sky into that dark garden of water
that lies between New York and the outer ocean. [*She
smiles ironically, understanding his meaning. He continues.*] I was a newsboy, and I had sold all my papers;
I was lying on the grass in Battery Park because that was
better than going to the place that I called home. I was
half asleep when I saw the lightning of the shooting
star. . . .

LADY HELEN—[*Looking at him again as he pauses.*]
And now what are you thinking of?

SOLOMON—I was thinking that there are better things
in life than cruising beneath the stars on the South Seas,
even.

LADY HELEN—It is very beautiful—cruising beneath the
stars on the South Seas; what is better?

SOLOMON—Purpose—for instance; the progress of one's
spirit upon a pilgrimage of achievement; the building of
one's life after the plan of one's dream. . . . When the
grass of Battery Park was my bed, an earl, to me, was as
legendary as the Santa Claus that drove his reindeer down
the chimney of more fortunate children at Christmas-time.
An earl's daughter was as remote as the farthest star in
the night. Yet here we are, Lady Helen—you and I.

LADY HELEN—Yes, here we are; you and I. . . .

SOLOMON—I suppose that I seem to you very conscious of all that I have got from life? Well, I am conscious of it. It's a great satisfaction to have got what one has wanted; and I've not stopped, you know, at getting money. I know the world, and all its finest things—its cities, its music, its literature and all its enjoyable games. I've thrust my hands into the past and touched history. In my house there are marbles and swords and fans, souvenirs of popes and emperors, warriors and queens, and immortal courtesans. I've touched the future, too. My money is building projects that will benefit generations not yet born.

LADY HELEN—It's power that you've really wanted—and have got, isn't it?

SOLOMON—Power—and the flavour of life at its rarest; and to know that, there is one thing more that I must have. I want you.

LADY HELEN—[*With uneasy irony.*] But I'm no longer a sufficiently precious object for the golden cabinet of your very successful life!

SOLOMON—[*Quietly.*] But I want you. . . .

LADY HELEN—That's rather ambiguous.

SOLOMON—I want an ambiguous thing—romance.

LADY HELEN—Oh, I see! [*There is a pause. A smile plays about her lips. He watches her closely. Presently she meets his eyes, and speaks a little sternly.*] But there is Alice Vance.

SOLOMON—[*Quietly.*] There *was* Alice Vance.

LADY HELEN—It means nothing to you at all, I suppose, that she cares for you?

SOLOMON—[*Very sincerely, then with lightness.*] If

she does, I'm sorry; but that's the usual tragedy of the heart, isn't it? Caring for someone who does not care for you?

LADY HELEN—[*With quiet and smiling irony as she quotes his words.*] I believe that it *is*—"the usual tragedy of the heart." And one tragedy, more or less, in a world of tragedies, doesn't matter . . . ?

SOLOMON—[*Choosing not to answer her directly; with delicate insinuation.*] We might go very far together—you and I.

LADY HELEN—And I'm not likely to go very far alone, I suppose.

SOLOMON—I don't know. I can't say. To me you seem singularly in need of someone to take care of you—to take care of you devotedly. I don't want you to disappear into the darkness, and there is a certain sort of outer darkness from which I can save you, always.

LADY HELEN—Poverty, you mean?

SOLOMON—Yes. You're very wonderful now, Lady Helen, but there's "tomorrow and tomorrow and tomorrow."

LADY HELEN—I know. And old age around the curve, and just one more pearl. . . . [*She looks at the ring on her finger, and laughs a little.*]

SOLOMON—One more pearl?

LADY HELEN—That's a joke you're not supposed to understand.

SOLOMON—[*Suddenly.*] Tell me—do you feel that I'd be a dull or repulsive companion on another cruise, for instance, on the South Seas?

LADY HELEN—It isn't what sort of companion you'd be. It's that I should have to cruise forever—among unknown islands, and on uncharted seas, if I once left port with you upon that journey.

SOLOMON—I see. Then try to think of me as the companion of more discreet pleasures; as a friend, very much at home, in the properly conducted life of a luxurious great lady.

LADY HELEN—[*After a pause.*] I wonder if I could. I'm afraid not.

SOLOMON—I wish that you'd be frank and explain to me just where the fine lines of your code are drawn.

LADY HELEN—Isn't it sufficient that they have been drawn so carelessly that you make me this ambiguous offer?

SOLOMON—You resent it?

LADY HELEN—Oh, no—no. . . . You probably know exactly what most things in the world are worth—even romance. Well—whatever is ahead for either of us, we have found life a strange adventure, haven't we? We've each come a long distance. The little newsboy has come a long way from his bed on the grass in Battery Park, and the child who was christened Victoria Helen Alexandria Varick has come a long way from the arms of that gracious Queen who was her godmother.

SOLOMON—And no one knows how much farther each of us has to go, Lady Helen, "tomorrow and tomorrow and tomorrow. . . ."

LADY HELEN—No, no one knows; but it's a part of the adventure to keep one's courage, and not to care too greatly how the wheel of fortune turns; for we must all go from the game, empty-handed at the end, and if we've played fairly I don't believe that we will mind, really, when the moment comes to blow out our candles, and sleep.

SOLOMON—You mean——?

LADY HELEN——I mean, my friend, that I am going to refuse your ambiguous offer, and all that it might lead to. And I really like you very much. And it's a temptation, too, to think of the sheer decency of having enough money again for one's whims—which seems so much more important, somehow, than one's needs. But it isn't quite cricket, according to my topsy-turvy ethics, to take away a woman's lover—though I suppose I shouldn't hesitate a moment if you were her husband! But Alice loves you; and there's something about love—true love—that's very touching to me; something at which even I cannot smile. . . . Another cigarette, Monsieur, s'il vous plaît. . . . [*Again he lights a cigarette for her. He watches the flame of the match burn down; then he speaks quietly.*]

SOLOMON—You must have been very much in love, once.

LADY HELEN——I was.

SOLOMON—And you must have been very much hurt.

LADY HELEN——I was.

SOLOMON—And then—what happened?

LADY HELEN——[*Smiling again, making an effort to veer away from the mood of emotion that has established itself between them.*] I ran very hard, and played very recklessly, and fell down and soiled my frock, and that's all.

SOLOMON—Didn't he care for you?

LADY HELEN——Not the least bit in the world.

SOLOMON—And that was why——!

LADY HELEN——[*Cutting him short.*] Oh, no! That wasn't why I played hard—and ran recklessly. I knew from the very beginning that he didn't care for me. I knew, at least, that the way he cared was nothing to the way I cared for him. So I had made up my mind to do what was best for him. I was married, you see. [*She*

pauses.   Then she speaks again with a smile and a shrug.]
I had made up my mind never to see him again—just to
be a "good influence" in his life!

SOLOMON—Don't tell me any more if you don't want to;
but I— [*He touches her hand.*]   I do want to know,
because I do care for you,—what happened then?

LADY HELEN—Then? Oh, then he cheated at cards.   I
couldn't bear that.

SOLOMON—And that ended it, of course?

LADY HELEN—It should have, but it didn't.   That's all.

SOLOMON—How long ago did this happen?

LADY HELEN—So long ago that it's not real now.   Let's
talk of something else.

SOLOMON—You've stopped thinking of him?

LADY HELEN—Oh, I still wonder sometimes why it was
that I—of all women, should have cared for him—of all
men.   I have stopped trying to explain to myself; but
now you know why I could never kill something in another woman's heart that might be as beautiful as the thing
that life killed in mine. . . . You told me over the telephone that you had an early dinner engagement.   Oughtn't
you to be going?

SOLOMON—[*Looking at his watch like a man who has
been a little lost in his own thoughts.*]   Yes, I should have
gone before.   May I take you or send you anywhere?

LADY HELEN—No, thank you.   Good-bye.

SOLOMON—Don't forget that you are dining at my new
house, a week from tonight.

LADY HELEN—I won't.

SOLOMON—[*Rising and bending over her hand, evidently
conquering a desire to be less casual.*]   We have not finished talking yet; and we have a great deal more to say

to each other.   Some day we will say it.   For you and I
—we have, each of us, something of the incommunicable
technique of magnificence. . . . Good-bye.   Although I
had hoped to see you quite alone today, I enjoyed your tea
party, Croatians included, very much. . . . I will telephone. . . . [*He leaves her quickly, going through the door
at the right.   The orchestra returns and assembles itself
on the balcony.   A waiter hovers near* LADY HELEN.   *She
signals to him.*]

LADY HELEN—Bring me some more cigarettes.   [*He
moves away quickly, knowing quite well, evidently, the
sort she wants.   The orchestra begins to play.   She listens.   Very quickly the waiter returns and places the
cigarettes before her.*]

THE WAITER—Anything more, my lady?

LADY HELEN—No . . . l'addition.   [*He presents the ac-
count.   She makes a movement to open her purse.   Then
she notices the amount of the bill.   She holds out her hand
and demands with a trace of impatience.*]   The pencil,
please.   [*After hesitating one instant he furnishes it; then
while she is writing her name he hurries to speak to the
maître d'hôtel who is passing.*]

WAITER—Her ladyship asked for a pencil.   The orders
are not to let her sign here any more.

[*From the corner of her eyes* LADY HELEN *sees them
whispering.   She is playing with the check, worrying it
into a tube as she rolls it nervously between her fingers.
Presently she catches the eye of the maître d'hôtel and signals to him.   He comes slowly, apologetically, pleasantly,
casually.*]

LADY HELEN—I wanted to speak to you about my maid,
Jean.   She's an excellent maid.   I've had her for years;

but I think she could get a great deal more money if she
went to someone else. They pay much more over here than
we do at home, don't they?

JEAN—Some get very good wages, my lady. Does she
want a place in New York?

LADY HELEN—She doesn't *want* a place anywhere except
with me; but she ought to take one. I pay her only fifty
pounds a year—how many dollars is that?

JEAN—Not quite two hundred and fifty, my lady.

LADY HELEN—Well, she can do much better than that.
I've told her so: but she's not very ambitious and if I try
to find a place for her she thinks it's because I want to
get rid of her. If you hear of anyone's wanting a maid
you might telephone me. You can't recommend her too
highly, Jean. . . . I don't know how I shall get along
without her.

JEAN—I'll not forget, my lady; and I'll telephone if I
hear of anything.

LADY HELEN—Thanks, Jean. Do you like America,
Jean?

JEAN—[*Slowly.*] It isn't Paris, and it isn't London;
and it isn't Cairo, my lady; but I do very well here. I
can't say that I'm not glad to be here, though there is
something about Cairo that one never forgets. It was in
Cairo that I first served your ladyship, and her party.

LADY HELEN—Was it? It's been so long. . . . Yes,
there's something about Cairo that one never forgets. . . .
The world and his wife will be coming in to dinner soon,
I expect?

JEAN—Yes, my lady. We'll begin to fill up very
quickly, now.

LADY HELEN—[*Slipping a ring off her finger and round*

the check which she has rolled into a small cylinder.]   I'll
give this to you—and will you give my waiter his tip
for me?

JEAN—[*Taking the check with the ring about it, amazement and concern in his eyes.*]   Certainly, my lady! Good
evening, my lady. [*She rises. He picks up her gloves
that have fallen to the floor. She accepts them with a
smile.*]

LADY HELEN—Good evening, Jean.

[*He is still bowing, his eyes on the ring about the check,
as she disappears—not too quickly—through the door at
the right.*]

THE CURTAIN FALLS

THE THIRD ACT

An evening, a week later.

A room, designed and furnished in the style of the late Italian Renaissance, in RUDOLPH SOLOMON's *house.*

At the back are two wide doorways, magnificently curtained; one leads to the hall; the other to a drawing-room. At the left is still another doorway, opening into the music-room. At the right are two windows, the mediæval iron shutters of which are set ajar so that one sees outside a lamplit area of upper Fifth Avenue.

ALICE VANCE *is standing at the end of a long table, talking to* RUDOLPH SOLOMON.

ALICE—[*With some difficulty, not looking at him.*] So you see—I'm going away— [*She breaks off.*]

SOLOMON—[*Quietly.*] I see.

ALICE—[*Suddenly moving as if to leave him.*] And that's all, I think.

SOLOMON—Wait— [*She pauses. He continues after an instant, rather hesitantly.*] You will let me help you in any way, at any time, that I can?

ALICE—Oh, yes. . . . [*She smiles.*]

SOLOMON—Remember! [*His voice is compassionate.*]

ALICE—[*Quickly.*] Don't be sorry for me, Rudolph! These things always end. I never expected anything else but this some day. [*He does not answer. She continues lightly, casually.*] And now I'm going to have a good

68

time at your party. I'm sorry I couldn't come earlier, but
I stayed to rehearse the girl who is to take my place in one
of the scenes that she's a little bit afraid of— Are there
many people here?

solomon—Most of those who came to dinner have gone;
but I suppose others will be drifting in from other parties
presently.

alice—Lady Helen and Mr. Charteris are still here, of
course? I'm to sing for him, and he's to play for me.

solomon—Yes, they are here. And the Wilderings.
Miss Ashley came after her play, and I was expecting another friend of Lady Helen's—Edward Thayer, the young
man I met the other day so unexpectedly at the Ritz, if
you remember. He was to come to dinner, but he couldn't
get here; however, I hope he'll turn up. It will probably
be a pleasant surprise for her to find another old friend
among those surrounding her tonight.

alice—You think of her always now. But after I am
gone—you will think of me too sometimes, Rudolph, won't
you?

solomon—I will, of course. I will think of you very
often, Alice.

[lady helen *enters with* lady wildering *and* charlotte ashley *from the drawing-room at the back.*]

lady helen—[*To* solomon.] I'm racing Charlotte
about the house on a very impressionistic tour of inspection. [*To* alice.] I'm so glad you've come. You're
going to sing? [*To the others.*] Do you know Miss Vance?

lady wildering—Oh, yes. Good evening, Miss Vance.

alice—Good evening, Lady Wildering. [alice *and*
charlotte *exchange greetings.*]

lady helen—There's one thing more that I must show

you at once, Charlotte. [*She goes to the doorway of the music-room, and stands directing* CHARLOTTE's *attention to something on the far wall beyond.*]   Look at it from here.

CHARLOTTE—Oh, the Gainsborough! How amazing!

SOLOMON—Have you ever seen that particular picture before, Lady Helen? It's from the Kingston collection.

LADY HELEN—Well, rather. . . . It's my great-great-grandmother. I'm always meeting my relatives on other people's walls, and sometimes I have to be introduced to them—if they were sold off before my day, I mean—but not to Georgiana, Duchess of Staffordshire. She was our greatest favourite—and we kept her as long as we could possibly afford her, until I was six or seven at least! Edith and I have found something else that will interest you, Charlotte; King James' chair.

CHARLOTTE—King James' chair! From Varick Hall?

LADY HELEN—[*Turning to* SOLOMON.] Did I tell you that King James the First came to Varick Hall one time, and everything went so merrily that he sent for the court painter to come and do a portrait of him, to be presented as a souvenir to his host? He was painted sitting in that very chair, and for three hundred years the chair stood against the wall, just under the picture.

SOLOMON—I should like to have the portrait, too. Where is it now?

LADY HELEN—I don't know.

SOLOMON—I should like to have it hang above the chair.

LADY HELEN—[*Gaily.*] If you really want it, my friend, you'll get it!

CHARLOTTE—Where is King James' chair?

SOLOMON—Let me show you.

LADY HELEN—And take a look at the tapestries in the

same room, Charlotte. I maintain that they are not good. They are almost the only things in the house that aren't, I admit, but take a glass and examine them, and see what you think.

SOLOMON—Lady Helen and I have had a controversy about those tapestries. It may be that she is right. I hope not. This way——

[CHARLOTTE *follows him through the doorway at the left.* LADY WILDERING *is examining through a reading glass some drawings from a portfolio on the table.* LADY HELEN *sits on the carved walnut bench in front of the table, and leans against it as if a little tired;* ALICE VANCE, *who has been listening, comes and sits at the other end.*]

ALICE—[*To* LADY HELEN.] It seems to me that you know something about everything in the world, Lady Helen.

LADY HELEN—Oh, no. Englishwomen aren't educated, you know; our brothers are, but we aren't. My father used to say that my education cost him less than his oysters.

LADY WILDERING—[*Looking up.*] But his capacity for oysters was unlimited.

LADY HELEN—Even so, I don't believe that I was ever educated three hundred pounds' worth in my life. That is—how many dollars?

ALICE—About fifteen hundred dollars; yet you know everything.

LADY HELEN—Don't let me dazzle you, my child. I'm a very ignorant woman, as you'll find out in good time, if you see me often.

ALICE—I'll probably keep my illusions about you, then —for I'm to sail next week. I'm going to Paris to live.

LADY HELEN—[*Slowly.*] You are leaving New York?

ALICE—[*Quietly.*] Yes. I gave in my notice at the theatre a week ago.

LADY HELEN—But isn't that a very stupid thing for you to do—to leave when you're such a success?

ALICE—Singing every night is hurting my voice, and I want something more than a musical comedy career. I'm restless here. So I'm going back to my teacher in Paris, and the next time I'm a success I hope it will be as Mimi or Butterfly. [*She is very quiet and impersonal. There is the barest pause as* LADY HELEN *looks at her searchingly.* ALICE *adds lightly, rising.*] Don't you want some supper? I do. [*She moves toward the door.* LADY HELEN *catches her hand and detains her an instant.*]

LADY HELEN—The very best of luck—Butterfly—"one fine day." [ALICE *smiles at her steadily.*]

ALICE—Thanks. [*She goes quickly.* LADY WILDERING *finishes with the drawings, and rises.*]

LADY WILDERING—A charming girl, isn't she? Emmett and I must be going; he's very tired. One gets no rest in New York.

LADY HELEN—[*Rising and standing at the end of the table, looking down at it, speaking a little shyly in her warm, husky voice.*] I want to tell you, Edith, how sporting it was of you and Emmett to come tonight. Rudolph Solomon has everything except friends; and he loves giving parties, even these nondescript affairs to all sorts of odd people. I like them, myself, but I know, of course, that you and Emmett haven't my passion for odd people; and neither has Harry nor Charlotte. . . . So—thanks . . .

LADY WILDERING—We'd do anything for you, Helen; you know that. Besides, your friend is a very remarkable man. Meeting him has been a great pleasure for us.

LADY HELEN—Oh, Edith. . . . I understand what you're all about—bless you!

LADY WILDERING—[*A little self-consciously.*] What are we all about?

LADY HELEN—It's a conspiracy. You're determined to send my stock up so high that Rudolph Solomon will do me the honour of asking me to be his wife, although he doesn't want to in the least. Don't deny it, Edith! There *is* such a conspiracy; I know it, perhaps I will join it myself. . . . There's "tomorrow and tomorrow and tomorrow" to be got through with, somehow; and one must get used to the idea of the setting sun. [*She becomes conscious of the table which her finger-tips are touching.*] This table came from the Palazzo Cavalli. . . . The sun sets for cities and races, too. Venice is in the twilight of her greatness now. And the families that were glorious when she was glorious are only the ghosts that haunt her lagoons. . . . [*There is a suggestion of reverence in the way her fingers play on the wood. All her mocking gaiety is gone, and she speaks with deep feeling.*] I'm not very modern, I suppose. I love old things, things that one seems to share with time. . . . It gives me a strange, warm, homesick feeling to see my great-great-grandmother's picture there on that wall. [*She goes to look at the picture, through the doorway into the next room.*] How young she was once—my great-great-grandmother! The sun never set for her. She fell from her horse, in the hunt, and died when she was thirty, soon after Gainsborough had made her immortal.

LADY WILDERING—Where is Sargent's portrait of you?

LADY HELEN—[*Hurriedly coming back from the doorway.*] It was sold. I believe that I'm hanging in the

Luxembourg now. It's amusing, isn't it, how far and wide the winds of Fate sometimes carry the leaves from the same tree.

[CHARLOTTE *and* SOLOMON *return.*]

CHARLOTTE—I've seen the famous chair.

LADY HELEN—[*Gay again.*] You must have taken a very casual look at it. I suppose you didn't sit in it—as I did, for the first time in twenty years. It was rather thrilling—to sit there, thinking. . . . My brother and I used to play King and Queen in it—when we were children. We were a very royal pair and believed in having everybody flogged and thrown into the egg-shaped dungeon of our forefathers—particularly a religious aunt who was one of our rare white sheep, and was very much given to worrying about our poor little souls. . . .

[SIR EMMETT *and* HARRY CHARTERIS *enter from the drawing-room at the back.*]

SIR EMMETT—[*To* LADY WILDERING.] Oh, here you are. Are you ready to go?

LADY WILDERING—I have been waiting for you.

SIR EMMETT—[*To* SOLOMON.] It's very difficult to take one's self away from this delightful house of yours, Solomon. We've just been looking at the Chinese jades. I hope you will let us come again.

LADY WILDERING—[*To* LADY HELEN.] Don't forget about our plans for the summer—but we will see you before we return to Washington, of course.

LADY HELEN—[*Lingeringly.*] I won't forget, Edith dear. . . .

LADY WILDERING—[*To* SOLOMON.] And I hope that we will see you again—in Washington, perhaps.

SOLOMON—Thanks; you will, Lady Wildering.

LADY WILDERING—[*To others.*]   Good night.

CHARLOTTE AND HARRY—[*Together.*]   Good night.

LADY HELEN—Good night, Edith—Emmett—bless you.
[SIR EMMETT *also nods to the others as he shakes hands
with* SOLOMON, *near the doorway to the hall.*]

SIR EMMETT—Au revoir, then, and thanks again for the
pleasure of seeing your beautiful house.

SOLOMON—Au revoir.   [*The* WILDERINGS *go, attended by
a servant who has been waiting to usher them from the*
room.   SOLOMON *turns to* CHARLOTTE ASHLEY.]   But you've
had no supper, I believe, Miss Ashley?

CHARLOTTE—I was just going to ask you to take me in
and give me some.

SOLOMON—[*To* LADY HELEN *and* HARRY.]   Perhaps you
will come, too?

LADY HELEN—Not—just now.   [*She sits on the bench
again, glancing at* HARRY; *it is obvious that she wishes to
talk to him.*]

SOLOMON—[*Lingering an instant.*]   There's nothing you
want?

LADY HELEN—Nothing.   Oh—I would like some champagne, I think.

SOLOMON—You shall have it, at once.   [*To* CHARLOTTE.]
This way——

[*They go.   There is a pause.*   LADY HELEN *motions*
HARRY *to sit beside her.   He does so.*]

LADY HELEN—[*Laughing suddenly as* HARRY's *troubled
glance makes her a little self-conscious.*]   Harry dear, I
don't know whether I am more amused or touched by this
deep, dark plot to get me properly married and taken care
of! It makes me feel like an ugly duckling carefully
manœuvred by sympathetic relatives. But why do you all

take so much trouble about me? I'm not a débutante—and Rudolph Solomon is neither a shy nor an impressionable youth waiting for someone to give him his cue. He knows perfectly well what he's about—and he, too, knows that I'm not a débutante.

HARRY—There has been no manœuvring. It is true that we are concerned about you, and that we've not hesitated at showing our affection for you; but why shouldn't we wear our hearts on our sleeves, for your sake?

[*A servant enters.*]

LADY HELEN—[*Quickly.*] Here's the champagne. I'm frightfully thirsty. Don't you want some? [*They are served. She glances at the servant, speaking with an assumption of carelessness.*] You might leave it there.

SERVANT—Yes, my lady. [*He leaves the tray, with the bottle, on the table, and goes.* LADY HELEN *drinks rather eagerly.*]

LADY HELEN—It's very good, isn't it? It would be—in Rudolph Solomon's house. [*There is the sound of dance music somewhere in the distance.* LADY HELEN *talks swiftly, a little hectically—as if to forbid certain emotions that might intrude upon the moment.*] They're going to dance. But I'm in no mood for dancing tonight; however, one evening not long ago I was. I don't know why, but I wanted to dance, and it always seems to me rather shabby not to respect one's own mood. But I had no one to dance with, and nowhere to dance. Then I remembered how shocked Blossom had been because the telephone girl at some hotel where we had tarried a few days had suggested their going to a place where you bought a ticket, and got a partner with it—an "instructor," he's called. I always remember things, so I remembered the name of the place—

you couldn't very well forget it—it was known as the Garden of Eden. It's closed now; they eventually committed the first sin, I suppose; but it was still open the night I went.

HARRY—You don't mean to say——

LADY HELEN—[*Interrupting.*] Oh, yes! I went and danced until five o'clock in the morning, and got a prize!

HARRY—A prize!

LADY HELEN—Yes, for dancing longer than any other woman in the room. I danced for hours and hours and wore out three partners, and I wasn't a bit tired when everyone else, even the Swedish couples, had finished. The prize was a purse—not in the best of taste, of course, but it made the black girl who comes to wash the steps outside our flat every morning quite happy. I gave it to her as I was going in. I'd gone to breakfast at Child's with my last partner—a little boy from the Argentine who'd never been in New York before, and who was homesick for someone to talk Spanish with. . . . The black girl always calls me "honey," and she's always chewing a gum. A great many people chew a gum in America, I notice. I've tried it. It makes me feel rather like a cow. . . . Another glass, please. [*He pours the champagne. She adds in a very different voice.*] You, and Charlotte, and Edith, and Emmett, are all great dears—bless you. . . .

HARRY—Oh, Helen—I— [*She sets down her glass, her eyes compassionate at the hurt in his voice.*]

LADY HELEN—[*Quietly.*] What is it? Tell me, my dear.

HARRY—[*Hopelessly.*] You know I've always loved you. [*She is silent; he continues.*] But I'm not a mag-

nificent person—and magnificence is in your blood. I
can't afford you. Only—I can't bear to see you drift,
like this. You're like a lost child in an uncaring crowd.
You think it's fun—being lost in a crowd; but after a
while night will come, and you'll get tired, and maybe
frightened— [*He breaks off and tries to laugh; then resumes.*] I suppose I'm very sentimental, but— If only
you were safe! Not drifting, not lost! I can't bear it!
[*Again he breaks off.*]

LADY HELEN—[*Quietly.*] Don't bother about me. I'm
very clever at taking care of myself.

HARRY—That isn't true. I know all sorts of things
you've done that prove that you know nothing about taking
care of yourself. I happen to know that you sold some
pearls in London for a few hundred pounds or so, when
they were worth thousands. What you'll do when they
are all gone——

LADY HELEN—[*Interrupting with a smile, trying to answer lightly.*] Let us hope that I'll buy others. The
ones I had from Bruce couldn't have had any deep sentimental associations.

HARRY—Very well, then, let us hope that you will buy
others; but if it happens that you don't—after your last
pearl is gone— [*She looks at her bare fingers with widen-
ing eyes, but he does not see her moment of panic. He is
looking instead, with bent head, into his clasped, empty
hands, as he continues.*] I'm sorry that I can't offer you
myself and all my worldly possessions with something of
a fine flourish, but—there aren't any worldly possessions,
as I've told you, to speak of—and——

LADY HELEN—[*Interrupting warmly with sudden tears
in her eyes and a smile.*] And if there were do you think

I could ever litter your life with the broken-up fragments of my own—even if I drifted for ever——?

HARRY—[*Still not looking at her.*] I used to dream that some day you might let me pick up the pieces.

LADY HELEN—Harry—I've a very great, a very real affection for you; but if I were your mother I wouldn't let you marry *me!* I wouldn't have let you do it even when I was a girl, and you were a very romantic boy, and there were no other reasons than my extravagance and my—my recklessness. Some men can afford such extravagances, and cope with such recklessness . . . I thought Bruce was one; but not you, my dear——

HARRY—[*Passionately interrupting.*] If Rudolph Solomon is one—then in God's name marry *him!* But don't go on like this— [*He breaks off.*]

LADY HELEN—Another glass, please. [*He pours the champagne for her, frowningly. She continues quietly in answer to his look.*] Yes, the time has come when I sometimes take the unnecessary glass. But don't frown . . . I will make port if I can, and drift no longer. [*Suddenly she lifts her glass, her voice thrilling as she speaks.*] To England!

HARRY—[*Repeating solemnly.*] To England!

[*They drink; her eyes are shining and her lips quivering a little as she puts down her glass.* RUDOLPH SOLOMON *enters.*]

LADY HELEN—[*To* SOLOMON, *turning away from* HARRY, *who finishes draining his glass, sets it down, and goes out quickly as if to avoid their notice.*] Have the Wonderful Waltons come? And have you provided milk and pastries?

SOLOMON—[*Smiling as he comes and stands before her; she has not risen from her seat on the long bench in front of the refectory table against which she leans as she smiles up at him.*] I've told you before that you are very child-like, Lady Helen.

LADY HELEN—I remember—the soiled frock, and all the rest of it.

SOLOMON—You do remember the rest of it, then?

LADY HELEN—Yes—all of it.

SOLOMON—You remember an offer——

LADY HELEN—An ambiguous offer; yes.

SOLOMON—Which you refused?

LADY HELEN—Yes—though I admit to you frankly that I was tempted. It quite dazzled me to think that I should never have to bother about bills again, or try to do sums in dollars and then do them all over again in pounds.

SOLOMON—[*Not smiling.*] You remember the reason that you gave as the cause of your refusal?

LADY HELEN—Yes.

SOLOMON—That reason no longer exists. Alice Vance sails next week, to remain in Paris indefinitely.

LADY HELEN—I know. She told me.

SOLOMON—Well . . . ?

LADY HELEN—[*Quietly.*] You seem in hot haste, my friend, to be off with the old love and on with the new.

SOLOMON—[*Sitting on the bench, at the other end opposite her and speaking deliberately.*] I have thought of you, and you only, for months. I know you very well; at least, I think I know you very well. You fascinated me from the moment I met you three years ago, in London—when you used to let me invite you to luncheon sometimes—and nearly always forgot to come . . . or—when you came—forgot my name. You never could remember whether it was David or Abraham or Solomon. [*He smiles ironically.*]

LADY HELEN—I have always been stupid about names.

SOLOMON—[*His smile goes.*] Particularly about your own. [*She lifts her head and looks at him. He continues quickly.*] Oh, I know that if it were not so, you would still be forgetting mine; but if mine were yours, would you be as careless of it as you have been of your own? [*She stares at him; he stares at her; each searches the other's eyes. His voice is low and insistent.*] Would you?—I wonder?

LADY HELEN—[*Gravely.*] If your name were mine? Are you asking me to marry you?

SOLOMON—I want to ask you to marry me. But—I'm very proud of my name. That may seem a little silly to one whose ancestors have written themselves down, generation after generation, in the history of England, but I *am* proud of it. And it hurts me to give it into the keeping of one who has been as careless of the traditions and glories of her own—as you.

LADY HELEN—[*In a low voice.*] This is a strange wooing.

SOLOMON—Yes, it is a strange wooing, indeed. Strange for me. [*He takes both her hands and, crossing them, holds them a little roughly; there is an angry, impatient note, too, in his voice as he continues.*] I'm not a sentimentalist; and I'm not a weakling. When I've thought of marriage I've thought of a mother for the children that I've hoped to have. Health and dignity and simple goodness—these were to be her characteristics. I've known women well enough to realize that most of them determine their fates according to their temperaments. But you,

Helen,—what sort of woman are you? A mother who never had a child? An artist without a talent? A courtesan born to the purple? What are you?

LADY HELEN—[*Simply.*] It doesn't matter.

SOLOMON—[*Decisively.*] But it does matter! For I love you. And I think you ought to be my wife. [*She looks at him, startled for an instant. He is still holding her hands, looking at them, not at her, frowning. For an instant neither speaks; then he continues, more to himself than to her.*] I didn't know I loved you until that day when you refused— [*He breaks off, and then continues.*] But for a week, now, I have known, ever since that first intimate moment together when I found you capable of deep and exquisite feeling; when—[*he lifts his eyes to hers, and he smiles ironically as he adds*]—I looked into your heart and found there your love for another man— the thing, I suppose, that cut you adrift from your kind, and sent you, soiled and broken, to me. [*There is deep pain in his mood, not only for her but also for himself. She feels this, and although she answers gently there is something of the pain of a cry in her voice.*]

LADY HELEN—No, no—it wasn't that! It wasn't love for anyone that cut me adrift. Whatever has happened, it wasn't that. It's just that my life has been, from the very beginning, one of these mistakes that sometimes happen. No one is responsible—except myself . . . and I don't think it would be very wise of you to marry me, really.

SOLOMON—Hush! No other woman belongs here—in my house—except you. . . . Who was the man?

LADY HELEN—What man?

SOLOMON—The one you cared for?

LADY HELEN—It doesn't matter, does it? . . . A name means nothing.

SOLOMON—You are right. It's only the fact itself that is important. But do you—do you ever see him now?

LADY HELEN—No. I don't even know where he is. I have never heard of him since that dreadful night when he cheated at cards. Everything ended then. And if ever I should see him again we would not—we could not—even speak,—not as strangers speak, even.

SOLOMON—All the same he is the ghost in your heart. How do you know what might happen if ever you should see him again?

LADY HELEN—[*With greater concern for him than for herself.*] Rudolph—it was such a little love—it died so soon, that it was like a child from that Never Never Land where nothing is quite real. . . . And if its ghost has walked in my heart perhaps that is because ghosts have a way of haunting empty places. [*She is smiling.*]

SOLOMON—[*With sudden resolution.*] Will you marry me? [*She does not instantly answer. He continues, humbly, anxiously.*] Do you care for me—at all?

LADY HELEN—[*Hesitantly, being very honest.*] I—I like you. I've great respect for you. And I can see how life with you would be very easy—very easy and very beautiful. I do, really, and of course you know that if you want me to marry you I should be quite mad if I refused.

[SOLOMON'S *silence and the glance between them indicates that he finds her answer enough. Then, after an instant, he takes a key from his pocket, picks up a small metal box from the table, opens it, replaces the key, and holds the box toward her, trying to speak casually.*]

SOLOMON—You've been selling these, one by one. They

were given to you by your family—not your husband—
and you kept them as long as you could. Put them on
again.

LADY HELEN—[*In a low, astonished voice as she lifts a
string of pearls from the box and, bending her head, winds
it about her throat.*] Thanks. . . .

SOLOMON—[*Again seizing her hands.*] You *will* be good,
won't you? You're so reckless; but you will take care—
won't you? And let all the old miserable gossip die?

LADY HELEN—I'll take care; I promise. I *will* be good.
I'll be quite a reformed character, Rudolph, if you talk to
me like that!

SOLOMON—[*In a low voice, now.*] Thanks. . . . [*She
turns away, afraid to let him see her face, and read all that
she feels at the moment. The introduction of the Fisher-
Girl song, played on the piano, floats out.* LADY HELEN,
to steady herself, reaches for her glass of champagne.
SOLOMON *sees the gesture, and whispers*] No, dear . . .
[*as he catches back her hand and lifts it to his lips. She
is content to let him hold it so for an instant. The music
fills the pause. Suddenly she lifts her head.*]

LADY HELEN—Poor Harry! [*She releases herself from
his handclasp and rises, her eyes filled with tears as she
whispers.*] I'll be back—in a moment.

[*She goes swiftly out through the doorway into the hall.*
ALICE VANCE *begins singing. . . . As the first stanza of the
Fisher-Girl song ends,* CHARLOTTE ASHLEY *enters from the
door of the drawing-room at the back.* ZELLITO *follows
her presently.*]

SOLOMON—[*Rising.*] I hope you "did yourself well,"
as you English say, Miss Ashley.

CHARLOTTE—Much too well, Mr. Solomon. A woman's first business these days is not to do herself well. [*She moves toward the music-room.*] That was Miss Vance singing, wasn't it?

SOLOMON—Yes.

CHARLOTTE—And Harry Charteris is playing for her, I'm sure. [*She goes into the room at the left as* ZELLITO *strolls toward* SOLOMON. *The second stanza begins. Both* SOLOMON *and* ZELLITO *are gripped by its poignant beauty.*]

ZELLITO—[*As the song ends.*] Poor Alice! [SOLOMON *looks up.*]

SOLOMON—She will be an artist some day, Zellito.

ZELLITO—So, you are letting her go?

SOLOMON—She wishes to go.

ZELLITO—You know why. *Eh bien,* everyone cannot be loved; but if you cannot make her happy, you can at least make her rich. That is something.

SOLOMON—[*A little awkwardly.*] She knows there is nothing I would not do for her.

ZELLITO—That is good. I, myself, prefaire generous men to faithful. But Alice—! [*She shrugs her shoulders, pityingly, and goes into the music-room.*]

[*A servant enters from the hall.*]

THE SERVANT—Mr. Edward Thayer.

[SOLOMON *turns, a little eagerly, as* EDWARD THAYER *enters. He wears business clothes, and his general appearance is that of strength and manliness.*]

SOLOMON—Thayer! I'm delighted. I was afraid you wouldn't get here.

THAYER—I've come direct from a fourteen-hour day at hard labor. I haven't had time to dress, you see, but I thought you wouldn't mind from what you said over the telephone.

SOLOMON—Of course not. . . . But you must tell me something more about yourself than I had from you in that telephone conversation this morning.

THAYER—[*Hesitantly.*] There's nothing much to tell. I've been in South Africa all this time—and I found I could stand the heat better than the cold. [*He puts in as if by way of explanation.*] Once I went prospecting in Alaska—but that was no good. [*He smiles to himself, and then continues briefly.*] But in South Africa where I went seeking my fortune I happened to find it. That's all.

SOLOMON—In true romantic fashion: a diamond mine, you said.

THAYER—Yes.

SOLOMON—[*Curiously.*] What sent you out there? When I met you with Rena Leslie in London, you seemed a pretty soft sort of chap to me—attractive, and all that; but scarcely one to go through the South African grind.

THAYER—[*Again hesitating as he speaks.*] You're quite right. Certain circumstances sent me there—things that you mustn't expect me to explain; and I went, hating it. I went because it was my only chance. For a while I drifted about, then I began to work. I worked at anything and everything—wherever a man was needed. After a while I found that some of the things I'd learned at the Boston Tech were useful after all; and then one day I stumbled upon my mine. It took time to work it—and I had to share it with the people whom I went to, on my knees, for the money needed to develop it. It just happened that they thought I'd made a pretty good record down there. I got the money and I've other mines now. And—that's all . . . I heard someone singing as I came in. Who is she? She has a lovely voice.

SOLOMON—[*With a start, evidently deeply impressed by* THAYER's *story.*] Alice Vance. I'm forgetting that you've been away so long that you probably know none of my guests. By the way, are you hungry?

THAYER—Very.

SOLOMON—Then come with me and have some supper first. There's one person here, however, to whom you will not have to be introduced.

THAYER—Who is that?

SOLOMON—[*Proudly.*] You had the privilege of know-ing her rather well in London once. Lady Helen Haden.

THAYER—Lady Helen Haden!

SOLOMON—You remember that I first met her with you and Rena Leslie?

THAYER—[*Flushing.*] Of course—but—I've heard— [*He pauses, self-consciously.*]

SOLOMON—[*Quietly, quickly, misunderstanding his con-fusion.*] I don't know what you've heard. But Lady Helen was divorced from Sir Bruce Haden some time ago, and is to become my wife—very soon, I hope.

THAYER—[*After a pause, also quietly.*] I am glad that I am to have the opportunity of meeting Lady Helen again, and of offering her my congratulations and best wishes. I hope that you will both be very happy.

SOLOMON—Thank you. You will see her presently. Shall we go to the dining-room now?

[*He leads the way.* THAYER *follows slowly, like a man a little lost in the maze of his own thoughts. The room is empty for an instant, then laughter is heard behind the curtains in the hall and a footman appears, ushering before him* MRS. LESLIE, *accompanied by a very young man—an Italian, obviously, who seeems vastly amused and entertained by all that she does.*]

MRS. LESLIE—[*To the servant; glancing about the room.*] This is all right; there's no one here. We'll wait while you tell Mr. Solomon.

THE SERVANT—What name, Madame?

MRS. LESLIE—Just say a "mysterious lady in black," and hurry.

SERVANT—Yes, Madame. [*He goes.*]

THE YOUNG MAN—How jolly you are! To drive by a house and stop just because you see lights! That *is* American.

MRS. LESLIE—[*Only half pleased by his attempt at a compliment.*] It isn't American exactly, but it *is* Rena Leslie. Of course, everyone can't do that sort of thing; but I——

[SOLOMON *enters, a little puzzled, but he smiles as he sees who is waiting. She breaks off speaking and stretches out both hands to him.*]

SOLOMON—Ah, Rena!

MRS. LESLIE—Rudolph! Count Paolo del Magiore, Mr. Rudolph Solomon. [*The men bow. She hurries with her chatter.*] I've just been back a week. I've been in the Orient, you know, for a year. I've been calling you up fifty times a day. You've been very wicked not to come to the telephone, but I know that you were out of town—or something. Somebody told me this was your new house, and the Count and I were passing, and decided to drop in on you. Are you having a party? And is it the sort that I can come to? Or have you a lot of queer people? If

it's very disreputable you must invite me to stay. The
Count wants to meet some American chorus girls.

SOLOMON—My dear Rena, I shall be delighted to have
you stay——

MRS. LESLIE—[*Interrupting.*] Then why didn't you
ask me properly, a week ago?

SOLOMON—I thought you'd only been back a week?

MRS. LESLIE—Yes, I have—and I want to make some
money right away. You must give me some tips on the
market. What shall I buy? And how much shall I pay?
And what shall I sell at? And how long will I have to
wait to get it? [*She breaks off as he laughs.*] What a
gorgeous house! You ought to like this room, Paolo. It's
Italian enough. I suppose everything in it is *real?* [*She
looks around with sharp, quick glances of inspection.*]

SOLOMON—I hope so! But if you want some tips you'll
have to wait until——

MRS. LESLIE—Oh! [*Her sharp utterance halts* SOLOMON'S
words. He turns about and, following her glance, sees that
LADY HELEN *has entered, followed by* HARRY CHARTERIS.
As they advance MRS. LESLIE *is like a snake coiled for defence or attack. There is a sharp pause.*]

SOLOMON—[*Pleasantly, seeing for the instant only* LADY
HELEN.] You know each other, of course?

LADY HELEN—Yes, it's Mrs. Leslie, isn't it? How do
you do?

[MRS. LESLIE *does not answer at once, nor does she see*
HARRY CHARTERIS *a little distance beyond* LADY HELEN.
SOLOMON *after an instant detects the strain of the moment,
and speaks sharply.*]

SOLOMON—I think you know Lady Helen Haden, Rena?
MRS. LESLIE—[*Also sharply, staring at* LADY HELEN.]

No, I don't! [*Then she turns to* SOLOMON.] I think I understand your not asking me to your party, after all. One hears a great many things in New York in a week. Come, Paolo! [*She makes a movement as if to go, but the young Italian has advanced quickly to* LADY HELEN *with a deep bow.*]

THE ITALIAN—Lady Helen—you do not remember me? [LADY HELEN *turns to him; her face is like marble, but her eyes concentrate upon him, gently, in a vain effort to remember. He hurries on charmingly.*] But how should you? When I was nine years old, you were my first love, Lady Helen. You came to Roma with my sister one Christmas from Switzerland where you both went to the same school.

MRS. LESLIE—I am going, Paolo!

HARRY—[*As she turns toward the door.*] One minute, Mrs. Leslie! [*She shrinks as she recognises him; he speaks sternly, angrily.*] If you do not remember Lady Helen Haden, perhaps you remember me! I was Lady Helen's partner at bridge the night that you——

LADY HELEN—[*Swiftly.*] Harry—it doesn't matter!

MRS. LESLIE—[*To* SOLOMON, *desperately.*] I don't know what these people are going to say, but must your old friends be insulted because they do not choose to recognise every woman who happens to come to your house?

SOLOMON—[*Quietly.*] Unless the lady who is to be my wife chooses to invite you to this house, Mrs. Leslie, you cannot expect me to be greatly concerned about the treatment you receive when you intrude.

MRS. LESLIE—Oh, so you're going to marry her! I *have* put my foot into it. Well, I'm sorry; and there's nothing more I can say, is there? Except good night. [*Again she makes a movement toward the door, but is intercepted by* HARRY.]

HARRY—You can say also, "I am sorry that I cheated at cards three years ago in Lady Helen Haden's house in London." You can say that, Mrs. Leslie, or I will take the trouble to tell the story to everyone who will listen to it in New York. You can promise also never to mention Lady Helen's name again, in return for her generosity in keeping silent about your—shall I call it your "mistake"?

[RUDOLPH SOLOMON *stares at* LADY HELEN *at the mention of cards. She faces him steadily, as if scarcely interested in what* MRS. LESLIE *is being made to say.*]

MRS. LESLIE—[*Bitterly, parroting* HARRY.] Very well, I promise. I won't mention her name again, and I am sorry that I cheated at cards three years ago in Lady Helen Haden's house in London. Is that sufficient?

HARRY—It will be when you have apologised for your rudeness to her tonight.

MRS. LESLIE—[*Haltingly.*] You're very difficult. But! —I apologise, Lady Helen. Come, Paolo. Good night— everybody!

[HARRY *turns away—as one who has finished a disgusting bit of business.*]

PAOLO—Good night, Lady Helen. [*He lifts her hand and kisses it with profound sympathy.*]

LADY HELEN—[*With the ghost of a smile.*] Good night, little Paolo.

MRS. LESLIE—[*From the doorway, venomously.*] You were quite right to call it a "mistake," Mr. Charteris; and Lady Helen's friend, Mr. Edward Thayer, was to blame for it, entirely.

HARRY—One cannot judge of that. [MRS. LESLIE, *followed by* PAOLO, *leaves the room.* HARRY *looks at* LADY HELEN, *who stands pale and trembling at one end of the long table; then at* SOLOMON, *who is as silent and rigid as she. He speaks first to one and then to the other.*] Well, that's done. I think she's learned her lesson and will remember it. . . . And now, good night. I won't wait for Charlotte. I don't want to hurry her away, and I must be about early in the morning. [*As there is no response from either of them, he hurries on, awkwardly.*] There's a ship sailing at noon and I'm going home. So this is good-bye as well as good night. You know, of course, that you have my best wishes for the best of luck, both of you.

SOLOMON—[*Gravely,—realising at last what he has heard.*] Thank you, Charteris. I think we both want Helen to be happy.

HARRY—Right-o. That's it. [*They shake hands;* CHARTERIS *goes to* HELEN.] Good-bye.

LADY HELEN—Good-bye, my Don Quixote. And I don't think you'll have to worry about one lady in distress, any more. [*She laughs a little.*]

HARRY—[*Sharply.*] Don't laugh! This is—forever. [*He bends and kisses her; then goes quickly from the room.*]

SOLOMON—[*After a pause.*] So it was Edward Thayer . . . ?

LADY HELEN—Yes.

SOLOMON—[*After a pause, speaking with some difficulty.*] Lady Helen— [*His tone is formal. She glances at him with sudden apprehension.*]

LADY HELEN—Yes? [*The word is barely whispered.*]

SOLOMON—I am going to say something which may seem strange to you. . . . I think it would be a mistake for us to go through with this marriage. . . . [*Her head goes up. He adds quickly.*] You don't understand—but you will in a moment. There is someone else who can explain better than I. Wait here— [*He goes toward the doorway, but she checks him with a gesture and a smile.*]

LADY HELEN—Don't bother to explain, my friend. It isn't necessary. I can imagine so many more reasons than anyone could possibly tell me. Good night—and I shall never regret those few moments when I felt that I knew a remarkable man very well indeed, and when I had the novel sensation of feeling safe and at peace. [*She bows her head again, by way of saying good night, and moves toward the hall, but he detains her before she reaches the door.*]

SOLOMON—Wait. . . . It is not always enough for a woman to feel safe and at peace. Do not go; there is someone here whom I want you to see. Please wait one moment.

LADY HELEN—If you insist, of course.

SOLOMON—[*In a low voice, hesitantly, with deep feeling.*] And I want you to know that—it was very difficult —for me—to do—what I am doing. [*He goes out quickly.*]

[*Left alone,* LADY HELEN *stares straight ahead of her, slightly bewildered. An orchestra begins to play for* ZEL-LITO *to dance in the music-room.* LADY HELEN *goes to the doorway and looks in. She is impersonal enough to appreciate the moment.*]

[*A servant enters and approaches her, offering his tray.*]
THE SERVANT—Some champagne, my lady?

LADY HELEN—[*With sudden weariness.*] Yes, please. [*Then she continues as he fills a glass for her.*] And will you tell Mr. Solomon that I was tired and did not wait to say good night?

THE SERVANT—Certainly, my lady. [*With a bow he leaves her, and continues on his way to the music-room.* LADY HELEN *moves toward the table like a person groping his way in a fog. Suddenly she sees the box from which* SOLOMON *took the pearls. She sets her glass, untouched, on the table; then, with a slow wintry smile, unwinds the pearls from her throat, drops them into the box, snaps it closely shut—and with one last lingering look about her —her head high—goes from the room, through the doorway into the hall. The music continues.* EDWARD THAYER *enters from the dining-room, looking for somebody. He is perplexed at not finding her. He goes to the doorway of the music-room, and looks inside, but turns away disappointed; then goes out through the door by which he entered. The music continues.* RUDOLPH SOLOMON *enters quickly. He is disconcerted at not finding* LADY HELEN *waiting, and goes into the hall, looking for her. Then he returns, as the music stops and there is a loud sound of hand-clapping from the next room, from which* ALICE VANCE *presently enters. He does not notice her until she speaks.*]

ALICE—[*Pausing as if only for a word on her way into the hall.*] Good night, Rudolph.

SOLOMON—[*Turning quickly.*] You're going?

ALICE—Yes.

SOLOMON—Do you know where Lady Helen is?

ALICE—I saw her there in the doorway a moment ago, while Zellito was dancing.

SOLOMON—[*With relief.*] Oh, I was afraid she'd gone.

[ALICE *turns to go. He watches her to the doorway, then
he calls her back in a low voice.*]   Alice . . . Come here.
[*She comes toward him slowly, a little amazed. He speaks
awkwardly.*]   I only want to tell you—I'm very unhappy,
myself—that I'm sorry if you've been unhappy, too; you
deserved better than you've had from me.

ALICE—[*Hopelessly, quietly.*]   You couldn't help it—
the way things have happened. I knew that. . . . Only
—I wish I could hate her, Rudolph. It would make it
easier, I think, but I can't.

SOLOMON—Don't try to hate Lady Helen, my dear. Her
life will soon concern neither you nor me.

ALICE—What do you mean?

SOLOMON—She was not for me. Like a fool I thought
I was the arbiter of her destiny; and all the time Fate
had happier plans for her. Fate has brought the one man
she has ever loved, here, to my house, of all places in the
wide world, to find her again.

ALICE—[*Drawing a sharp breath.*]   Rudolph! But—
[*She falters at the look on his face—her voice breaks
with anxiety as she continues.*]   But—that's why you're
unhappy, too! It's all right for me to be miserable—but
I can't bear it when you look like that.

SOLOMON—Don't worry. . . . It's . . . [*A servant enters
from the music-room.* ALICE *turns away quickly, and
walks to a window, staring out, trying to check her tears.*]

THE SERVANT—I was to give you a message from her
ladyship, sir; she wished me to say that she was tired and
would not wait to say good night.

SOLOMON—She's gone!

THE SERVANT—I think so, sir. Is there anything else,
sir?

SOLOMON—[*Wearily.*] Have you any champagne there?

THE SERVANT—Yes, sir. Shall I pour it, sir?

SOLOMON—No—just leave it.

THE SERVANT—Very good, sir.

[*He sets the tray on the table.* CHARLOTTE *and* ZELLITO *appear in the doorway of the music-room, laughing and talking.* ALICE *screams suddenly.*]

ALICE—Oh, my God!

SOLOMON—What is it?

ALICE—[*Staring out.*] A woman—run over!

[SOLOMON *hurries toward the window. The servant runs into the hall.* ZELLITO *and* CHARLOTTE *run to the second window.*]

CHARLOTTE *and* ZELLITO—[*Speaking together.*] What? Where?

SOLOMON—Was it a woman—I see something lying there——

ALICE—[*Hysterically.*] Yes, yes! I saw her go down! She was crossing the street for a taxi—but she wasn't quick enough! Good God! They ran over her and didn't even stop! There are some people now——!

CHARLOTTE—[*Peering out—*ZELLITO *moves away to the other side of the room, her face in her hands.*] They're lifting her up!

SOLOMON—[*Moving away toward the door.*] I must see what can be done for her.

ALICE—They're bringing her in here!

SOLOMON—[*Calmly to all of them as they turn toward him.*] Try not to think about it; I'll see that she's taken care of——

[*The servant appears in the doorway, white-faced and trembling.*]

THE SERVANT—Oh, sir——

ZELLITO—[*In a low, wailing voice, looking up, her eyes sombre.*] It was she—Lady Helen! I knew it was to happen some day!

THE SERVANT—[*Confirming* ZELLITO's *cry.*] Yes, sir— it was she—it was Lady Helen!

SOLOMON—Good God!

[*There is the sound of low, tortured laughter, and another servant enters carrying* LADY HELEN, *white and limp, in his arms. Her garments are torn and soiled, her hair is disarranged, and carries the damp and dirt of the street in its falling strands. Yet she is reassuringly composed as she directs the servant to place her on the bench in front of the table.*]

LADY HELEN—Just arrange me with my feet down, and my head up, please, so I can sit, like this. I don't want to lie down. [*He does as she directs.*] There—now I'm very comfortable. I've two perfectly good arms. [*She extends her arms along the table at the back and holds herself in place. The others, alarmed still and nervously concerned, recover a little from the sense of shock that for the moment bereft them of all power of thought and action.*]

SOLOMON—[*To the* SERVANT.] Telephone for a doctor at once.

SERVANT—Yes, sir. I think they're doing that now, sir —and somebody in a car went to find one, also. [*He goes out.*]

CHARLOTTE—Oh, Helen dear! Are you suffering?

LADY HELEN—[*With a sharp laugh and a long-drawn breath through tightly shut teeth.*] Well—rather! [*She almost falls backward—for an instant her head drops forward.* SOLOMON *hurries to her and forces some champagne from a glass on the table between her lips. There is grave concern about her.*]

SOLOMON—Helen—come—drink this! [*She lifts her head obediently and drinks, but does not seem to understand for the moment what is happening about her. A* SERVANT *enters.*]

SERVANT—A doctor will be here at once, sir.

SOLOMON—Have a bed made ready—

SERVANT—Yes, sir. [*He goes.* LADY HELEN *slowly comes out of her daze.*]

SOLOMON—[*To the others.*] I think you'd better wait in another room. She oughtn't to talk. [*The orchestra begins to play—a swift delicate air from Mozart.*] And tell them to stop that music! [*But the music has roused* LADY HELEN *to an understanding of what he is saying.*]

LADY HELEN—No—please—let them play. I love it. Mozart's so gay.

SOLOMON—[*With a significant glance at the others.*] Then—let them play.

[ALICE *hurries from the room, and although the music is suddenly softened as if at her suggestion, the gay dancing air goes on and on.* LADY HELEN *happens to see* ZELLITO *staring at her with brooding eyes.*]

LADY HELEN—[*With a twisted smile.*] So this is what —what you were keeping from me, Zellito, all the time?

ZELLITO—[*Uneasily.*] This—this is nothing—chérie.

LADY HELEN—I never believe lawyers and I never believe doctors—but I always believe fortune-tellers; only you

might have warned me, Zellito. . . . I would have picked
out a handsomer motor than that little noisy taxi—though
I don't believe a Rolls-Royce, with two men in front, could
have done a better job. . . . May I have—some champagne
—I'm getting— [*Her voice weakens.* SOLOMON *is quick
to hold a glass against her lips.* ZELLITO *with a sob hurries from the room.* CHARLOTTE *hovers near the doorway.*
LADY HELEN *sees her, and calls faintly.*] Charlotte.
[CHARLOTTE *comes near her.* LADY HELEN *turns her head
ever so little toward* SOLOMON.] Will you give me a cigarette—and light it—please? [*Still very casually, although
her voice is weak, to* CHARLOTTE *while he is doing so.*]
Don't worry about me. I hope it's the end. It ought to
be, at any rate—it would be such a regular Varick ending!
and one ought to have something in common with one's
family—even if it's only one's death. . . . Open that door
a little wider, Charlotte dear, so that I can see my great-
great-grandmother—there—across the river. . . . Where's
my cigarette? [CHARLOTTE, *choking back a sob, opens wide
the door, and hurries from the room.* LADY HELEN *smiles
up at* SOLOMON.] It's very considerate of you to have invited Georgiana, Duchess of Staffordshire, to meet me tonight. . . . [THAYER, *who has appeared in a doorway at
the back, in time to understand all that has happened, now
comes forward, trembling. She sees him and cries out.*]
It's—Ned! [*He flings himself down on the bench beside
her, and covers his face with his hands.*]

THAYER—[*In a whisper.*] Helen! [*She moves her arm
painfully to let it rest on his hair.*]

LADY HELEN—Ned—I don't understand—is it a dream,
my dear? It must be a dream.

SOLOMON—You are not dreaming. He has come back.

LADY HELEN—Now I understand why you— [*She looks at* SOLOMON *with sudden tears in her eyes.*]

SOLOMON—He's come back—a different man.

THAYER—[*Lifting his face.*] Yes—I've come back—a different man—a man who has wanted to thank you a million times. You did just the right thing for me—and oh, my God, I don't dare to think of what I did for you!

LADY HELEN—Don't think—now. Tell me—more—?

[SOLOMON *goes quietly out of the room.*]

THAYER—Not now.

LADY HELEN—Yes—tell me.

THAYER—[*Humouring her, but trying to be brief.*] I went to South Africa—but it doesn't matter where I went or what I did. The only thing that matters is that you saved me. I've worked. I've been honest. I've made good —and I don't know what I would have been except for you. And I've been in torture whenever I've thought of you. And one day—when I'd heard bad news of you—I decided to come and find you, if I could, and ask you if you'd forgive me—and marry me—and go back with me— [*She seems to bend her head. Glancing about, he realises that they are alone and hurries with all the things he is eager to say to her, not realising that, for the moment, she hears nothing.*] Of course I didn't know about Rudolph Solomon then . . . but I was glad when he told me you were going to marry him, for that set everything straight. You see, you were right, for I've found the girl you told me I'd find some springtime—only—you'd never have known about her if I had found that you needed me— [*He halts, a little confused at finding her so unresponsive, and looks up. Alarm is in his voice as he calls to her.*] Helen! Haven't you heard?

[SOLOMON *returns, impatient and anxious, a glass of brandy in his hand.*]

SOLOMON—[*Uneasily.*]   How is she?   Here's some brandy—it's stronger than champagne, and ought to dull the pain a little.   Helen——!

THAYER—[*Frightened.*]   I'm afraid she's fainted. . . . Helen!   [*Her eyelids stir and open.* SOLOMON *puts the brandy to her lips.*]

SOLOMON—Helen—drink!   [*She obeys.   Again she becomes conscious.*]

LADY HELEN—[*In a very small voice.*]   Ned—what were you telling me?   I'm all lost.   You came to find me, my dear. . . . What else?   It's so wonderful. . . . You said——?

THAYER—[*Steadily, realising at last all that it means to her.*]   I said that I'd come back to ask you to be my wife. [*A glance of understanding passes between him and* SOLOMON.]

LADY HELEN—[*Forcing back her pain; forcing back her emotion.*]   One more cigarette—and just one more glass of champagne—and—Rudolph——

SOLOMON—[*Catching up her limp hand, and holding it for an instant.*]   Yes?

LADY HELEN—Life with you would have been very easy and very beautiful, I know that; I was quite disappointed when you threw me over tonight.   I didn't know it was because Ned had come back.   And Ned——

THAYER—Yes?

LADY HELEN—Hold my hand. . . . We're drifting away together.   [ZELLITO, ALICE, *and* CHARLOTTE *have come back and have drawn together in a frightened, huddled group.* LADY HELEN *is smiling.* SOLOMON *is at one side of her and*

THAYER *at the other.   She speaks quite naturally but not very easily.*] Where's the champagne? You'll have to hold it, I'm afraid, Ned. My arms are tired— Hold it high. It's a toast. To England! . . . [THAYER *holds her glass so that she can touch it with her lips. She continues.*] "Oh, to be in England—now that April's there—" Only it isn't April—is it? My cigarette keeps going out. [THAYER *takes the glass from her. She clings to him convulsively, staring straight ahead of her.*] Just you—and my young great-great-grandmother, in her big hat—there —across the river. And the gay music! Everything else— is—going. It's like the theatre—when they turn out the lights before the curtain rises—on the next act. . . . [*Her heads falls forward. The last shudder tears her breath from her lips.*]

CHARLOTTE—[*With a cry, as she looks on.*] Helen!

SOLOMON—Helen! [*But there is no answer.*]

THAYER—[*Whispering.*] Helen! [*There is a sharp pause. He bends his head.*]

SOLOMON—Tell them they can stop the music now.

[ALICE, *who is standing in the doorway, signals into the next room by lifting her hand, and the music stops sharply, leaving a phrase broken.*]

CURTAIN

DADDY'S GONE A-HUNTING

DADDY'S GONE A-HUNTING

Produced at the Plymouth Theatre, New York, August 31, 1921, with the following cast:

JULIEN FIELDS	Frank Conroy
EDITH, his wife	Marjorie Rambeau
JANET, their child	Frances Victory
WALTER GREENOUGH	Lee Baker
THEODORE STEWART	Hugh Dillman
MRS. DAHLGREN	Helen Robbins
MRS. PRICE	Winifred Wellington
OSCAR	Manart Kippen
OLGA	Olga Olonova
LAURA	Jean Wardley
KNIGHT	John Robb

DADDY'S GONE
A-HUNTING

THE FIRST ACT

*A sitting-room which is also the dining-room of a flat
in that part of New York known as Harlem.*
It is the late afternoon of an autumn day.
JANET, *a little girl, nine years old, very conscious of
her new frock, is moving about a table which has been
set for three. Her place is designated by a chair
higher than the others. She is gravely interested and
pleased because of the unusual state with which it has
been arranged. She fingers the pink shades on the
four candlesticks and touches the little roses in the
low bowl. A buzzer rings. She races to the wall to
answer it through a speaking-tube, shouting down to
someone at the door, outside.*

JANET—Hello. Hello. . . . What do you want? . . .
This is me. . . . What? . . . Yes, I'm Janet. Who are
you? [*Her voices takes on a warmer note.*] Oh, Mr.
Greenough! No—mother's not here. No, nobody's here
but me and Mrs. Price, but mother's coming right back.
. . . Oh, please, please, please come up! [*A young, rather
pretty woman of a common type opens the swinging door
from the kitchen and hangs half-way around it, listening.*
JANET *continues.*] No, you won't be in the way, *at all.*
I'm pressing the button—now try. [*She clicks the button
that opens the door below and waits.*]

MRS. PRICE—Good gracious—who's that? The ice cream?

JANET—[*Through the tube to the person below.*] Try again. . . . Now . . . all right. [*She clicks the button again and again and then waits and turns to* MRS. PRICE *in delight.*] It's Mr. Greenough! It's Mr. Greenough! It's Mr. Greenough! I let him in. I let him in.

MRS. PRICE—Mr. Greenough! Be still—child—stop your noise and your dancing about—and tell me what——

JANET—[*Singing out.*] He's coming up and I'm going to show him the candles and the flowers and the new window curtains! [*She has raced to the door at the back and opened it; beyond is a narrow hall with a gas-jet burning on the other side.* JANET *stands outside the door looking down, singing.*] He's coming, coming, coming up the stairs——

MRS. PRICE—[*Following her and bringing her back into the room by a firm grasp on her shoulder.*] Hush! 'Sh! Don't yell like that. Your mamma wouldn't want such goings-on before Mr. Greenough! [*She shakes her into sobriety.*] Besides, Mr. Greenough don't care about the candles and the flowers. He has such things on his table every night. And you can't expect other people to be as excited as you are just because your papa's coming home.

JANET—Oh, but he's coming so far, Mrs. Price! All the way from Paris—clear across the ocean. And besides it's his birthday and mother's, too—and— [*Men's voices are heard from the stairs outside.* JANET *hushes and both she and* MRS. PRICE *listen attentively. Suddenly.*] That's him!

MRS. PRICE—[*Listening.*] He's got somebody with him. Gracious, I'm a sight! [*She catches a glimpse of herself in a mirror, then runs into the next room, already fingering her hair as two young men arrive at the open door.*]

JANET—[*Flashing toward them, but stopping short, suddenly shy.*] Come in.

[*They do so, a little amused. They are obviously not the sort of young men one meets in Harlem flats.* WALTER GREENOUGH *looks as if he might be romantic.* THEODORE STEWART *doesn't. But both give an instant impression of breeding and experience in the large world.* GREENOUGH *has a long box of flowers under one arm and another package under the other.* STEWART *is carrying a paper-wrapped basket.*]

GREENOUGH—Hello. [*He leads the way inside and indicates* JANET.] This is Miss Fields, Ned—Miss Janet Fields. [*She stands by, a little awkwardly. He proceeds to her.*] May I introduce a cousin of mine—? Mr. Theodore Stewart. He's very anxious to know you, Miss Fields.

STEWART—[*Gravely to the embarrassed but delighted child.*] How do you do, Miss Janet Fields— May I call you Janet? It's a nice name—and you mustn't mind. I call everybody Janet the minute I meet them.

JANET—[*Gravely still.*] Hello. [*There is just the barest pause while the men glance at each other. Then she continues quickly.*] Mother's not home.

GREENOUGH—So you told me—but you'll let us wait, won't you?

JANET—Sure. . . . Won't you sit down?

STEWART—Perhaps this is a fitting moment to present Miss Fields with a certain small token of admiration . . . ?

GREENOUGH—[*Presenting a large box to* JANET.] For once, Monsieur Stewart, I consider your well-known habit of giving advice inoffensive. Here's something for a good girl, Miss Janet Fields.

JANET—Oh—what a big box! Is it chocolates?

GREENOUGH—I was assured that it was chocolates, and I hope that there are enough to give you a fairly satisfactory pain in your tum-tum.

JANET—Oh! [*She doesn't know whether to open it or not—but proceeds to do so.*] Oh! Have some?

GREENOUGH—Thank you, no. But don't mind us. Open it and spoil your dinner if you wish.

JANET—[*Putting the box on the table and glancing at it.*] No, I don't think mother would like that. We're going to have such a good dinner. [*She pauses as they laugh, and then continues politely.*] If mother thinks there's enough to go around maybe she'll ask you to stay. Father's coming home.

GREENOUGH—So I heard, and thanks very much, but we couldn't possibly intrude.

STEWART—Yes, I'm afraid we'd be very much in the way tonight—even if there should be enough dinner to go around. If you were my daughter and I hadn't seen you for a whole year I wouldn't want anyone but you—and your mother, of course—at our first party after I came home. [STEWART *glances at* GREENOUGH *as he finishes, as if suddenly a little suspicious of his cousin's real interest in this household.*]

GREENOUGH—[*Rather quickly.*] And by the way, Janet, here's some fruit for your mother.

JANET—[*Eyeing the long box also.*] Oh, thank you. And more flowers?

GREENOUGH—Yes—but they will keep— [*He puts the box aside, on a table.*] However, there's something here that we might put on the ice—something that usually makes a party just a bit more—of a party. [*He has taken the*

*paper off the basket, pushed the fruit aside, and taken out
three quart-bottles of champagne.*]

JANET—Oh— Cider!

GREENOUGH—We'll call it that——

STEWART—What's in a name, anyway, these days?

GREENOUGH—And do you think we can put these on ice?
They ought to be cold.

JANET—Oh, I'll do it.

GREENOUGH—We'll help you.

JANET—Oh, no. Mrs. Price will. She's in the kitchen
watching the dinner for mother. [*She takes one of the
bottles and starts to take another.*]

STEWART—Careful—one at a time, Miss. That cider's
precious stuff.

JANET—I won't drop it. [*She backs through the swinging door.*]

[STEWART *looks at* GREENOUGH *quizzically.*]

GREENOUGH—Well? What's on your mind?

STEWART—Only that you're very much at home round
here.

GREENOUGH—Does it really seem like that to you? And
there's not a place in the world where I mind my P's and
Q's so carefully— Or where I feel more in the way. Nice
little thing, isn't she——?

STEWART—The child—you mean?

GREENOUGH—Yes, of course.

STEWART—Yes, yes, of course. [JANET *comes back into
the room during the pause that falls instantly.*]

JANET—Now.

GREENOUGH—[*Giving her another bottle.*] Here's another. [*She takes it and starts out, but pauses near the
table.*]

JANET—We're going to light these candles tonight at dinner.

GREENOUGH—Oh—really?

STEWART—I see— How jolly. [JANET *again goes through the swinging door.*] Great preparations have been going on, I see—even to those little roses in that bowl— [*He goes and looks down at the table.*] I'll wager there's just a dozen, even, and—you see the stems are very short—that they cost a dollar and a half around the corner.

GREENOUGH—I'll wager there's an extra one or two that the florists threw in. . . . She's like that——

STEWART—Who?

GREENOUGH—Edith—Mrs. Fields— Count 'em——

STEWART—One-two-three . . . eight-nine-ten— You're right—fourteen. I'm glad it wasn't thirteen. I rather like all this. I wouldn't want these people to have any bad luck. . . . Why didn't she go to meet the ship?

GREENOUGH—Her husband had written her not to try it. I suppose he knew that ships aren't always punctual. . . . At any rate, I offered her my motor but she didn't want it.

JANET—[*Returning.*] There's just room for the other one—Mrs. Price had to take some things out, though.

GREENOUGH—Here you are. [*He gives her the other.*]

JANET—Mrs. Price says it's not cider, but——

GREENOUGH—We'll leave that to your father. He'll know what it is. Aren't we going to see Mrs. Price?

JANET—Yes, sir, she's coming in a minute. [*She goes again.*]

STEWART—[*Suddenly, quietly.*] Is Mrs. Fields *very* beautiful?

GREENOUGH—Very beautiful? [*A little puzzled.*] Did I ever say she was beautiful?

STEWART—She must be. Isn't she?

GREENOUGH—I don't think so. Yes, perhaps she is— I don't really know!

STEWART—Who's Mrs. Price?

GREENOUGH—The wife of one of my employees—Earle Price. An extraordinarily good engineer.

STEWART—And, as I understand it, being an inquisitive employer was what brought you into the Prices' social circle in Harlem.

GREENOUGH—Exactly. The uplifters would approve of me. As they would put it, I "take an interest" in my men.

STEWART—Funny how you can know a man all your life —your own cousin, for instance—and find out new things about him every day. I might never have known of this interesting phase of yours, now, if I hadn't run into you coming out of Maillard's and begged to be taken wherever you were going.

GREENOUGH—I hope you're going to prove so useful that I'm not going to be sorry I brought you.

STEWART—Oh—I'm to be useful? To whom?

GREENOUGH—To Mrs. Fields, I hope.

STEWART—[*Suspiciously.*] And you . . . ? There are forms of usefulness that I've certain prejudices against, Walter.

GREENOUGH—Damn it, Ned—get rid of your silly suspicions that I'm here in the rôle of a villain. Or keep them—if you like—only get it out of your head that you're to preside at a scandal. . . . When I have a scandal —if I ever do—you won't be called in to assist.

STEWART—Thanks. I really don't like messes. Not

messy messes—where everybody concerned is much too good for that sort of thing, you know—and ought not to have got in so deep. . . . Things do happen, sometimes. Usually the people who get into messes are the people that don't matter. But I've seen any number of good men —and one or two good women—in my time—blunder right into hell before they had any idea of what they were up to . . . and . . . I don't like . . . to look on. . . . [*His voice has trailed off a bit uncertainly.*]

GREENOUGH—[*Drily.*] I don't think you need to worry, in this case. [*There is an instant's pause. Then he speaks, decisively.*] Fields doesn't happen to be an engineer. I can't help him. He happens to be a painter. You take an interest in that sort of thing. I don't—particularly. And when I ran into you today it occurred to me that I might bring you along and introduce you to Mrs. Fields—and that you might keep an eye open in order to help her husband—if he's any good. I don't know one single thing about him except that some mysterious benefactor sent him to Paris to study for a year and that Mrs. Fields has shown the most enormous pluck in supporting herself and her child by sewing during his absence.

STEWART—That's rather interesting. [*He looks about.*] A painter emerging from wall-paper like this—the "Angelus" on one wall—and "Hope" on another. What's his name—the young painter's?

GREENOUGH—Julien Fields.

STEWART—Seems to me I have heard it sometime or other —somewhere—or other——

[MRS. PRICE *enters, with* JANET *following.*]

MRS. PRICE—How do you do, Mr. Greenough?

GREENOUGH—Oh, hello.   May I introduce my cousin, Theodore Stewart, Mrs. Price?

MRS. PRICE—[*Putting out her hand.*]   Pleased to meet you, Mr. Stewart.   I've seen your name in the papers.

STEWART—That's rather alarming.   You make me think that you know all about me.   And I hope you don't.   I hope nobody does.

MRS. PRICE—[*Just a little awkwardly.*]   Oh, yes; you're very well known.   You both are, for that matter.

GREENOUGH—Really. . . .   How's your husband, Mrs. Price?   I haven't seen him for a few days.

MRS. PRICE—I don't see him much myself.   He's going to that school at nights that you recommended.

GREENOUGH—You won't blame me for that five years from now.

MRS. PRICE—Oh, no, sir; please don't think I was blaming you——

GREENOUGH—I know that. . . .   We just stopped to see Mrs. Fields a moment.   Have you any idea how long she'll be—or just when her husband is expected?   We don't want to be in the way.

MRS. PRICE—Oh, Edith won't be long now.   I'm sure of that.   She just asked me to step upstairs—[*to* STEWART] I live on the next floor—and watch the chicken that's roasting while she ran around the corner.   Knowing that she wanted everything very nice tonight, I was glad to oblige her.   I know she'll be put out if you don't wait.

GREENOUGH—We'll wait, all right, if you think she——

MRS. PRICE—[*Interrupting.*]   Oh, I know she'll be delighted.   [*To* STEWART.]   You can't imagine how nice Mr. Greenough has been to Mrs. Fields.   He's been simply lovely to her——

GREENOUGH—[*Quickly.*] I rather imagine everyone likes to "be nice"—as you call it—to Mrs. Fields.

MRS. PRICE—But you've sent her such lovely things and taken her on such lovely rides and you've been so lovely to Janet—I was just saying last night to Mr. Price: "I do hope Mr. Fields takes Mr. Greenough's kindness to his wife in the right spirit and appreciates it." And do you know what Mr. Price said—?

GREENOUGH—[*Drily.*] I haven't the least idea.

MRS. PRICE—"If he don't, he's a fool," he said, and then I said, "But some men can't help having jealous natures—" [*She pauses. No one speaks. She hurries on.*] There —maybe I've said something I shouldn't! But I only thought——

GREENOUGH—[*Briefly.*] You must give Price my regards and tell him that my secretary has a couple of books for him that I think he'll enjoy reading.

MRS. PRICE—Oh, thank you, sir, I will. . . . I guess I'd better look at that chicken again . . . if you'll excuse me.

GREENOUGH—Certainly— [*She goes toward the door.*]

MRS. PRICE—[*To* JANET, *who is at a window looking out.*] Come on, kiddie—I've got some work for you.

JANET—All right. [*To* STEWART, *indicating the window curtains.*] Mother just finished making these yesterday. They're new.

STEWART—So I see. They're pretty, aren't they? [*She nods and then follows* MRS. PRICE *into the kitchen.* STEWART *watches for the door to close and then speaks with energetic distaste.*] Well, I will say one thing, Walter. I don't believe you or any other fairly civilised man could work up a romantic interest in the Venus de Milo—or

Cleopatra—or Helen of Troy in the perfectly respectable lower-middle-class environment of a Harlem flat.

[*A bit of a song is heard coming near.*]

GREENOUGH—Somebody's coming. Wait—I think——

[*The door opens and* EDITH FIELDS *enters. The song leaves her lips as she sees her guests—but the radiance is still upon her face. Her arms are full of autumn leaves and brown asters. She pauses sharply and then advances quickly toward* GREENOUGH.]

EDITH—Oh—Mr. Greenough! I thought that was your car downstairs.

GREENOUGH—Yes—I hope you don't mind our running in like this—for a moment. Mrs. Fields, I think you've heard me mention Ned Stewart—my cousin?

EDITH—[*Giving him her hand.*] Oh, yes. How do you do, Mr. Stewart? [*To* GREENOUGH.] You said once you wanted Julien to know him, didn't you? [GREENOUGH *nods.* EDITH *hurries on, her voice suddenly dreamy with happiness.*] Isn't it too wonderful? . . . He's coming. . . . [*Both men glance at each other, then at her, and both are held speechless by the look in her face. Then her thoughts come back and she glances a little impatiently at the clock.*] What time is it? Only six! . . . I telephoned from the drug store. The ship is in. Nothing happened to it, thank God. . . . He's somewhere in this very city now, hurrying home. . . . I've been everywhere trying to find some autumn leaves—and I found these, at last; he loves them. Aren't they wonderful? And these asters? I must put them in water. . . . [*She goes toward the kitchen door—looking back as she is about to leave them.*] You'll pardon me—a moment?

STEWART—Of course. . . . [*She goes out. There is a*

pause. Then GREENOUGH *looks at his watch mechanically.*]

GREENOUGH—[*Without expression.*] The ship's in. He's coming—we must go.

STEWART—[*With a look that has something of sympathy in it.*] Yes; it's not likely that he'd want to find *us* here.

GREENOUGH—[*Suddenly, apropos of nothing.*] There's something about her that's extraordinarily—that's— [*He gropes for the word.*] That's——

STEWART—You mean that—is——

GREENOUGH—I mean that is *heart-warming.* I like to think that there are such things in the world as her devotion and courage and simplicity. I don't believe anything that could happen to her could spoil or change her.

STEWART—The thing you don't realise is that every other woman you know is just as capable as Mrs. Fields of devotion and courage and simplicity.

GREENOUGH—I don't believe it.

STEWART—Oh, yes, they are. It's rather the fashion to hide these things, I admit. But don't think you can't find them all over the place if you care to look. There's my mother, now. After fifty years she feels exactly like that about my puffy little father. And our cousin, Alice——

GREENOUGH—Perhaps—only——

STEWART—Only you're damned sentimental about Mrs. Julien Fields, Walter, and I'm very glad for your sake that the wandering husband arrives today.

GREENOUGH—Don't you think it's perfectly possible for a man to appreciate another man's garden—or pictures— or jewels without wanting to steal them? [EDITH *enters again, carrying a vase filled with leaves and flowers.*] Let me help you. [*He takes the vase.*] Where shall I put it?

EDITH—Suppose we try it here—there!

STEWART—That's very successful, I think.

EDITH—Yes,—isn't it? [*To* GREENOUGH.] I've such a lot to thank you for—and here are more flowers— [*She picks up the box and opens it as they talk.*]

GREENOUGH—I took the privilege of remembering that this was a great day for the household.

EDITH—You never forget anything. The flowers are lovely, of course,—but it's the champagne you brought for Julien— [*She pauses, looking up from the box of flowers, and smiles radiantly.*]

GREENOUGH—It's always fun to help give a party.

EDITH—You see, I know Julien likes champagne. But the poor boy has never had it often. He likes so many things that are dreadfully expensive and rare and fine. I wish he could have exactly what he wants all his life. He'd always choose the best.

STEWART—We can believe that—seeing that he chose you.

EDITH—That's a nice thing to say—but I'm not sure who did the choosing in that case. I rather think I did. And I was the one who showed that I liked the best that time.

GREENOUGH—I suppose when two people are born on the same day and brought up next door to each other as intimately as you and your husband were, it is difficult to say who did the choosing—it's so natural that you should care for each other under the circumstances.

STEWART—Were you really born on the same day—and brought up together?

EDITH—[*Gravely.*] Oh, yes. But that's not very strange, is it? Our mothers were friends. They lived in a little town in Indiana. Afterward both had their troubles—Julien's father and mine were killed in the same railroad wreck, and our mothers went to a larger town and went into dressmaking together. Of course there was a certain closeness in the way that Julien and I grew up—and I suppose it does seem natural for us to have cared for each other—only— [*She pauses, as if about to say something that she's not sure she should say.*]

GREENOUGH—Go on—what were you going to say?

EDITH—[*Unexpectedly.*] Are you married, Mr. Stewart?

STEWART—I—I? [*Hesitates just an instant.* GREENOUGH *flashes him a look of sympathy, but he continues calmly.*] Yes—I am married.

EDITH—Then you will understand what I mean—Mr. Greenough would think it a little silly, I'm afraid. [*She turns directly to* GREENOUGH, *smiling.*] Unless you've been married you really wouldn't understand. What I was about to say is—[*she turns to* STEWART *again*]—that in spite of its all seeming so natural—our having been boy and girl together and caring for each other always—as if it were *meant,* somehow—I've found—and I suppose you have, too—that there's a great strangeness about love. . . . [*There is a bare pause. She rests from gathering the flowers in her hands, and her eyes see far-off things as she continues in a lower voice.*] Yes, I'm very sure that love is the strangest thing in the world—much stranger than death—or—or just life.

GREENOUGH—I understand that, I think.

EDITH—[*Suddenly, earnestly, swiftly.*] Oh, but do you understand things like this—things that come out of the terrible clairvoyance of love? Things that— Once just before Julien and I were married I began to walk with a

limp. He was away that week. When he came back he
was on crutches. He'd broken his leg, but he hadn't let
me know—— Then, of course, there have been all sorts of
more usual things—like our getting up to write to each
other at the same hour of the night . . . and messages
and telephone calls that were like answers to an instant
need.

STEWART—[*A little awkwardly.*] This separation must
have been very difficult for you—both.

EDITH—We made up our minds that it was his great
chance.

STEWART—I don't think that it was necessary for my
cousin to point out to me that I might be of some service
to your husband. I think this meeting with you would
have made me anxious to be of any use possible.

EDITH—Thanks; I don't know just what there is that
anyone can do—— [*She halts.*]

STEWART—Do you know what his plans are for the immediate future? If he wants people to see his work?

EDITH—I don't really know just what he means to do.
You see, I don't know anything about painters—or art.
Julien never meant to be an artist at all. That just hap-
pened to him.

GREENOUGH—[*To* STEWART.] Did I tell you that he
was with an advertising firm—doing what's called com-
mercial drawing—when someone with discernment offered
him this year of real study in Paris?

STEWART—No; I understood that some picture of his had
attracted attention——

EDITH—That's true, too. It was one he'd painted—just
for fun—in oils—of Janet and me. Wait, I'll get his
scrap-book and show you some of the things he did the

last year he was with his firm. [*She is about to go out of the room, but pauses to take a booklet from the table.*] Here's a pamphlet that he illustrated—if you'd like to look at it.

STEWART—Thanks. [*She goes. Both men glance over the pamphlet.*]

GREENOUGH—[*Reading.*] "How to spend your vacation"— The handsome lady and the handsome gentleman starting off on horseback aren't half bad—are they?

STEWART—No; for this banal sort of stuff I should say they were exceptionally well done. Did he ever study anywhere?

GREENOUGH—I believe he went to the Art League—for a time.

STEWART—I should have thought this sort of thing his natural *milieu*—well done—without the glimmer of an idea or a thought.

GREENOUGH—Possibly ideas and thoughts were forbidden.

STEWART—Possibly. One can't judge fairly by this——

GREENOUGH—I suppose there was something unusual about his picture of his wife and child, or the mysterious benefactor who saw it in the window of the shop—where his firm had sent it to be framed—would not have taken the trouble to be a fairy godfather—if there are such things as fairy godfathers as well as fairy godmothers.

STEWART—[*Suddenly.*] Look here—I think I know who that fairy godmother was—for it was a *she* instead of a *he,* if I'm right. I think Hester Dahlgren told me something about discovering a young man quite satisfactorily poor and ignorant and talented.

GREENOUGH—Hester Dahlgren! But does she know what's what?

STEWART—Not a damned thing! She's one of those women with fool enthusiasms who like to meddle with other people's lives. . . . If she's the one— [*He shrugs his shoulders.*]

GREENOUGH—Well—I don't suppose Hester's romantic meddling—if it was Hester—has hurt anything. She may not have discovered a genius, but——

STEWART—At the worst she's probably let a good draughtsman waste some time. [*They glance through the pamphlet.*] Here's a child on the beach that's rather nice.

[EDITH *returns carrying a big book.*]

EDITH—Here are all sorts of things that I've kept——

STEWART—I've seen enough to know that your husband is very clever. Whether he's on the right road as an artist —or whether he's an artist at all, or not—is another story. You must let me meet him very soon.

EDITH—Oh, if you'll come any time—any time after tomorrow. Tomorrow will be a sort of holiday.

STEWART—I understand; and now I think we'd better go and leave you alone with your happy thoughts.

EDITH—Good-bye, then; and thanks so much for coming. [*To* GREENOUGH.] And thanks so much for everything—particularly Julien's champagne. [JANET *enters—* EDITH *addresses her.*] Thank Mr. Greenough again for the candy, darling, and tell him and Mr. Stewart good-bye.

JANET—Thanks again,—and——

GREENOUGH—Perhaps your mother will let you take your usual trip as far as the corner with me.

JANET—Oh, may I, mother? Please!

EDITH—Yes—I think so—if——

GREENOUGH—[*Quickly.*]   Then come along! [*She runs and opens the door.* STEWART *joins her on the threshold.* GREENOUGH *holds* EDITH'S *hand an instant.*] Good-bye, then—and good luck—and many happy returns of both birthdays.

EDITH—Good-bye, Mr. . . . I always want to call you "Mr. Santa Claus" instead of Mr. Greenough.

GREENOUGH—You've not much reason to do so—but I'll drive my reindeer to your chimney any time you'll let me —whether it's Christmas—or Easter—or only April fool's day—any time at all.   Don't forget that. . . . [*He leaves her and joins* JANET *and* STEWART *in the doorway—turning back to wave his hand again.   Then all three call back "good-bye"—the door shuts, and they are gone.   There is an instant's pause.* EDITH *moves toward the window and stands looking out.*

[MRS. PRICE *enters from the next room.   She has to speak twice before* EDITH *is aware of her.*]

MRS. PRICE—Are they gone . . . ?   I said—did the gentlemen go?

EDITH—[*Turning.*]   Oh, yes—they've gone.

MRS. PRICE—Well—it's a good thing you had me to depend on.   If you hadn't you never would have gotten anything done in the kitchen—not with your head in the clouds like it's been all day.

EDITH—I'm sure of that.   You've been a great comfort, Ada.

MRS. PRICE—It's not as if you had a regular hour when you knew you was going to sit down. . . . However, there's nothing there that will spoil, even if it's not eaten until ten tonight. Do you suppose Mr. Fields will take a taxi or come up in the subway?

EDITH—I don't know. He'll have all his things to carry. I suppose he'll have to take a taxi.

MRS. PRICE—Well, there's no telling when he'll get here —and as I knew that I made Janet drink a glass of milk and eat a piece of bread and butter a minute ago. It's her dinner-time now and I didn't think the child ought to be allowed to go hungry.

EDITH—I suppose you were right.

MRS. PRICE—Don't you think you'd better have something yourself?

EDITH—Oh, no—I'll wait for Julien. [*There is just a tiny pause.*]

MRS. PRICE—Well, I'll go along. If you need me to help you any more, you know just to call.

EDITH—You've done enough today. . . . I won't bother you any more. And I'll never forget it, Ada.

MRS. PRICE—And why shouldn't I? Haven't you helped me make everything I have that's fit to wear? I often wish there was more. Give Mr. Fields my best regards.

EDITH—I will.

MRS. PRICE—And you tell him for me that no matter how famous or rich he's going to get he's not a bit too good for you.

EDITH—Oh—nonsense, Ada! I'll tell him nothing of the sort.

MRS. PRICE—I will, then. . . . I've watched you very close, Edith. You're not a woman who can get her head turned easy—and a husband ought to appreciate that. . . . It's getting dark. Well, good night, dear.

EDITH—Good-night. [*They kiss—and* MRS. PRICE *opens*

the door to leave. But JANET's *voice shrills from the stairs.*]

JANET—[*Outside.*] Oh, mother—mother! He's come!

MRS. PRICE—[*As* EDITH *turns radiantly about.*] That settles it. I'm going to stay right here and see that this dinner gets put on the table. [*She turns toward the kitchen.*]

JANET—Mother—father's here— [*She is in the doorway now.*] He's getting out of an automobile!

MRS. PRICE—Go down and meet him.

EDITH—[*Still in a radiant daze, to* MRS. PRICE, *who is lighting the candles on the table.*] Oh, please don't——

MRS. PRICE—Run on down. I'll attend to everything here and not get in your way, either——

EDITH—Oh, but—but— [*She would like to be alone, but suddenly she laughs and catches at* JANET's *hand.*] Then come, darling! Let's see who will get the first kiss!

[*She races from the room and down the hall,* JANET *hurrying to keep up with her.* MRS. PRICE *finishes with the candles, hurries out, and returns with a vase containing the white roses that* GREENOUGH *brought. She places these on a side table, hurries out, and brings in the bread and butter. Then she goes into the kitchen and does not at once return. There is a brief pause.* JANET *comes back, almost creeping into the room. She stands huddled and a little frightened by the door, waiting. Then* EDITH *returns—silent and slow of movement and lost and uncertain. Voices float up from the stairway.* EDITH *stands near the door, her eyes wide with disappointment, amazement.* JANET *goes and puts her hand in hers. They wait near the open door.* JULIEN FIELDS, *burdened with bags, etc., appears in the hall just outside, and pauses under the gas-jet.*]

JULIEN—[*Calling down the stairway.*] Courage, Olga. Only one more flight! We arrive, Oscar—*nous sommes ici!*

[*He enters. He is a blithe young man, extravagantly dressed—fashionably rather than artistically—yet with a certain suggestion of the Quartier Latin in both manners and clothes. His hat is crushed under his arm—his coat hangs over one shoulder and he carries a big portfolio and a bag. Immediately behind him follows a bare-headed, wildly dressed young man, very big and blond, and laden wih luggage.*]

JULIEN—[*Indicating* EDITH, *but speaking to* OSCAR.] Enter, my friend—and permit me to inform you that this charming creature who precipitated herself into my arms on the sidewalk is my wife. Edith, my child, this is Oscar, a scoundrel, a Swede, and a philosopher.

OSCAR—Greetings, Edith and— [*He looks at* JANET.]

JULIEN—You may have heard me mention in my unguarded moments that there was a child. Her name is Janet.

OSCAR—Thank God it's not Muriel. Salutations, Janet.

JULIEN—That's his idea of humour, Edith. Don't mind anything he says. [*To* OSCAR.] Where's Olga?

OSCAR—Sitting on the top step of the floor below, rolling a cigarette. If you had looked back as Lot's wife and I did, you would have seen a considerable crowd gathering to observe her. Or perhaps they were observing Dame Dahlgren's impressive footman laden with your possessions trying to decide whether to step over her or wait respectfully for her to proceed before him. You will have to be patient with Olga, Edith. She is mad, a nomad, and a musician. . . . A mad, nomad musician—yes—that will serve as a description of Olga. Also she is a child—

a child as primitive as her Russian plains. [*He has grad-ually unburdened himself, so that the room is cluttered up with luggage.* JULIEN, *seeing* EDITH *so unresponsive and hurt, suddenly speaks in a different, businesslike voice, kicking at the bags on the floor.*]

JULIEN—Where do you want these things put, Edith?

EDITH—[*In a low, tight voice.*]   In—in the other room, I suppose. [JULIEN *stoops and picks up two of the pieces that* OSCAR *has just deposited. He looks about the room curiously as though he had never seen it before—as he speaks very casually to* OSCAR.]

JULIEN—I'll take care of these—while you lend a hand to the footman that's Olga stalled on the stairs.

OSCAR—*Très bien*—why not? He's probably a poor man with eleven children. . . . I hope you approve of non-sense, Edith. [*He goes out—through the door that has been standing open.*]

JULIEN—[*Staring about still and speaking half-bitterly, half-humorously to himself as he stands holding a travel-ing bag in each hand.*]   And I lived here seven years . . . with the Angelus and— [*He turns suddenly to* EDITH.] Did we always have this wall-paper, Edith?

EDITH—[*Still in a low, tight voice.*]   I suppose it is rather soiled and faded, but the landlord wasn't willing to put on new—and I— [*She halts and then changes the subject with sudden courage.*]   Are these people going to stay here, with us, Julien?

JULIEN—[*Uncomfortably but with coolness.*]   Oh, I see. . . . You don't like my friends. I'm sorry. But they won't stay long—only until they can find another place. I hope you'll not mind that.

EDITH—[*With painful matter-of-factness.*]   Then I'd better lay two more places at the table.

JULIEN—Good heavens—nobody wants dinner at this hour.

EDITH—[*Apologetically.*]   Then we won't have it yet. I just had it ready—so that if you were hungry . . . [*She stops, not quite able to go on.*]

JULIEN—Oh, well—just as you like, of course.   We might as well have it now—if it's ready.   You'll get used to Oscar.   He's really an amusing fellow.   [*He starts toward the closed door of the bedroom—and pauses, his hands full.*]   Open this door for me, Janet—will you? [*She runs and obeys him in silence.   He stares at her an instant.*]   Three times as tall as you were a year ago—*at least!*   Do you forgive your father for trying to be a famous man, Janet,—instead of the nice stay-at-home regular kind?   [*She is too much at sea to answer.   JULIEN, still looking at her, laughs suddenly as he moves away.*] I'm afraid you don't.   [*He goes into the next room.   JANET runs to her mother.*]

JANET—[*In a low, alarmed voice.*]   What's wrong, mother?

EDITH—'Ssh. . . . Nothing, dear, nothing. . . .

JANET—May I go downstairs and play on the steps?   I don't want any dinner.   I'm not hungry, mother.   Please— [*Her mother does not instantly answer her.   She continues to plead uneasily.*]   Won't you let me go downstairs?

EDITH—You might as well.   Yes, go downstairs if you want to, child.

[*MRS. PRICE hurries into the room carrying a dish upon which is a roasted chicken.   JANET, after a wavering look at her mother, slips out of the room and downstairs.*]

MRS. PRICE—Here's the chicken.   I'll put it here for Mr. Fields to carve.   Well—?   [*She is immensely curious.*] I thought I heard several voices.

EDITH—Julien brought some friends.   I'll do the rest— [*She starts toward the kitchen door.*]

MRS. PRICE—[*Hesitating, then yielding to the set determination in* EDITH's *face.*]   Well, everything's all ready. Maybe I'd better go down, anyway, and see about Earle. He wasn't coming home, but maybe he's changed his mind. Hadn't I better get some extra plates, first?

EDITH—No, I'll do it.

MRS. PRICE—All right.   I—I'll see you in the morning, I guess.

EDITH—Oh, yes.

[MRS. PRICE, *very well aware that something uncomfortable has happened, hesitates, then takes off her apron and goes as* EDITH *moves toward the kitchen. Almost at once* EDITH *returns with two covered dishes which she puts on the able.* JULIEN *also returns, and busies himself with the luggage.*]

JULIEN—[*Wryly—but trying to make the best of a situation.*]   I'll stack these things up—over here.   [*He moves them against the wall.*]   There's really not enough room, I suppose, for Oscar and Olga, and if they once got unpacked they would probably decide to stay forever.

EDITH—Is she his wife?

JULIEN—Olga?—Oscar's wife?   Good heavens! No.

EDITH—Isn't it rather strange, then——?

JULIEN—Our having her along?   I suppose it is—to you.

[JULIEN *arranges the luggage and then turns again to* EDITH.   *At her hurt bewilderment he laughs, but unsteadily and uneasily, and speaks with sudden humorous compassion.*] Poor Edith! You shouldn't have made me go.

[OSCAR *again looms in the doorway, laden with bags, and stooping forward.*]

OSCAR—Let the camel kneel and be unburdened. Lend a hand—Julien! [*He gives the name a French pronunciation;* JULIEN *helps relieve him.*]

JULIEN—Drop the things here. . . . [JULIEN *indicates the corner where he has piled the rest of the luggage.*]

[*A young woman, very picturesque and eccentric-looking, appears in the doorway—a cigarette in a long holder between her lips. Her hair is short, and she carries a samovar and under one arm an untidy lot of music sheets.*]

OLGA—Ah— [*She strolls into the room, staring about her, explaining blandly in an accented voice.*] One page of ze manuscript in Zito's new concerto I have lost. It is possible that it remains in the motor. The servant searches there now.

OSCAR—Cease to lament, Olga. That concerto isn't worth a damn, anyway.

OLGA—[*With a radiant smile at* EDITH.] Men are without compunction and scruple—always. Is it not so, Madame? Are you really the wife of our shocking little Julien, *chérie?* Or do they make a joke to me?

EDITH—They have made no joke. It is quite true that I am Julien's wife.

OLGA—Then I pity you, Madame. He is quite mad. He himself knows it. But there is a talent somewhere in those lazy fingers of his. Where is ze piano?

JULIEN—There isn't one.

OLGA—No piano!

JULIEN—We apologise—but there isn't a piano.

OLGA—Zen I do not remain. A piano I must have. And tonight. [*To* OSCAR.] Take ze things that are mine again to the motor before it departs. [*To* EDITH.] I have a thousand regrets that I go—but I will come again, Madame, when my technique and my mood do not require zat I play.

JULIEN—But you do not know where to go to find a piano tonight.

OLGA—Zat is not important. I will search.

OSCAR—Then I'll go with you. And a piano you shall have. [*To* EDITH.] My regrets, Edith—it is difficult to leave both you and that charming fowl. [*He indicates the chicken.*] However—genius is imperative and must be obeyed. We may return anon. [*He kisses* EDITH's *hand.*]

OLGA—[*Kissing* JULIEN.] Au 'voir, my friend. At my first concert bring your beau-ful, serious wife. Au 'voir, Madame.

JULIEN—Well, good luck with the piano, you crazy pair!

[EDITH *has bowed her head to* OSCAR *and whispered "good-bye" to* OLGA, *who now go rattling down the stairs in a clamour of French.* JULIEN *follows them out, calling down "A bientôt!" after them. Then he returns, and closes the door. He pauses awkwardly and then moves toward the table.*] I suppose we might as well begin. Do you want me to cut this chicken?

EDITH—Yes—or I'll do it, if you don't want to——

JULIEN—I will. [*He cuts it.*]

EDITH—Is the knife sharp enough?

JULIEN—It'll do. [*He serves her silently, giving all his*

attention to doing so.] Is that all right? [*She nods "yes."*]

EDITH—[*After a pause in which he serves himself.*] Here are the potatoes—and the beans. [*She indicates the vegetable dishes and offers to serve them.*]

JULIEN—Thank you. [*He holds his plate. She takes some, but neither touches the food. He speaks suddenly.*] I suppose there's not such a thing as a drop of wine in the place?

EDITH—[*Rising suddenly.*] I forgot! [*She hurries into the kitchen. His head drops between his hands. She returns with a bottle of champagne.*] Here's some——

JULIEN—[*Taking sudden notice.*] Good heavens— champagne? Where did you ever get it?

EDITH—Someone sent it—for you.

JULIEN—Good heavens! Who——

EDITH—A man named Greenough. Ada Price's husband works in one of his engine plants. He's always doing nice things for people.

JULIEN—[*More to himself than her.*] Well, we'll take what the gods send—and ask no questions. [*He pours a glass.*] Have some? [*She shakes her head miserably to say "no" and her head drops between her hands. He drinks.*]

EDITH—[*Suddenly, with a sob in her voice.*] Oh, Julien! [*He drains his glass before he answers.*]

JULIEN—Come, come. Let's not be tragic. There's nothing to be tragic about. . . . [*She lifts her face, wet with tears.*] For God's sake, don't cry! Be reasonable.

EDITH—[*Again, brokenly.*] Oh, Julien!

JULIEN—[*Pouring another glass of wine; almost violently.*] I've come back. Yes—I've changed. I'll try to do my best. But I'm different, of course. . . . You didn't expect me to come back unchanged, did you?

EDITH—So you do not love me any longer. . . .

JULIEN—Love! What in the name of God has Love got to do with it? It's life! Just life. Life has a way of picking people up and tearing them apart—and taking them on—different ways—and no man knows what's to happen to any of us next.

EDITH—But can't you tell me what's happened to you, Julien?

JULIEN—Everything. . . . Talking's no good.

EDITH—But, Julien—you and I—all our lives—we've been so——

JULIEN—I know. I know.

EDITH—We weren't like other husbands and wives who just happened to meet and like each other and get married. We were each other's always.

JULIEN—Yes—we were each other's. Too much each other's.

EDITH—And now—I'm still yours—but you aren't mine——

JULIEN—You can't talk about these things. They happen. Nobody wants them to happen. They just happen.

EDITH—I don't know what you've done—or what's happened to you. I only know you've come back a stranger —and that I can't bear it! [*She lays her face in her folded arms. For an instant there is silence between them.*]

JULIEN—[*Slowly.*] I've changed. I said I had changed. But what can we do about it? You sent me away. You wanted me to get on . . . a man can't go and find out what the world is and remain tied to his wife's apron strings. . . . Good God! These readjustments! How long have I been away? A year or a lifetime?

EDITH—[*Looking up gravely.*] You're being terribly cruel, Julien.

JULIEN—I'm trying to be honest. I can't bring back what I used to feel for you, Edith. What do you want me to do? Pretend? I'm sorry, but . . . [*He pauses, shrugging.*]

EDITH—[*Still gravely.*] Do you love some other woman?

JULIEN—[*Rising.*] No! My God! No! I never have and I never will. Love! Love! Love! I've had enough of love. Love's not everything—as you women think. Love is damned little—when a man's got work to do.

EDITH—[*Relaxing a little.*] Then you've been faithful, at least. That's a great load off my heart. [*There is another pause. He paces the floor nervously and then comes back and sits in his chair at the table.*]

JULIEN—No—not even that. [*He takes up a candle— blows it out—strikes match after match, and then remembers what he is doing and lights the candle and sets it back. EDITH rises blindly. He catches at her hand.*] Sit down. [*She obeys. He speaks again.*] I wonder if I can make you understand. . . . These—these affairs with other women haven't meant anything to me. You've been the only woman, Edith. You've had the best of me. You've had all my youth. Be content with that. You had the years when I should have been free. And we wronged each other—you and I—because you should have had your freedom, too.

EDITH—Freedom? Weren't we free? How could we have wronged each other? When we only loved each other?

JULIEN—It was wrong for me to know nothing—nothing of life—except what I learned in a little office filled with drab workingmen at their desks—and what I found here—here in a little four-room flat in Harlem. Here . . . where our everlasting conversation was about an increase in salary—or the price of eggs—or what to name the baby. For thirty years I was yours, Edith— Since the day we were both born you've stood between me and the freedom my soul needed if it was to find—to find the things that the soul of every man ought to hunt for—the things that have nothing at all to do with the price of eggs or the money in his pocket or even his child's name. Do you understand?

EDITH—[*Shaking her head blindly.*] Only that you want to be free—so—you'd better—go—now—tonight.

JULIEN—You *don't* understand. . . . But—do you want me to go?

EDITH—Do you want to go?

JULIEN—Not unless I must. [*There is another pause. He rises—and stands by the window and continues presently.*] There's a world outside this window that you don't know anything about. . . . We can't live like babes in a wood again. . . . I can come back to you and come back to this room—but there's no way back to our yesterdays—and if there were—we ought not to want to take it.

EDITH—Be patient with me, Julien. All I can understand is that you don't love me and that you don't want to love me . . . and there isn't anything at all left in your heart—for me.

JULIEN—I've come back—haven't I?

EDITH—I wonder why?

JULIEN—I had to come sometime—I didn't quite remem-

ber that you were like this.   I didn't mean it to be such
a tragedy. . . . You ought not to have let me go.

EDITH—No—I ought not to have let you go—my—
—my precious— [*A sob checks her.*]

JULIEN—Please don't—it hurts—please— [*Her sobs
cease, but she does not speak. He moves impatiently.*]   I
can't stand this. [*He finds his hat and cloak and goes to
the door. As he opens it she rises, and cries out desperately.*]

EDITH—Where—where are you going?

JULIEN—[*Also desperately—in a low, hard voice.*]   I
don't know. . . . I don't care. . . . I'll be back later, I
suppose. [*The door closes behind him. EDITH goes
toward it, but sits suddenly—huddling into a large chair.
She is very still. A clock strikes. The moments go by . . .
Presently JANET enters.*]

EDITH—[*Not seeing who it is—and starting up as she
hears the door open and close.*]   Julien!

JANET—It's me, mother. [*She goes and sits on her
mother's lap.*]

EDITH—Are you tired, dear?

JANET—A little. [*JANET clings to her.*]

EDITH—What's the matter with mother's big girl?

JANET—Nothing.—Let's play I'm a little baby.

EDITH—All right. You're a little baby now.

JANET—Sing "Bye-o" to your little baby.

EDITH—[*Singing.*] "Bye-o, baby buntin'—Daddy's
gone a-hunting——" [*She halts.*]

JANET—Go on, go on. . . . Hunting what?

EDITH—[*With a sob.*] God knows. . . .

THE CURTAIN FALLS

THE SECOND ACT

A year later.

A rather big, shabby room in an old house that was once magnificent, near Washington Square. At the back there are two doors. One, larger than the other, leads out into the wide, high hallway of the house; the other into a small hall bedroom. At the left there are the two big windows usual in such rooms in such houses. At the right a sliding door leads into the room that JULIEN *uses as a studio. At the side of a rather large round table painted orange colour is an immense chair upholstered in shabby, faded stuff that was once brilliantly flowered chintz. A lamp with a crudely devised yellow shade stands on the table. Two low, built-in bookcases are filled mainly with china and glasses. Another table, square and painted black and set about with four painted chairs, stands in the right-hand corner. A stencilled cloth runs like a brilliant streak across it. A seven-armed brass candlestick is at one end and a vase filled with leafy white roses at the other. Except for strips of red stuff at each side of the window there are no curtains. An incongruously handsome chandelier hangs from the ceiling in the centre—but later when the lights are turned on only two of the dozen bulbs flare.*

JULIEN *is talking to* MRS. PRICE. *She seems on the point of taking her departure—somewhat reluctantly.*

JULIEN—[*As if continuing a conversation.*]   Oh, she'll be here all right—any moment. . . . Edith was wondering what had become of you only the other day.

MRS. PRICE—[*Looking about curiously as she speaks.*] Isn't that funny?   I was thinking of her, too, only the other day; and I says to Earle, "I'm just going to take the elevated some day and go straight down and see Edith Fields."   And he said, "I wonder what's become of her and her husband and little Janet?   I suppose she's grown a good deal in the last six months."

JULIEN—I think I have heard her mother mention that her frocks had to come down a bit at the knees.   But I haven't noticed that she looks much different.

MRS. PRICE—Isn't it funny how soon you can lose track of people in New York?   Only the other night at a picture show I saw a man and woman speaking to Earle and I; and I didn't know them till they come up and told us who they was.   It was a couple that lived right across the hall from us in the same boarding-house for two years when we first came to the city.   To tell you the truth, I had lost Edith's address, but I had intended asking Earle if he could get it through Mr. Greenough—though I suppose you don't see so much of him now.

JULIEN—Oh, yes, we see him now and then.

MRS. PRICE—[*Interested.*]   Oh . . . I thought maybe— He was always so lovely to Edith—being as she was alone, and a friend of ours.   He's very much interested in Earle.

JULIEN—And how is your husband?

MRS. PRICE—Fine.   He's got an idea of some kind that Mr. Greenough is going to have patented for him.   And he's had another raise.

JULIEN—That's good.

[MRS. PRICE *stares about. For an instant the conversation drops.*]

MRS. PRICE—This looks like a nice *roomy* place.

JULIEN—Yes—it is—rather *roomy*—as far as it goes. There are only two of them, however.

MRS. PRICE—Only two rooms!

JULIEN—Yes—this and my studio—in there. [*He indicates the big door at the right.*] And a bedroom—such as it is— [*He indicates by a glance the door at the back to the left.*]

MRS. PRICE—Oh! Can I peep?

JULIEN—Certainly—though there's not much to see.

MRS. PRICE—[*From the doorway.*] This looks more familiar. Edith has kept some of her things, I see.

JULIEN—Yes—a few. We sold most of them. They didn't fit in very well—here. [*His annoyance is increasing.*]

MRS. PRICE—She's got the same white bureau—and her bed and Janet's little one—it was hard work getting them both in there, wasn't it? With the sewing machine, too.

JULIEN—She has considerable ingenuity about such things.

MRS. PRICE—I should say she had—and she's as neat as a pin. [*She closes the bedroom and comes forward. She looks at the couch.*] I suppose that opens out to make a bed at night.

JULIEN—I don't think so.

MRS. PRICE—[*Going to the couch and feeling it.*] Don't tell me Edith makes you sleep out here on a hard, narrow——

JULIEN—No—the studio is my domain. I'm very comfortable there. [*The conversation drops again.*] Won't you sit down?

MRS. PRICE—You're sure she's coming down?

JULIEN—She's coming—I know that. But I can't say just how soon.

MRS. PRICE—Well, I do want to see her. When I saw your address in the paper this morning—I made up my mind to come right down. But I didn't get started as early as I meant to—and I spent half an hour finding the place—so I'm afraid I can't wait.

JULIEN—As a matter of fact, perhaps you'd better not. I've got to go out, myself, in a few minutes. Of course you can wait if you don't mind being left alone.

MRS. PRICE—No, I want to get started so's to be ahead of that awful jam going uptown. The cars will all be crowded pretty soon—even if they aren't already. Well— [*She looks about reluctantly.*] I don't feel my trip was all in vain. I'm glad to have seen your new home. Edith don't mind it not being very modern, I suppose.

JULIEN—We have most of the conveniences—though the house is an old one, of course.

MRS. PRICE—Artistic things are very much the style now, anyway. [*She glances about again.*] Oh—you must have a kitchen somewhere, haven't you?

JULIEN—[*Impatiently.*] There's a kitchenette—off a little passage beyond the studio. I wouldn't dare to show you that. Edith's very much ashamed of it. . . . I'll tell her how sorry you were not to see her. You must come some other time. [*He is trying to manœuvre her out.*]

MRS. PRICE—I will—and you tell Edith about me losing

the address—but she's had no excuse for not coming to see me. She knew where I was.

JULIEN—I'll tell her.

MRS. PRICE—Tell her to drop me a postal making a date.

JULIEN—I will. Good-bye. Give my regards to your husband.

MRS. PRICE—I will. And—and— [*She hesitates, a little embarrassed.*] And you tell Edith I said not to mind what the newspapers say. Nobody does.

JULIEN—[*Airily.*] Oh—that! [*He waves his hand.*] She's much too sensible.

MRS. PRICE—Well, I hope so. But knowing how foolish she always was over you—I—it worried me. I——

JULIEN—Good-bye.

MRS. PRICE—[*Who cannot delay any longer.*] Good-bye.
[*With another reluctant, curious glance about, she goes. JULIEN closes the door after her almost viciously. He goes back to his couch. He picks up his book, lights another cigarette, and settles himself to read again. OSCAR enters, from the studio. He carries a large manuscript envelope and looks as though he had just dressed. His hat is in his hand—and a coat over his arm.*]

OSCAR—*Bon jour—mon cher* Julien.

JULIEN—[*Looking up.*] Oh, hello. Going?

OSCAR—[*Sitting down.*] Starting. However—there's always time for a cigarette. Got one?

JULIEN—Here. [*He throws a box. OSCAR catches it.*] Got matches?

OSCAR—Think so. [*He finds matches and lights a cigarette.*] Here. . . . [*Looking toward the windows, as he tosses the cigarettes back to JULIEN.*] By yonder street lamps I take it that the day begins to wane.

JULIEN—Yes. It's almost time for breakfast. I hope you feel more like it than I do.

OSCAR—I never felt more like coffee, eggs, and bacon in my life—not even at five A.M. on the old farm in Nebraska. Have you had anything?

JULIEN—No.

OSCAR—Edith not about?

JULIEN—Very much so.

OSCAR—Cross?

JULIEN—Worse than that. Hell-of-a-mess.

OSCAR—Jealous? Some girl—or something?

JULIEN—"Some girl" is right. I'm distinguished for life. Dahlgren's after a divorce. Hester and I are all over the newspapers.

OSCAR—Edith's not cut up about it, is she? Did she say much?

JULIEN—She said nothing. That's worse.

OSCAR—But didn't you have it out with her—that you were both to be perfectly free—and all that?

JULIEN—Oh, yes.

OSCAR—Well, if she understood what was going on she hasn't anything to kick about now. She can't blame you because Hester's husband got nasty.

JULIEN—Women aren't very logical.

OSCAR—You oughtn't to have gone to Palm Beach with Hester.

JULIEN—She had half a dozen other people staying at the cottage all the time.

OSCAR—Yes—but different ones. They all came and went except you. You were the fixture. That was a fool thing for you to do.

JULIEN—I know that now. . . .

oscar—I think she's in love with you. . . .

julien—No, thank God. She's not. She's never been in love with anyone.

oscar—Women are funny. Olga wants me to marry her.

julien—Good heavens—why? [oscar *shrugs.*] It seems very difficult to dodge the "grand passion" these days.

oscar—It will be worse in about two weeks. April will be here then. However, it's not the "grand passion" with Olga. It's plain Russian-Jewess business sense.

julien—Don't you flatter yourself?

oscar—No. . . . I've got talent. And if she married me she'd make me turn out a short story every month. Then she'd get them sold. She says she's discovered that a woman needs both money and a marriage certificate in America.

julien—Going to oblige her?

oscar—Good God! No! [*But during the pause that follows he is not so sure, adding humorously.*] Oh—well, perhaps. I'm fond of Olga.

julien—There are worse things than having a wife. And then children are always rather wonderful.

oscar—Then, of course, in a case like yours a wife's a protection. Hester Dahlgren can't expect you to marry *her*. That would be awful, wouldn't it? I suppose she'll have no money. . . .

julien—Pretty awful.

oscar—Well, I'm off. Won't you come along?

julien—Where are you going?

oscar—Anywhere—where there's coffee. We might try Olga's first. . . . If she's amiable she'll fix us up.

JULIEN—No, she might play something. [*He puts his hand to his head.*]

OSCAR—Oh, well—somewhere else, then—unless— [*He looks about.*]

JULIEN—We'd better not mess things up around here. Edith prepared breakfast at ten—and again at one—called us each time and each time we said we were getting up——

OSCAR—You mean you said it. I never rallied once.

JULIEN—And then again when I did get up—about an hour ago. But I happened to see the paper first—and lost my appetite. So——

OSCAR—Then we might as well travel—unless you want to lie around here. [*He rises.*]

JULIEN—No, I'll go.

OSCAR—If we run into Olga later be sort of tactful.

JULIEN—She knows you had some sort of party last night.

OSCAR—Oh, we'll admit that. Only we'll slow up on the details. Also she doesn't know about the check I got for those two poems yesterday.

JULIEN—Too trivial to mention, I suppose.

OSCAR—You can laugh. But you've got a wife. It's all right to tell a wife the brutal truth, but you've got to go sort of easy with your lady-love. You know that as well as I do.

JULIEN—All the same, you don't have to stand for any of that nonsense from Olga.

OSCAR—Don't I? Olga's mad, of course—but not every woman—no matter how much sense she has about other things—knows how to stable a man properly. And Olga's as clever as Edith about that.

JULIEN—That's true. Heaven only knows how they

manage—Edith particularly—on what she has to spend,
—but . . . let's get along. I'll get my things. [*He goes
into the studio—and returns immediately with his hat and
coat and stick.*]

OSCAR—By the way, when are you going to get to work?

JULIEN—It will surprise you very much—but—tomorrow.

OSCAR—[*Cynically.*] We'll see——

[*The door opens as they go toward it, and* EDITH *and*
JANET *enter, several small bundles in their arms.* EDITH
*wears a short blue skirt, a white blouse, a boyish jersey,
and a tam on her head.* JANET *also wears a tam and a
jersey over her blue serge frock.* JULIEN *halts, greeting
them.*]

JULIEN—Hello.

EDITH AND JANET—[*Together.*] Hello.

JULIEN—[*To* JANET.] You don't get by, young lady,
with a cool, airy "hello" to me.

JANET—That's not all of it. [*She holds up her face to
be kissed.*]

JULIEN—I should say it isn't! [*He catches her up in
his arms and then stands her quickly but tenderly on a
chair.*] Have you been weighed lately?

JANET—No. [*She is smiling and happy.* EDITH *puts
her bundles on the table.* OSCAR *follows her.*]

OSCAR—Thanks for putting me up every other night or
two—I suppose I should say every other day or two—
like this.

JULIEN—[*To* JANET, *who is standing on a chair with her
arms around his neck.*] I've got a secret to tell you.

JANET—What? [*He whispers in her ear. She laughs
and whispers back. Then they kiss.*]

oscar—[*Continuing to* edith.]   I hear that we accepted two invitations to breakfast and failed to keep either—or even send our regrets.   I apologise.

edith—Did you want another now?   [*She smiles absently.*]

oscar—A thousand thanks—but——

julien—Come along, Oscar.   [*To* edith, *as he sets* janet *back down on the floor.*]   We're off for a walk.

edith—Will you be back for dinner?

julien—I don't know.   Don't bother about me.   But I've just made an engagement with a certain young lady to take her to a picture show tonight—if you'll permit such a dissipation.

edith—If she's home by half-past nine I think she might go.

julien—Then that's settled, Janet.   Haven't I a model child, Oscar?   She's never said a "cunning" thing in all her prim, quaint little life. . . . Good-bye, darling!   [*Again he kisses her—nods to* edith *and goes.*]

oscar—Peace be on the household!   *A bientôt, mes enfants.*   [*He goes.*]

janet—[*To her mother, who is gathering up the packages.*]   Do you want me to put the butter in the refrigerator, mother?   [*She has picked up a bag and peered into it.*]

edith—Yes, darling, you can help me put all these things away—and then, if you're to go to the picture show tonight you must go in the bedroom and shut the door and study until dinner-time.

janet—Can't I study in father's studio?   Father doesn't mind if I sit at his desk.   I'll only turn on one light.

EDITH—It's rather cold in there. Besides, I have to clean it up.

JANET—I'll keep my sweater on. And all you have to do is to fold up the bed-clothes and put the day-covers on the couches. I'll do that. It won't take a minute.

EDITH—Very well. Put these things away and then come back and get your books.

JANET—Thanks, mother. [*She insists upon kissing her.*] I love to sit at father's desk.

[EDITH *says nothing, and* JANET *goes out at the right with the packages.* EDITH *takes off her tam, and picks it and* JANET'*s up from a chair where it has fallen. She takes them into the bedroom and then returns, a tissue-wrapped package in her hands. She opens it and takes out a bit of pink organdie upon which she prepares to sew.* JANET *returns.*]

JANET—[*Coming close to* EDITH.] Why don't you come to the picture show, too, mother?

EDITH—I've something else to do.

JANET—[*After meditating a moment—speaking wistfully.*] Father's awfully nice, mother, when you get to know him well.

EDITH—I'm sure he is, darling. I'm glad you've got to know him well.

JANET—But he's not any nicer than you. I like you both exactly alike. I like you both all there is to like.

EDITH—[*Suddenly putting an arm about her and drawing her close, kisses her, speaking softly.*] Who's mother's blessed comfort . . . ?

JANET—[*Smiling at their joke.*] Janet May Fields is Mrs. Edith Fields' blessed comfort.

EDITH—That's right. Now run along, Janet May Fields.

[JANET *goes to the bookcases and takes out a small stack of books, pencils, tablets, etc. Then she starts out at the right.*]

JANET—Call me if you want anything, mother. [EDITH *nods and* JANET *goes, closing the door behind her. Almost at the same instant there is a knock on the hall door.* EDITH *goes, listlessly.*]

EDITH—Oh, Mr. Stewart!

STEWART'S VOICE—Hello—may we come in——

EDITH—Of course——

[*He enters with a woman, veiled and magnificently dressed.*]

STEWART—I've brought Mrs. Dahlgren, Mrs. Fields,—at her request—very much at *her* request.

[*His voice is light but serious.* EDITH *is amazed and a little stern.* MRS. DAHLGREN *laughs and speaks in an easy, rich voice.*]

MRS. DAHLGREN—How do you do . . . There really didn't seem to be anything to do about it except to come straight up and knock. How do you ever manage to say "not at home"?

EDITH—We don't.

MRS. DAHLGREN—That's probably very fortunate for me. Or else— [*She changes the subject quickly.*] Poor Teddy Stewart is miserable. He didn't want to bring me without a warning. But I knew that he knew you and— [*She again changes the subject, addressing* STEWART.] You promised me ten minutes alone with Mrs. Fields, Teddy.

STEWART—Very well. I'll go down and wait in the motor.

Then I want a moment or two with her myself. [*He goes over to* EDITH, *and takes her hand.*]   *Au revoir.* . . . There are times when we all skate on thin ice, Mrs. Fields. Mrs. Dahlgren is an expert. I'm not. But I hope that you won't be sorry we came. I think that she wants to suggest something that is for your ultimate happiness as well as her own.

[*He goes. The door closes.* EDITH *moves about, painfully awkward and dumb.* MRS. DAHLGREN *lifts her veil, looks about, and makes herself comfortable in the big chair near the doorway to the studio. She pulls off her gloves, and finds a cigarette with such deliberation that* EDITH *comes to a halt behind the other big chair by the table and addresses her with desperate uneasiness.*]

EDITH—Hadn't you better tell me what you came for?

MRS. DAHLGREN—Pardon me. I was just looking round. Rooms always interest me.

EDITH—We don't have to beat about the bush, do we?

MRS. DAHLGREN—Certainly not. . . . [*But she continues in the same irrelevant tone.*] I've always wondered what sort of person you were, Mrs. Fields. Of course, Julien's told me *something*. Men always like to talk about one woman to another. I suppose he's told you a good bit about me. Hasn't he, now? We might as well be honest with each other.

EDITH—We've never mentioned your name.

MRS. DAHLGREN—Really?

EDITH—Or the names of any of the other women——

MRS. DAHLGREN—Oh! Isn't that a little catty?

EDITH—Is it? You knew there were other women, of course? As you say—we might as well be honest.

MRS. DAHLGREN—[*Uncomfortably.*]   Men are such cads!

EDITH—If you don't mind—I'm waiting to hear what you wanted to say to me.

MRS. DAHLGREN—You're one of those very direct persons, I see. Direct people, to me, are like houses set close to the road. Now I am like a house behind all sorts of hedges and trees—approached by a long, winding poplar-bordered avenue. . . . Do you understand what I mean? At all?

EDITH—[*Gravely.*] I think I might understand if I could keep my mind on what you are saying. But I've a good many thoughts of my own today—and when I think I'm listening to someone—I suddenly find myself listening instead to something that's going on here. [*Touching her head at the back. Then she continues.*] If you had come any other time—yesterday, or the day before, or the day before that—I might have been able to imagine some reason for it. But now that the cat's out of the bag I can't see how anything I can do can help matters for either of us. So——?

MRS. DAHLGREN—[*Suddenly becoming business-like and alert.*] The cat may be out of the bag, as you say—but it hasn't got away yet. And that's what I want to prevent. I don't want to be divorced. In the first place, I don't *believe* in divorce——

EDITH—No? Is there anything that you do believe in? Surely you do not believe in marriage.

MRS. DAHLGREN—Oh, but I do! We can't all be good wives and good husbands—but marriage is so correct—so absolutely necessary. I believe every woman should get married and stay married—no matter what happens. You look astonished. Don't you believe in marriage?

EDITH—Not when it means shutting one's eyes for fear of what one is going to see.

MRS. DAHLGREN—How quaint! Shutting one's eyes is an art, my dear. I suppose there's no use trying to make you see that—but that's the only way one *can* stay married. Most attractive wives have their—little temptations—and all men. . . . Don't you know that every woman, practically, goes through sometime what you're going through today?

EDITH—I don't believe that—not what *I'm* going through. [*Her tone is significant.*]

MRS. DAHLGREN—[*Uneasily.*] Oh, well, of course, there are different ways of taking things. But surely you knew —*something?*

EDITH—Yes, I knew *something.*

[*A pause falls between them.* MRS. DAHLGREN *moves restlessly.* EDITH *is motionless behind the chair, staring at her.*]

MRS. DAHLGREN—[*Nervously.*] I wish you'd sit down! [*Indicating her unlighted cigarette.*] May I smoke?

EDITH—[*Ignoring her first remark.*] There are matches on that shelf—to your left.

MRS. DAHLGREN—[*Shortly.*] Thanks. [*She lights her cigarette, and begins abruptly.*] It's all strange to me— the way you feel about this sort of thing, evidently. I have a motto that I made myself—"Take everything exactly as if it happened every day." It's not a bad way of doing. One gets on very well by taking whatever happens casually. . . . I said I didn't want to be divorced. I don't. My husband is up in the air and has done what he's threatened to do a hundred times, at last. He's sued. I don't believe he'll go through with it—not if you don't get up in the air, too—and start divorcing Julien.

EDITH—Oh!

MRS. DAHLGREN—I came to try to persuade you that it would be silly to do so.   I was afraid you might have some romantic idea that you ought to set Julien free so that he could marry me—after all this talk.

EDITH—No.   I don't believe that I've thought of you, at all.   Or of him.

MRS. DAHLGREN—[*Sympathetically.*]   I understand. You were thinking of your child.

EDITH—[*Coldly.*]   No, I've been thinking of myself. [*There is another pause.* MRS. DAHLGREN *puts out her cigarette before speaking.*]

MRS. DAHLGREN—And what do you think you are going to do?

EDITH—[*Decisively.*]   That will concern only Julien and me.

MRS. DAHLGREN—[*Getting up, impatiently.*]   But, don't you see, whatever you do must concern *me,* too!   If you sue for a divorce, that will make my husband sure he was right.   At present all he knows is that everything looks wrong—but he knows, too, that it's like me to have everything looking wrong, when it's really all right.   He's very wobbly since it really came out in the papers today. . . . He's fond of me. . . . I amuse him.   But—if you're going to do stunts, too, he'll have to go through with it.   Only I don't think that would be quite fair of you—because Julien—[*she hesitates and then comes out with it*]—Julien told me you weren't jealous—that you knew he was interested in someone else—and that it didn't make any difference.

EDITH—[*Quietly.*]   You were very credulous—even I would never have believed that—and I'm not nearly so experienced as you.

MRS. DAHLGREN—But why not? I didn't know you. And I did know that Walter Greenough was here all the time. Naturally I supposed——

EDITH—[*Interrupting with a gesture.*] Let me get that straight. . . . [*She thinks an instant, and then continues, her voice amused and bitter, and then decisive.*] I see . . . naturally. . . . No, Mrs. Dahlgren—whatever else happens I am not going to get a divorce.

MRS. DAHLGREN—Oh! Thank heavens! But— [*She is suddenly wary.*] If my husband should try to get you as a witness——

EDITH—I don't believe that he will need me——

MRS. DAHLGREN—But if he does, you'll say that you never objected to our—friendship—? [*She halts over the word.*] And that you knew all about it?

EDITH—You've put it very well for me. I'll remember the way you've worded it. I never objected—and I did know all about it. . . .

MRS. DAHLGREN—You *are* a brick!

EDITH—Your ten minutes must be up. [*She goes deliberately to the door and opens it.*]

MRS. DAHLGREN—Oh, I see—you want me to go, evidently. Aren't you going to let me thank you?

EDITH—That isn't necessary. Good-bye.

MRS. DAHLGREN—[*Opposite* EDITH *near the doorway.*] Good-bye. And you'll never be sorry for being sensible about this, my dear. It will always give you a wonderful weapon against Julien—that you knew and didn't make a fuss. If only I could get something on *my* husband— but poor Willy never looks at another woman! And remember my advice, my dear—it's the advice of a woman of the world, remember. *Stay married.* Once is enough.

If you can't make the first marriage go you're not likely to have better luck with the second—or the third. Besides getting divorced and remarried all the time is so *dégagé*. Don't you agree?

EDITH—[*With a flicker of amused and bitter irony.*] Frightfully *dégagé*, Mrs. Dahlgren. . . . Good-bye. [*Both hands are behind her and her attitude forbids further conversation.*]

MRS. DAHLGREN—Good-bye. I'm not sorry I came—although you seem so—so *hostile*. I suppose Teddy Stewart will want to come up now. I hope no reporters will see me outside in the motor.

EDITH—I don't think you need to worry about that. They've been here—and gone. But if Mr. Stewart doesn't mind I'd rather see him some other time.

MRS. DAHLGREN—I'm glad. I hate waiting. I'll tell him. Good-bye.

[EDITH *closes the door after* MRS. DAHLGREN. *She moves about the room, making a nervous, absent-minded inspection. She straightens the books on the shelves—and finds a stitch needed in the lamp-shade. She chooses her thread carefully from a sewing-box and repairs the shade—lifting it nervously from the lamp. Then she lights two lamps on the wall, carefully examining their shades. She is almost like a busy, frantic insect hurrying in one direction and then another.* JANET *enters.* EDITH *twitches nervously at the unexpected opening of the door.*]

EDITH—[*Seeing* JANET, *and relaxing.*] Oh——!

JANET—You're terribly jumpy today, mother.

EDITH—Am I? Well—I thought you were studying?

JANET—What time is it?

EDITH—[*Indicating a little clock on the farthest shelf.*] Look and see.   [JANET *goes closely to see.*]

JANET—[*In a disappointed tone.*]   Oh!

EDITH—What time is it?

JANET—Only ten minutes after five.   I thought it must be half-past six, anyway.

EDITH—You haven't finished getting your lessons, have you?

JANET—No, but——

EDITH—You'd better go back, then, and study until you have.

JANET—All   right. . . . [*She   hesitates.*]   You don't think father will forget about the picture show, do you?

EDITH—He often forgets, doesn't he?   Don't be disappointed if he does.

JANET—But father never *means* to forget.   [*She goes over to the window and stands a moment and then cries out happily.*]   He's not forgetting!   He's coming across the square now—with Olga and Oscar.

[*There is a knock on the door.* EDITH *opens it.* GREEN- OUGH *is there.*]

GREENOUGH—Hello.

EDITH—Hello.   Come in.

GREENOUGH—[*Entering.*]   I couldn't resist stopping a moment. . . . Hello, Janet!

JANET—Hello.

GREENOUGH—How are you?

JANET—Fine.   [*To her mother.*]   I guess I'd better go back and study now.

EDITH—I think you had.   [*To* GREENOUGH.]   She has some lessons to be learned.

GREENOUGH—That's hard luck—isn't it, at a time when you and your mother might come for a ride with me?

JANET—[*Going.*] Oh, but I'm going to a picture show with father after dinner. So I don't mind.

GREENOUGH—I see. That's different.

JANET—[*At the door, to* GREENOUGH.] Good-bye.

GREENOUGH—Good-bye. [JANET *goes. The door closes after her.*]

EDITH—Won't you sit down?

GREENOUGH—If you will. [*They sit—he on the sofa—she opposite on the other side of the table. A pause falls. He begins recklessly.*] I don't know what I'm doing here. [*She looks at him, but does not speak. He continues recklessly.*] This is one day when I might have had the decency to stay away. . . . You can't want anyone about today.

EDITH—It doesn't seem to matter much whether anybody's about, or not.

GREENOUGH—I saw the papers. . . . [*With sudden compassion.*] Tell me, Edith, are you very much cut up? Does this thing hit you as hard as I'm afraid it does?

EDITH—I don't know *how* hard it's hitting me.

GREENOUGH—[*Getting up and walking about.*] I can see that it hurts—that it hurts damnably hard. It does—doesn't it?

EDITH—[*Bending her head, nodding, barely able to speak.*] Oh, yes.

GREENOUGH—[*Coming to a halt beside her chair.*] And here I am—so damned much in love with you that I could kill anybody—even another man—for making you suffer one single instant. Yes, here I am, up against something that I can't do a single thing about! . . . Absolutely help-

less to help you. . . . You know, Edith, love's a pretty
·big thing when it can make a man feel like this. I'm not
thinking of myself at all. Not now.

[*The door opens noisily, and* JULIEN, OSCAR *and* OLGA
enter. There is something half-modish about OLGA *now.
Her wild hair seems to be less eccentric and she has acquired
smart shoes and a smart serge frock. She wears no hat,
and a short, shabby cape, but she strides about with a
certain style and with the assurance of a person who knows
she is getting somewhere.* GREENOUGH *moves away from*
EDITH's *chair and makes himself as amiable and impersonal
as possible to the others.*]

OLGA—[*Gaily, first to* EDITH *and then to* GREENOUGH.]
Hello. . . . Hello. . . . [OSCAR *and* JULIEN *each toss a
greeting at him.*]

EDITH—Hello.

GREENOUGH—How do you do? [*He nods to the men.*
OSCAR *goes to* EDITH. JULIEN *busies himself in the back of
the room.* OLGA *goes, with a certain impudence, for*
GREENOUGH.]

OSCAR—[*To* EDITH.] You see, we return.

OLGA—[*To* GREENOUGH.] Will you tell me, my rich
friend, why never you keep your promise to come to hear
me play?

GREENOUGH—I've been intending to. . . .

OLGA—But the intention only gets one nowhere. You
should . . .

OSCAR—[*To* EDITH.] It was discovered with regret at
the very entrance to a tavern that neither Julien nor I had
been to our banker today.

EDITH—Oh—so you haven't had your breakfast yet?
[JULIEN *comes and listens.*] Don't you want me—?
[*She looks toward* JULIEN.]

JULIEN—[*Interrupting.*]   No, no.   Don't bother.   Not again.   We'll make ourselves some coffee——

OLGA—[*Catching the drift of the conversation and speaking across to* EDITH.]   Julien means that I will make it for them.   That was why they invite me here when I meet them in the Square.   They are very, very helpless.

OSCAR—And Olga is very, very helpful when a man's starving.   You don't think there's an egg anywhere about —do you, Edith?   Any egg will do.

EDITH—Look in the ice-box, Olga.

OLGA—Then come, *mes enfants*—I will not go alone.   If I am to make coffee for you, you must make conversation for me—   [*They move toward the door.   She continues half in jest, half in earnest.*]   —and it must be very good conversation if you are to make me forget that I am very, very cross.   Where do you think they were last night, Edith, that Oscar was afraid to come home?

EDITH—I don't know.

OSCAR—I'll tell you.   We sat up most of the night with Jack McBurney and half a dozen others——

OLGA—Girls?

OSCAR—No—all men.   And we all drank too much and talked too loud and stayed too long.   Then we went out and rode on a milk-wagon up Fifth Avenue to the Park. And in the Park we watched the day arrive and discussed the Soul of Man and prayed to the Rising Sun for just one more good round of good "likker"—which we didn't get.   Don't you believe me?

OLGA—[*With a shrug.*]   Perhaps. . . . It may be true —it is very like you—   [*To* GREENOUGH.]   They are what you call "loafers": anything they may do—except the work.   But they do not bore me and they have something

of the spirit. That is saying much for any man. Shall
you desire coffee, too, monsieur? My coffee is such as
you often do not taste.

GREENOUGH—Thanks, very much—but I'm going in a
moment.

OLGA—And you, Edith?

EDITH—I think not. If I want any, I'll come and
get it.

OSCAR—[*Placing his arm about* OLGA *and leading her
toward the kitchen.*] Then ho! for the kitchenette and
the shining lyrical kettle! Coming, Julien?

JULIEN—[*Quietly.*] Yes, I'm coming. [*He follows
them with a backward look at* GREENOUGH *and* EDITH.]
See you later, I suppose. [*He goes. There is a little
pause after he leaves the room.*]

GREENOUGH—[*Rather awkwardly.*] I suppose I ought
to go . . . I suppose I ought not to stay . . . I suppose
you don't care whether I go or stay? But—in God's name
Edith, haven't you had enough? Aren't you tired of this?
Is there anything more that a man can do to a woman to
humiliate her and distress her—? When I saw the papers
this morning, I said, "This ends it." And it does end it
doesn't it?

EDITH—I suppose you're thinking that I ought to leave
him?

GREENOUGH—What else is there to do?

EDITH—And get a divorce—like her husband's doing—
I suppose?

GREENOUGH—Of course . . . and I'm not one who believes in divorces usually. . . . And I'm not thinking of
myself, either—or what your being free might mean to
me, some day. I tell you I'm thinking only of you. Oh

I know what he's meant to you. But I've been watching ever since he came home. I know how things have gone from day to day—and I tell you, Edith, I swear to you that I don't believe the woman lives who could be married to Julien Fields—and be happy. There's nothing in it for you, my dear,—nothing but a miserable half-squalid Bohemian existence—that's against all your clean, orderly instincts—here—in a home that isn't a home—as a slave to a husband who isn't a husband. Life owes you something more—and you owe it to yourself to take it.

EDITH—[*Vehemently.*] And don't you suppose that I've said all this to myself a hundred times!

GREENOUGH—Then if you see it, too——

EDITH—[*With a sob.*] I do see it! [*There is a sharp pause. Then she breaks out passionately.*] But there's some more than just that! I see that Julien is right.

GREENOUGH—Right! To treat you as——

EDITH—Yes, he's right. In *his* mind he's right. That's what is so important. It may be all wrong in another way. And it's been hard to bear—and is hard to bear—as far as I'm concerned—all these new ways of his. But I'm willing to bear them because I know there's something very fine back of all his nonsense and his cruelty and his idleness and his selfishness. I know there's something he's been trying to make me understand—a little bit. It's that he's going through something, and he's got to go through it to get where he wants to be.

GREENOUGH—I see what you mean. You think this is a phase—that he'll settle down and have a real career some day. Well, he's paying too big a price for it. And you're paying too big a price.

EDITH—It's not the career. That will come, too, maybe.

But it's something more important that he's hunting—and that he'll surely find. It's something of the spirit—like Olga said. It's something that would be like religion if religion meant doing everything you want to do—and laughing about it—and learning from it—instead of not doing it. . . . Do you see?

GREENOUGH—I see—but not with your idealism. I see only a young man with no great talent—idling away—but— [*Pausing.*] There's no use talking. You love him. And no matter what he does you're not willing to blame him. You'd forgive him for anything.

EDITH—I can see how you think that. But I don't think it's true. There have been times when I've wanted to run out of this house, screaming, and I wouldn't have cared where I went either—to the river—anywhere——

GREENOUGH—[*Turning to her suddenly.*] Edith——!

EDITH—Oh, it was only that I was so terribly hurt, sometimes, and so terribly ashamed—that I wanted to run where it was dark and cold. . . . But that's over, thank God. Now I know that what I must have is patience. . . . Patience. . . . [*She is silent for an instant. Then she speaks suddenly out of a reverie.*] Poor Julien! I wish I weren't so heavy-hearted all the time! But when I try to be gay—I—I'm so stupid about it. [GREENOUGH *draws his hand sharply across his eyes and then goes to the window, looking out.* EDITH *continues presently, humbly, but with shining eyes.*] I'm not clever. . . . You say Julien is idling away his time. That's true. But I've worked all my life and I don't know that keeping oneself busy is such a wonderful thing. I often wonder what he must be thinking of when he lies on the sofa, there, smoking. I've a great respect for anyone who can lie still and

think. I have to be doing little things all the time. As
for the rest of his faults—I don't deny them. But when
I go to places and see other women with other men—men
who look tame and sleek and contented—I think of Julien,
and I'm glad he's not like them—whether they're good
husbands or not. At least there's something very *free*
about everything he says and does—and I'm sure it's a very
fine thing for a man to be free, that way, whether it makes
a woman happy or not. [*Then she adds, more to herself
than to him.*] Yes, I'm sure that it's a fine thing for a
man to be free to think and act as it suits him—whether
it makes some woman unhappy or not.

GREENOUGH—[*Coming back toward her.*] And what
do you think your husband would say or do if you chose
to be as free as he does?

EDITH—He's explained that many times. He thinks we
ought both to be free. He doesn't think our being married to each other ought to make the least difference—to
either of us. Julien's fair.

GREENOUGH—Is he? [*Suddenly he puts his hand in his
coat pocket.*] Are you brave enough to prove to yourself
whether he's fair or not? [*She looks amazed. He continues, sternly.*] Are you?

EDITH—Why should I prove what I know?

GREENOUGH—If you're afraid——?

EDITH—Afraid?

GREENOUGH—I think you ought to get rid of him. *Now,*
when your opportunity is here at your hand ready-made.
You've a lot of ideas about him that won't stand testing
out. I'm going to a family dinner tonight. It's one of
my cousins' birthdays. I'm very fond of her, and today
I **went** through some things of my mother's that I have at

the bank—looking for an old miniature that I knew Alice, my cousin, had always wanted.   There was a lot of stuff there. . . .   There was this box among several others . . . My mother had very beautiful hands.   She was fond of wearing bracelets.   Some of these were old-fashioned, some quite new when she died—five years ago.   They made me think of your hands.   I brought them away—on a purely fantastic impulse.   [*He has given her the box, which she has opened.*]

EDITH—Oh!   [*She stares at them.*]   They're very beautiful, aren't they?   [*He watches her a moment—and then she starts to give them back.*]

GREENOUGH—No, I want you to put them on.

EDITH—But I——

GREENOUGH—I'm not asking you to keep them.   Please.

EDITH—But why——?

GREENOUGH—Let me help. . . .   Please.   [*He takes the box from her hands, places it on the table, and puts half a dozen glittering bracelets on each of her arms.*]   There. . . . You see, some will go on without being unclasped. You have small hands.

EDITH—[*Holding both her hands up so that the light flashes from the jewels.*]   Oh, but—how fine I am!   Oh, look!   [*Her gestures flash them back and forth.   She laughs and stops short.*]   Oh, but—how silly they make me!   For a moment I felt like a child—so excited!   Please help me take them off.

GREENOUGH—Please keep them on.

EDITH—Oh, no.   Certainly not.   [*She is decisive.*]

GREENOUGH—I wonder what your husband would say if he saw them on your arms?

EDITH—I think it would hurt him very much to see them

on my arms, and to think what he'd have to think, but I know that he'd say I had just as much a right to them as he's had to the things he's done. And I think—[*she grows a little excited again*]—that I'll let him see them there— if you'll lend them to me—for it might be very good for him to feel that sort of hurt.

GREENOUGH—Keep them, then, and see. But I think you'll find— [*He pauses sharply—then speaks wearily.*] I'll go now. Probably I've said exactly the wrong things —and I thought I had my arguments all arranged in invincible formation. At any rate, it's something to see you now and then. You're very good. . . . Life would be a very simple thing today, wouldn't it—if you cared for me as I care for you?

EDITH—There'd still be Julien—and I'd still think him right—in all the dreadful things he's done—whether I cared for someone else or not—and I'd still be a faithful wife as long as I felt—as I do—that he does still need me. Good-bye. [*She has suddenly forgotten the bracelets.*]

GREENOUGH—[*Quietly.*] Good-bye, my dear. You don't rail at your "yoke of inauspicious stars"—so all I can do is to bear mine—as gracefully as possible.

[*He finds his things, and goes in silence. EDITH stands still an instant, then goes into her bedroom at the back, closing the door behind her. The stage is empty for a moment, then JULIEN enters, two cups of coffee on a small tray. It is evident that he has been expecting to find someone. However, seeing no one, he sets the tray down by the table, makes himself comfortable, and prepares to drink the coffee himself. EDITH enters. She wears her cap and her sweater. As she closes the door behind her JULIEN looks about.*]

JULIEN—Oh. . . . Going out?

EDITH—Yes. It's time to think about dinner. Olga and Oscar will stay, I suppose?

JULIEN—I suppose so—if you ask them.

EDITH—You can ask them. I'll go to the market and get some more things.

JULIEN—Olga sent you and Greenough this coffee. She thought you might want it, after all.

EDITH—He's gone—and I don't believe I want any, thanks.

JULIEN—I'll drink it, then. [*She starts toward the door, but turns back.*]

EDITH—Julien——

JULIEN—Yes?

EDITH—You won't forget about the picture show, will you? Janet's counting on it.

JULIEN—I don't know why I mentioned it. I ought to go to sleep instead of going out.

EDITH—But you promised.

JULIEN—Oh, I'll take her. I don't like to disappoint Janet. You know that. [EDITH *comes away from the door and hovers near the table.*]

EDITH—[*Timidly.*] Julien——

JULIEN—Well, what is it?

EDITH—Don't you think—if you come home early to-night—and sleep well—that you might start in tomorrow morning and do those drawings for your old firm——

JULIEN—God! How I hate that job.

EDITH—I know. But we're spending such a lot, Julien. If you could only make something now and then, so that everything we had saved wouldn't go——

JULIEN—I'm going to do it, all right. You know that. For God's sake don't keep worrying about money. [*He drinks his coffee. She comes and sits in the chair across the room from him. He eyes her uncomfortably.*] I thought you were going to the market.

EDITH—I am. [*But she does not move.*]

JULIEN—[*Finishing his coffee, and lighting a cigarette.*] Well, what have you got on your mind?

EDITH—I don't know how to say just what I would like to say.

JULIEN—I suppose you're thinking of that stuff in the papers today. Well—everything was all twisted—and exaggerated. But—suppose we forget it? It's a mess—and I'm sorry I ever got into it, but—you'll forget it, won't you, Edith?

EDITH—It isn't that.

JULIEN—No? What, then? [*She is frowning in her concentration. With a sudden laugh.*] To watch you think is like watching a lot of fellows heaving a block of marble into place. Nothing in the world is worth all that effort, Edith. Whatever it is, don't bother.

EDITH—[*As if she hadn't heard.*] Julien——

JULIEN—Well—go on.

EDITH—Julien, you've talked a lot about freedom. And experience. . . . And doing as one wants to do.

JULIEN—Yes—I suppose I've talked more than was really necessary about a thing that most men take for granted.

EDITH—And when you said it was all right for you to go where you pleased and do what you pleased—with other women——

JULIEN—You exaggerate the other women, Edith. You always have. They were simply incidents.

EDITH—Perhaps. But you did mean that I had the same right to have the same sort of incidents in my life?

JULIEN—You! [*He suddenly laughs.*] What are you driving at?

EDITH—You said we were both to be free.

JULIEN—Poor Edith! Don't tell me you've been having your little temptations.

EDITH—Would that be so very amusing?

JULIEN—[*Her gravity causes him to stop smiling, but he still takes her very lightly.*] Now this begins to sound serious. . . . I'm afraid you've been letting Greenough really make love to you.

EDITH—I'm afraid I have. [*She lifts her hands and holds them out so that the bracelets catch the full light beneath his eyes. He bends over sharply to look at them, as she adds simply.*] Does it matter?

JULIEN—Good heavens! Those things are worth a fortune—if— Did Greenough really give them to you? [*She nods "yes." He looks at her with a slowly changing expression as she sits staring at her lifted hands in the lamplight.*] I can't believe it—of you. [*A bit unsteadily.*] By George—women always fool men. Even you! [*With an effort.*] Fair . . . ? [*Then, recklessly.*] Why not? Sauce for the gander is sauce for the goose. I've always said that. [*They sit in silence a moment. She touches his hand.*]

EDITH—Shall I take them off, now?

JULIEN—Take them off? Why? [*She doesn't answer at once. He continues easily.*] You spoke of being fair. Well, I hope I've proved to you that I meant what I said

about freedom.   I've not asked for anything I'm not willing to let you have. . . . I—I congratulate you.   As a
woman you're a great success.   I hope you get another
dozen or two like them.   They make your hands look very
charming.   [*She still doesn't answer.   Then suddenly she
stands up, blazing.*]

EDITH—Fair!   But this—this is—horrible!   [*A sob
tears from her lips.*]

JULIEN—Are you crazy?   Didn't I say what you expected me to say?

EDITH—[*Moaning.*]   Oh, but this is the end!   This is
the end!

JULIEN—The end!   Are you crazy?

EDITH—[*Starting toward the door.*]   The end!   I'm
going now——

[JULIEN *is before her and holds the door shut.*]

JULIEN—What do you mean?   Are you crazy?   Going
where?

EDITH—I don't know. . . . Oh, Julien!   [*He takes her
wrists and pulls her down toward the couch.   She is
sobbing.*]

JULIEN—You little idiot—hush!   What in the name
of God is the matter with you?

EDITH—[*Holding out her hands—still in his grip.*]
Don't you know?   You should have torn them off!   You
should have beaten me!   But you didn't care!   You
didn't care.   [*He drops her hands quickly.   She goes to
the door.   She opens it, and turns back—no longer sobbing,
but wide-eyed with grief.*]   I don't know what you'll make
of yourself—but now I know what it is you'd be willing to
let me make of myself.   And that's what I can't bear—
—that you're willing to—see *me*—that low!

[*She goes, quickly. The door slams behind her.* JULIEN *is like a man dazed.* JANET *comes into the room, her books under her arms. She goes and arranges them very neatly on a shelf and then comes to her father and touches his hand.*]

JULIEN—Oh—hello.

JANET—I've got all my lessons, father.

JULIEN—Have you? That's good.

JANET—We can go to the picture show now.

JULIEN—Yes, yes—so we can.

JANET—How's your headache, father? . . . Does it hurt—still?

JULIEN—It's all right. [*He moves impatiently to the window.* JANET *follows him, slipping her hand into his.*]

JANET—Do you think it's going to rain, father?

JULIEN—Perhaps. [*There is silence for an instant.*]

JANET—[*Excitedly.*] That's mother running! She's crossing on the other side of the Square. See! Where's she going, father? Where's she going! Running like that?

JULIEN—God knows! . . .

CURTAIN

THE THIRD ACT

Three years later. A spring afternoon.

*A small exquisite room high up in an apartment over-
looking the Park. At the back there is a row of windows with a small balcony just outside. Window boxes
of flowers brilliantly in bloom have just been placed
there. A very blue sky built about with white clouds
is the background for a radiant glimpse of the budding
trees and the towers beyond the Park.*

*At one side there is a fireplace, in which a fire has been
laid but not lighted. Beyond it is a doorway to
another room. Opposite there is a wider doorway to
the hall. There are several cases of books, and delightful pieces of painted furniture. The general impression is that of a delicate but luxurious setting for a
woman of sensitive taste.*

LAURA, *a maid—a pleasant-looking, intelligent young
woman—is talking to a young man who is there, obviously, on business. He is not exactly shabby, but one
is not surprised to find that he is a florist's assistant.*

LAURA—[*Indicating the tulips.*] I never saw a finer lot,
Mr. Knight.

KNIGHT—No, ma'am; I don't think you ever did. And
they look very handsome grouped like that.

LAURA—You don't think it's too early to put them outside?

KNIGHT—If it had been put up to me I'd have said "wait

one more week." Even tulips don't like the nights too cool, but your lady was so eager to have them right off that I figured out I wouldn't get any thanks by saying anything more than I did against it. People don't want too much advice, I've found.

LAURA—That's true enough of most, but not so much of her as you might think. Mrs. Fields is very willing to hear both sides always, even when it means that she's to be disappointed in something she's set her heart on. She'd have minded what you said about waiting a little longer if she hadn't been so excited and happy about her little girl.

KNIGHT—That's what she said to me herself. "I want everything lovely, Knight," she said, "so it'll look gay and beautiful when she comes home." Well, it's better than an even chance she's got with her window boxes. The weather's been warm for ten days now, and all we can do is to hope for good luck with them. I guess I'd better be getting along. [But he doesn't go.]

LAURA—Perhaps you'd like a cup of coffee and a bite of something to eat? I'm sure Mrs. Fields would like me to offer it to you—being as you've been working around without stopping at all for any proper lunch since morning.

KNIGHT—I might rest a bit, and drink the coffee, if it's no trouble to get, and you've a minute to spare——

LAURA—There's nothing to do now but listen to the telephone and the door-bell—and keep her from being awakened by anyone.

KNIGHT—The way the bells have been ringing all day makes that a harder job than it sounds.

LAURA—That's true. You can understand that we—[significantly as she lowers her voice]—live very quiet, as

a usual thing. But since the little girl's been in the hospital it seems as if people have turned up, right and left,
to show their kind feelings for the mother. And now that
the danger's all past and Miss Janet is being brought home,
Mrs. Fields is like somebody who—who—[*she hesitates
and then goes on*]—well, it expresses it to say she's like
somebody with a friendly jag on after drinking a little too
much. She wants to talk to everybody. She almost wants
to hug them. She heard me telling the man at the grocer's,
over the 'phone, how much better the child was—and got
out of bed herself to thank him for asking.

KNIGHT—I've always thought her a very nice lady,
myself, although . . .

LAURA—[*Nods.*] She's a lady in every respect, Mr.
Knight—or I wouldn't have stayed a year in a household
where things were not strictly regular.

KNIGHT—[*Nodding regretfully.*] She should appreciate
you.

LAURA—*I* appreciate her. [*She pauses, troubled.*]

KNIGHT—Of course we're talking confidential, and if
there's anything that's bothering you, and I could help
you——?

LAURA—No, it's not that you can help. It's only that
a person calling himself *Mr.* Fields has been calling up,
trying to see her. [*Her tone is ominous.*] What do you
make out of that, Mr. Knight?

KNIGHT—Could it be—a husband? What did he sound
like?

LAURA—Like—like—like anybody. Very dignified.
Very short. And I know she has a husband—and that he
let her have the child. [*A door is heard opening outside,
then men's voices. They move toward the door to the*

hall.] There's somebody coming in now. I guess it's Mr. Greenough. Just walk on out to the kitchen, while I see if anything's wanted. You don't mind, Mr. Knight? I'll be with you in a minute. You know where it is?

KNIGHT—I ought to—oughtn't I?

LAURA—Don't try to pretend that you're here often.

KNIGHT—[*Boldly as they go out.*] If I'm not whose fault is it? Not mine——

LAURA—'Ssh. . . .

[*They go. The stage is empty for a few moments. Then* GREENOUGH *enters with* STEWART. LAURA *follows them in.*]

LAURA—Shall I light the fire, sir?

GREENOUGH—[*Briefly.*] No, it's too warm.

LAURA—And the windows——?

GREENOUGH—Leave them open. [*To* STEWART.] It's really warmer outside than in. . . . Are you thirsty? After that walk— [*To the maid.*] Bring us something to drink.

LAURA—Yes, sir. [*She starts out, but turns back at his next words, spoken from the window.*]

GREENOUGH—Knight put these out today, I suppose.

LAURA—The flowers, sir? Yes, sir. [*She goes.* GREENOUGH *steps out upon the balcony.*]

GREENOUGH—[*Calling to* STEWART, *inside.*] What a day! [*Then he comes back into the room, continuing.*] By the way, have you the afternoon papers?

STEWART—I left two out in the hall. Want them?

GREENOUGH—If I do I'll get them later. I just remembered that I'd not seen one. Nothing new, I suppose?

STEWART—Stocks went down, generally, during the morning—then rallied—if that interests you.

GREENOUGH—It doesn't. Have you been in the market lately?

STEWART—Yes, unfortunately.

GREENOUGH—Did Uncle William decide to sell his steel, after all?

STEWART—Yes—unfortunately . . . again. It's gone up since. [*There is a bare pause.*]

GREENOUGH—[*Restlessly.*] I should think you'd want to get out of town—with the weather like this. [*He goes and looks out of the window.*]

STEWART—[*Rising and joining him, also restlessly.*] Those flowers are very pretty, aren't they . . . ? [*There is no answer and he continues in the same casual manner.*] I saw Julien Fields at the hospital today.

[GREENOUGH *looks up sharply but does not answer.* LAURA *enters with a bottle of whiskey and some soda and two glasses on a tray.*]

LAURA—Is there anything else, sir?

GREENOUGH—[*Quietly.*] You said Mrs. Fields was still asleep, didn't you?

LAURA—Yes, sir.

GREENOUGH—When she awakens tell her I'm home.

LAURA—Yes, sir. [*She goes out.* GREENOUGH *pours himself a drink.*]

GREENOUGH—Here you are. You like to mix your own.

STEWART—Thanks. [*He mixes himself a drink. Presently.*] Edith's all in, I suppose.

GREENOUGH—She's well enough now—only she can't seem to get enough sleep. It's the reaction—now that everything's all right.

STEWART—I suppose she went through hell.

GREENOUGH—I know she did.

STEWART—I said I saw him today—Fields.

GREENOUGH—I heard you.

STEWART—He's looking as if he'd been through hell, too. [*There is an instant's silence.* GREENOUGH *makes no comment.*] I suppose—after the child is brought here—that you'll have to have him about, now and then. She'll want him, and . . . It's rather a situation, isn't it?

GREENOUGH—He can't come here.

STEWART—But—she'll want him. He's her father.

GREENOUGH—He can't come here. That's settled.

STEWART—You and Edith could avoid seeing him.

GREENOUGH—He's not coming. [*There is a pause.* GREENOUGH *drinks his highball.*]

STEWART—A moment ago you asked me why I didn't get away; well, that's what I think you ought to do. [GREENOUGH *does not at once answer and* STEWART *continues, going to the window and staring out.*] With the weather like this and the whole land turning green I feel that the town is very much like the Augean stables, and one gets tired of marble stalls, even when they're clean.

GREENOUGH—There's nothing to keep you from turning yourself out to pasture.

STEWART—No, nothing. . . . I'll be off in a day or two, now.

GREENOUGH—Have you decided where to go?

STEWART—The Adirondacks. Your camp. I've invited myself. I wish you were coming along. Leave Edith here to work it out herself. That's what she's got to do—sooner or later.

GREENOUGH—I almost broke your head once—in our nursery days—for interfering with something I wanted to do. But you still interfere on every possible occasion with everybody and everything. I suppose no one will ever break you of the habit.

STEWART—You'll have to pardon these intrusions of mine if we're to go on being friends as well as relatives, Walter. When a man's headed wrong somebody's going to tell him so. . . . And there's one thing— [*He speaks with sudden heat.*] If you knew how often every member of the family —and every friend you have—and even men who are simply associated with you in a business way—had put it up to me that I ought to—to talk to you—you'd realise that I stood by you and Edith with a good deal of delicacy.

GREENOUGH—Oh, yes. I can imagine that. Thanks very much.

STEWART—I'm not asking for thanks. All I want is the privilege of saying to you—what I'd be jolly well glad to have you say to me under the circumstances—that you're not looking well, that you need a change, that you've been through a good bit, and that you must realise that Edith has a big situation to face—a very trying one—no matter how fond she is of you—and that it would be a good thing for both of you if you left her alone for the next three or four weeks.

GREENOUGH—Where's any situation? I don't——

STEWART—[*Quoting, with a shrug.*] "There's none so blind . . . "

GREENOUGH—But I *can* see how a sentimentalist—like you—who is always talking about the old-fashioned sanctities—for other people—might work himself up into thinking that a woman will throw over everything and go back to a miserable marriage that she ran away from years before—just because she and her child's father have been watching together at the child's bedside. . . . [*He laughs, but unhappily.*] Good God—that's the sob stuff they used to make sentimental songs of! . . . Life's different. "Baby hands" don't happen to, really, hold together men and women who have got through with one another, and gone different—and happier—ways for years.

STEWART—[*Quietly.*] There's something in what you say, of course. "Baby hands" haven't the enormous influence in real life that they've always had in the songs of the vaudeville singers. Neither has "mother." But there's something there—something that must make the sob stuff go down so easily—or they wouldn't keep on handing it out. But— [*Again he speaks with heat.*] Take the facts—then—and throw away the time-honoured sentiments. There *is something* damned touching about a sick child. You saw Janet—and all any of us could do was to go about trying to find things we could buy her —that she could have. If she'd wanted the moon for a locket you'd have managed to get it for her. Don't you think Edith felt something of the sort? Don't you think she still feels . . . [*He pauses.*]

GREENOUGH—[*Almost to himself.*] She'll never go back to him. I don't care who . . . [*He breaks off, then begins again.*] He had his chance. And I've nothing to blame myself for—I was on the square. I never said a word until . . . She won't go back to him. I'm satisfied of that.

STEWART—Maybe not. [*Something in his voice makes* GREENOUGH *look up quickly.*]

GREENOUGH—You don't think—you can't think that she *should,* Walter!

STEWART—I don't know. . . .

GREENOUGH—But——

STEWART—You see, after all, no matter how broad-minded one is—or is not—about this sort of thing—[*he waves his hand to indicate the establishment*]—one wants things a bit more regular where a child is concerned. There's something that Julien Fields can give his wife and daughter that you can't, Walter, with all your money.

GREENOUGH—The water's gone over the dam, Ned. . . . He drove her away. She's not going back.

STEWART—[*Changing the subject casually.*] When are you going to open the house at Westbury?

GREENOUGH—It's being put in order now. Edith and I are going out late this afternoon and have a look around. Then we'll move as soon as the doctors have finished with Janet.

STEWART—They want you to get her to the country as soon as possible, I suppose.

GREENOUGH—Oh, yes, of course. But it may be two or three weeks yet.

[LAURA *enters, a little uneasy.*]

GREENOUGH—[*Looking up.*] Well?

LAURA—It's a man—to see you, sir.

GREENOUGH—Well, who is it? Didn't he give his name?

LAURA—He said it—it was—Mr. Fields.

GREENOUGH—[*After a bare pause.*] Take him into the library—and ask him to wait.

LAURA—Yes, sir.

[*She goes. There is a silence. Then* GREENOUGH *speaks sharply.*]

GREENOUGH—You know him. You always had a good deal more to say to him than I did. Will you—will you —see him for me now?

STEWART—Don't you think he must have something

that he wants to say to you pretty badly—since he's come here—like this?

GREENOUGH—If he has he can say it to you. There's nothing I care to talk about to him. Good God! He can't think he's got anybody to blame but himself—can he?

STEWART—Very well. I'll see him. There's nothing you want me to say to him, is there?

GREENOUGH—You can tell him for me—you can say to him—that . . . But, what's the use? He knows as well as I do that all he can decently do, now, is to keep away . . . and he knows, of course, that there's nothing that won't be done for Janet.

STEWART—I think he appreciates it. I know he does, in fact. . . . [*He starts out.*] But I suppose the least I can do is to listen to what he has to say and make him understand your position.

GREENOUGH—Yes. . . . He might think of that.

[STEWART *goes. There is a long pause. Then* GREEN-OUGH *goes and rings the bell.* LAURA *comes presently.*]

LAURA—[*As she enters.*] Mrs. Fields is awake, sir; I was just coming to tell you when I heard the bell. [GREENOUGH *looks about with a sudden uneasy glance.* LAURA *hurries on.*] She rang for Clara about twenty minutes ago, but I didn't happen to know it at the time. I must have been brushing up the balcony after the florist's man had finished. I'm sorry, sir, I——

GREENOUGH—Never mind. Is William about?

LAURA—I think so, sir. I'll see.

GREENOUGH—Tell him to put some things in a bag and find out the first train I can get accommodations on—going to the camp. Then get them by long distance.

LAURA—The camp, sir?

GREENOUGH—The caretaker—William will understand.

LAURA—Very well, sir. [*She starts out.*]

GREENOUGH—And Laura——

LAURA—Yes, sir.

GREENOUGH—If Mr. Stewart wants me I shall be in Mrs. Fields' room.

LAURA—Very well, sir.

[LAURA *goes out in one direction;* GREENOUGH, *after the slightest hesitation, in the other. There is an instant's pause. Then* LAURA *returns, ushering before her* OSCAR *and* MRS. PRICE. LAURA *has in her arms two florist's boxes that they have evidently just given her.* OSCAR *is very smart, with a moustache and gloves, these days, although his shirts still have the look of the Nebraska farm—a look that he has managed to retain by having them made of too bright-coloured linen at a fashionable shop. And his suit of rough grey tweed has undoubtedly come from the hands of an English tailor.* MRS. PRICE, *much prettier than one has remembered her, is also amazingly smart in a simple frock and hat.*]

LAURA—If you'll wait here, please——

OSCAR—And please make a point of saying to Mrs. Fields that we've only come to say we couldn't come—and to ask when we may come instead.

LAURA—I'll tell her, sir, and she may want you to wait——

OSCAR—[*Briefly.*] That wouldn't be possible, today. We're on our way to a concert. But any other time, tomorrow or the next day, that she says.

LAURA—Yes, sir. I'll explain that, sir. [*She goes.* MRS. PRICE *waits for an instant for her to get out of ear-shot, and then turns about in amazement.*]

MRS. PRICE—But why on earth did you say a thing like that! I telephoned that we'd be here—and she said she'd love to see us! She's expecting us——!

OSCAR—[*With the manner one uses to a child.*] 'Ssh. . . . Tact, my dear. Tact. [*He indicates the hallway.*] There were voices in a room that we passed. And one of those voices was Julien Fields'.

MRS. PRICE—Oh!

OSCAR—Something's going on here. Don't you feel it? I could—even if I hadn't heard what I did.

MRS. PRICE—But——

OSCAR—'Ssh. . . . It behooves us to get out as delicately and as quickly as possible. [*She looks a little blank at this. He laughs indulgently.*] And that's an awful blow to your feminine curiosity, isn't it?

MRS. PRICE—You needn't make fun of me. Who wouldn't be curious? Aren't you?

OSCAR—Absurdly and tormentingly curious.

MRS. PRICE—[*Ingenuously.*] Then we might have hung around—a little while.

OSCAR—Now that's just the sort of thing that I'd consider a mortal sin. [*She looks at him curiously.*] Don't try to understand. You can't.

MRS. PRICE—I wonder why I put up with you. Except that you do understand certain things about my being lonely.

OSCAR—Pouf! You know why you put up with me and why I put up with you. It's springtime—the loveliest springtime that this particular year has ever seen—but we needn't lie about it. Oh, it's not because your husband had been so busy with his lucky inventions and his sudden flood of gold that he turned you loose with a full purse

to go out and buy what you liked—and let it go at
that. . . . It wasn't because you were opulent and lonely
that you waited and asked me to come to see you after
you'd come to one of my lectures.

mrs. price—If I hadn't been lonely I'd never have gone
to your lecture. I didn't know it was you, anyway. I
didn't know it when I read your book. I never even knew
you had a last name when I used to run into you at
Edith's—in those days when we both lived in that dreadful little flat in Harlem. [*She shudders delicately.*]

oscar—That dreadful little flat in Harlem. [*He smiles
and then changes the subject.*] Oh, I don't doubt you had
to be very lonely in order to get through with that book
of mine at all——

mrs. price—No—there was something about it I liked.
I've lived in a little town in Nebraska, too; and it brought
back something. You don't give me credit for any brains
—but I did like it. And that was why I went to hear your
lecture. And that was why I asked you to come to see me.
That and——

oscar—What?—go on.

mrs. price—You won't give *me* credit for having any
delicacy, I suppose, but I have. I never thought of anybody really making money out of writing books—and I
thought you might be poor still—and like to have some
place to go. You used to always enjoy a good home dinner
at Edith's.

oscar—So you thought you might give me one. I see.
[*He stares at her, a smile playing about his lips.*]

mrs. price—[*After a pause.*] What were you going to
say—? About it not being loneliness. You—you don't
flatter yourself that I'm in love with you, do you—just
because I keep on seeing you all the time?

OSCAR—Oh, no. The answer's much simpler. You're a woman. I'm a man.

MRS. PRICE—There are lots of men. . . . I've never . . .

OSCAR—I know. This is your first flirtation. But it won't be your last.

MRS. PRICE—It's not a flirtation. You're married. And so am I.

OSCAR—Good God—you don't think it's an intellectual companionship—do you? [*She doesn't answer this, but changes the subject coolly.*]

MRS. PRICE—How long has it been since you've seen Julien Fields?

OSCAR—I don't know . . . months . . . years.

MRS. PRICE—Olga told me that he was one of the ones she made you drop as soon as you were married—but that he'd always been a sort of hanger-on.

OSCAR—[*Apropos of nothing.*] Poor old Julien! The mills of the high gods do grind exceedingly small, at times. I wonder that they bother.

MRS. PRICE—Poor Julien—nothing! Poor Edith, I say! . . . And Mr. Greenough might have married her once. Now it's too late. Everybody knows he's kept her. Earle says he started out by trying to protect her—and he still pretends to live at a club in town. But they went to Europe together—first; then they took to living together openly in the country; and now— [*She shrugs.*] He's here all the time . . . and everybody knows—and even marriage couldn't make things really all right for her. Poor Edith—she was born soft. But as for her husband —he's only himself to blame.

OSCAR—Of course. Himself—and the mischief-making high gods that beckoned him along an impossible road.

Eh bien. . . . How smug and comfortable we get in this world when the dice fall right for us. You and I are very, very superior human beings, my child. Your husband had a talent for tinkering with engines; and my wife—once she *was* my wife—set her heart on a grey squirrel coat. So we are successes. Let us salute ourselves. [*He lifts her face between his hands and is about to kiss it.*]

MRS. PRICE—[*Warningly and angrily.*] Don't do that! I don't like it!

[*OSCAR laughs and moves away.* MRS. PRICE *goes and stares out of the window.* LAURA *enters.*]

LAURA—Mrs. Fields thanks you very much for the flowers and for asking about Miss Janet, and she says she's sorry not to see you—but she hopes you'll find it convenient to come another time—any time at all, but you can make sure of finding her if you'll telephone.

OSCAR—We will. Tomorrow perhaps, if it's convenient. At any rate, we'll telephone. [*To* MRS. PRICE.] Ready?

MRS. PRICE—Yes. [*To* LAURA, *who is leading the way out.*] Do tell Mrs. Fields how glad we are about her little girl. . . . [*They go, their voices dying away down the hall.*]

[GREENOUGH *enters presently and sits down, his face between his hands—a sullen, unhappy look on his face. After a few moments* EDITH *follows—coming and kneeling beside him, her arm about his neck, her attitude full of tenderness and compassion.*]

EDITH—[*Very gently, as if continuing an argument.*] Oh—but we mustn't quarrel! [GREENOUGH *does not answer at once.* EDITH *is radiant from a long sleep, although her eyes are, for the instant, troubled. She has wrapped herself in a tea-gown—delicate and aërial in the effect of its pale colours and falls of lace. About her neck is a long string of pearls. Her hair is freshly massed upon her head, and she is no longer the half-awkward, badly dressed, immature young woman of three years before—but is exquisite and gracious with something rare and wonderful about her. She repeats her appeal.]* We won't quarrel—will we? *[*GREENOUGH *rises suddenly and closes the door to the hall.* EDITH *rises and goes to the fireplace. He returns to his chair. She resumes.]* You've been so wonderful, Walter—through it all. . . . But you're making me feel very—very awkward. . . . Of course I didn't want to see him. . . . I think you know that after that night when you came up to me and put your hand on my shoulder—and said—"Stop . . . stop—where do you think you're going—running like this—" *[She stops and does not for an instant go on. Then she speaks again with great sweetness.]* Thank God you'd walked away from our house that night—just ahead of me! I think you know that—that—from that time on there began for me a new life. . . . *[He doesn't answer She continues.]* I don't say that from that moment the new life was a happy life. One gets used to great changes slowly. But I *have* been happy, Walter. And I've the very deepest respect for you . . . and a gratitude that's like nothing else—exactly—in the world. *[Again silence falls between them. And then again she goes over to him and is kneeling beside him.]* You made life all over for me. You've been so generous. . . . Please be generous now.

GREENOUGH—Kiss me. *[For an instant his lips are on hers. Then he speaks roughly.]* Have it your way. Have him here when you want him here—after she comes—as long as she's not able to go to the country. I don't suppose

that even you will think I ought to ask him to visit us there.
[*His tone is bitter.* EDITH *is silent.* GREENOUGH *continues.*] But I'll not be around. I'm going to the camp.
I'll stay until you're settled in the country.

EDITH—No—don't leave me! I don't want you to be
driven away like that!

GREENOUGH—Why not?

EDITH—Because . . . [*She rises and her mind takes
a new direction.*] You're right, I suppose. It's too awkward for him to be coming here. We'll keep her in the hospital where he can see her——

GREENOUGH—Nonsense. She'll be better off here. You
want her here. She'll come home. That's settled. But
I'll get out. . . . I need a change anyway. Only— [*He
rises and takes her by the shoulders.*] Once you said something—about the terrible clairvoyance of love. You were
talking about yourself—and him. Well, I've got that—
that clairvoyance. I'll *know* if anything happens to change
you.

EDITH—Nothing can happen. Everything happened that
could happen a long time ago.

GREENOUGH—But he and you—this—this sort of thing
never happened before. . . .

EDITH—Don't you realize, Walter, that there's only a
stone-cold feeling in my heart for Julien Fields? I've seen
him there—sitting by Janet's bed—drawing pictures for
her—holding her hand, trying, even, to pray to something
that he didn't believe in—and I felt nothing—nothing for
him, at all—except——

GREENOUGH—Except what?

EDITH—Except how terribly sad it was that I felt
nothing.

GREENOUGH—I'm afraid. There's a certain door that you won't shut——

EDITH—Walter—I'm very sensible! You're much more sentimental about this than I am. Please believe me.

GREENOUGH—There's one thing I'd believe against all the evidence in the world—and that's your word. . . . I'm going away. I can't say to you "feel this and that"—or "don't feel this and that." You'll feel what you're going to feel. But I can say to you, "Give me your word that you'll never go back to him." Will you do that?

EDITH—Go back to him! But— [*Her amazement is almost touched with humour as she promises ironically.*] I give you my word, my dear. I'll never go back to him. . . . Now?

[*For answer he holds her in his arms an instant, and kisses her, speaking with sudden gentleness, close to tears.*]

GREENOUGH—I'm so sorry—dearest—about all this. . . . We'd better arrange it so we can be married. . . . It will be better for Janet, you know—she's growing up. It will be better in every way, for us both. Don't you think so, too? [*She nods "yes." He goes on, suddenly, almost buoyantly.*] That's sensible—at any rate. No more of this apologetic uncomfortable semi-clandestine stuff. We'll be Mr. and Mrs., and those that like it can come and see how happy we are . . . and those that don't can go to the devil with our compliments. If we're going to look round the place at Westbury before dark, we'd better be starting pretty soon. I've telephoned them to have some dinner for us. . . . I want to get back in time to catch my train.

EDITH—You're really going to the camp?

GREENOUGH—Yes—but I'm going with a much happier mind than I thought possible half an hour ago. I'll let you dress now—while I see if William has attended to everything.

EDITH—Very well, I'll— [*But as he starts to walk with her to the door she sees the window boxes and pauses, standing in the window.*] Oh! So Knight came—and filled the window boxes!

GREENOUGH—Come away from that open window. You'll take cold in that thin thing.

EDITH—Nonsense. . . . Oh, Walter— [*She holds her arms up in the air.*] This is like June! It's not like April, at all.

GREENOUGH—Come on—come on.

EDITH—In a moment. I won't be an instant getting into my frock.

GREENOUGH—All right. But it's nearly four—and it takes an hour and twenty minutes—the best we can do.

EDITH—I know. I'll be down and in the car waiting for you ten minutes before you're ready. . . . Janet's a good little thing—isn't she? [*Her voice breaks suddenly, as she adds.*] She looked too lovely today. . . . She's going to be pretty, Walter. [*She comes away from the balcony reluctantly.*]

GREENOUGH—She's damned plucky. I'll say that.

[EDITH *goes to a desk.* GREENOUGH *pauses at the door to look back inquiringly.*]

EDITH—Don't wait, dear. I'm only looking for a list I made out—things I want the housekeeper to attend to.

GREENOUGH—It's nearly four—remember.

[*He goes.* EDITH *looks about, searching for her list. The door opens and* STEWART *enters.*]

STEWART—Oh—pardon me. . . . I left Walter here a moment ago. Am I intruding?

EDITH—Come in. . . . No—I'm just going, too. Walter is packing, I believe.

STEWART—Is he going somewhere?

EDITH—To the Adirondacks for a few weeks.

STEWART—Good. . . . [*She looks a little surprised. He hurries on.*] Edith——

EDITH—Yes?

STEWART—There's someone here I think you ought to see—for a moment.

EDITH—Who?

STEWART—Julien.

EDITH—Julien!

STEWART—Yes.

EDITH—But why——?

STEWART—Let him tell you.

[GREENOUGH *enters, and stands near the doorway, listening.*]

EDITH—It isn't necessary.

STEWART—He's going away. He won't come here again. He had something that he meant to say to Walter,—but Walter won't see him.

GREENOUGH—[*Advancing.*] This is about enough. Tell him to come in—if he's still here. We'll both see him—and that will end it.

STEWART—I'll bring him. [*He goes quickly.*]

GREENOUGH—[*To himself more than to* EDITH.] That's best, I think.

[EDITH *says nothing.* GREENOUGH *walks half-angrily, half-nervously about the room.* EDITH *goes and sits down on the far side of the room.* GREENOUGH *glances at her sharply.* LAURA *enters.*]

LAURA—[*To* GREENOUGH.] Pardon me, sir, but— [*Sh*

includes EDITH *in her look.*] There haven't been any orders given about dinner yet.

GREENOUGH—No one will be here.

LAURA—That's all the cook wanted to know. We weren't sure. [*She starts to go.*]

GREENOUGH—Bring Mrs. Fields something to put around her, first.

LAURA—Yes, sir. [*She turns about and goes out by a different door.*]

EDITH—[*Absently, pulling her pearls out from her throat.*] But I'm not cold. . . .

[*He does not answer.* LAURA *returns with a long chiffon scarf edged with fur, and goes to* EDITH.]

LAURA—Shall I put this around you, Madame?

EDITH—Thanks, Laura. And have everything ready for me to dress to go to the country.

LAURA—Yes, Madame. Everything's laid out. And I'm going to put your heavy wraps in the car, now.

[*She goes out again through the door into* EDITH'S *room. Almost at the same moment* STEWART *enters from the hall, with* JULIEN *following. There is silence as they come into the room and as* GREENOUGH *and* JULIEN *nod to each other —and then* JULIEN *and* EDITH. JULIEN *has the unhappy, shabby look of one of the millions of men whom life has cowed. But there is still in him something of courage for the great quest—and something of his old indifference to fortune, happiness and the peace of others.*]

JULIEN—[*To* GREENOUGH, *impatiently, out of the pause.*] Naturally I didn't know when I came here that you were going to regard a simple conversation between us in the light of a social *faux pas.* I suppose, however, an apology is in order for this intrusion. . . . I apologise.

[LAURA *enters, closing the door a bit noisily behind her, carrying a fur coat and a tissue-wrapped package.*]

EDITH—[*Quickly, from her place on the other side of the room, lifting her hand to hurry* LAURA *out.*] Put those things there—on a chair. [LAURA *puts them down quickly, and instead of passing through the room retreats quickly— closing the door behind her.*]

EDITH—Sit down, Ned. . . . You might sit down, Julien. . . Walter. . . . [*She glances at a chair. The three men sit.* EDITH *turns to* JULIEN *expectantly.*] Now . . . ?

JULIEN—It's not so easy to talk now. Everything's got too difficult, somehow. What I came for—[*he speaks to* GREENOUGH *with sudden energy*] was to thank you, first, for all that your money has done for my daughter.

GREENOUGH—That's not necessary.

JULIEN—No—but she's had the best—when she needed it worst. I realise that. You—you were able to buy Death off. Money's a fine thing to have at a time like that. . . . I'm sorry my own pockets were empty—as usual.

[EDITH's *eyes are suddenly turned miserably away from* JULIEN. GREENOUGH, *too, looks away.*]

STEWART—[*After a pause.*] By the way—perhaps this isn't exactly the time to mention it—but if you want some work to do——

JULIEN—[*With a quick gesture, stopping him.*] I can't settle to anything. . . . It's no use, thank you.

EDITH—[*Almost crying out.*] But, Julien—how do you get along? You must——

JULIEN—Don't worry. One odd job keeps me going to another. Besides, my old firm—they still remember that I sat at a desk there in a very regular fashion for ten years —that was your doing, Edith—and they're not afraid to trust me with all the work I'm willing to undertake.   [*He laughs.*]   They even offered to take me back the other day, again, and start me in where I left off five years ago. That's fine progress, isn't it?

EDITH—[*Quietly.*]   You ought to go.

JULIEN—Why?

EDITH—It may not be anything—very—very brilliant, just now—but it would be better than just drifting—aimlessly—doing nothing at all.

JULIEN—I'm not so sure. *You'd* think that, of course. [*He smiles.*]   But there are worse things than being free —to drift. You never know what's just round the corner. Probably it's somebody you owe money to—but it might be a bird of paradise flashing like a rainbow through an alley.

EDITH—So you're still hunting——?

JULIEN—[*Interrupting.*]   For birds of paradise?   You might put it that way. . . . No, there's a chance of finding that one's got something in him as long as he holds himself free to do his best. But to tie myself up to a desk, now, would be the end of everything—for me.

STEWART—I think you're wrong, Fields.

GREENOUGH—[*Impatiently.*]   You can't expect me to take a very sympathetic point of view—and I hope you'll pardon me for saying it, but, as far as I can make out, you're trying to explain to yourself, and to us, an inactivity that may be—— Are you sure you're not—just lazy?

JULIEN—I am lazy—but that—that's not the main difficulty. [*With sudden scorn.*]   You wouldn't call a man standing still in a fog lazy—would you? However—there's no use of your bothering about me. I'm going away so I won't have to put any unnecessary strain on your hospitality—and Janet might not understand why I don't come round unless she knows I'm not in town. So thanks again —and good-bye.

GREENOUGH—Wait a minute. There's one thing more. The sort of life that Edith and I have been living isn't exactly to our taste. She wouldn't bother about a divorce in the beginning——

JULIEN—And you'd like one now, so you can be married? I see. That ought to be easily arranged. I'll do anything that you suggest——

GREENOUGH—Then before you go—since you're leaving town—suppose you talk over the details with my cousin? [*He indicates* STEWART.]

JULIEN—Certainly. . . . I suppose there are facts you ought to get. . . . [*A pause falls.* JULIEN *turns to* STEWART.] You and I might go back to that room with the Romney over the mantelpiece. [*He turns to* GREEN-OUGH.] Then I'll be on my way. . . . That's a fine Romney. Next to having money for the doctors and the nurses when there's a child ill, I'd like it to spend for things like that.

GREENOUGH—[*Briefly.*] It's a good picture, they tell me.

JULIEN—[*To* EDITH, *who rises.*] This is good-bye, Edith. [*She holds out her hand. He takes it, speaking with sudden simplicity.*] There's no use getting senti-mental, but you know that if you and Janet needed me now I'd be willing to be a galley-slave at that desk I hate so much—the rest of my life. It was good of you to send for me—and let me see her—so often. But I know you're both better off than you ever were with me.

EDITH—Good-bye, Julien. I want you and Janet to go on being the best of friends, always.

JULIEN—Thanks. You're very generous. [*He drops her hand and turns quickly to* STEWART.] Shall we go?

STEWART—Yes. [*To* GREENOUGH.] I'll see you later, Walter.

[JULIEN *and* GREENOUGH *nod to each other, and then* JULIEN *follows* STEWART *from the room.* EDITH *comes over and stands by the mantelpiece.* GREENOUGH *waits for her to speak, which she does presently, in a voice touched with compassion and tenderness.*]

EDITH—Julien's a child, really. . . .

GREENOUGH—Well, that's done.

EDITH—Yes. That's done. You understand, don't you, how impossible it is to keep from feeling sorry for Julien? And to keep from worrying a little about him. He's so wrong-headed. . . . He's very charming with Janet. Yesterday they were playing that she was his mother— [LAURA *enters, her face averted. She stops, as if she had something to say, and then starts to hurry out.*] Laura— [LAURA *stops, her face still averted, her eyes lowered.* EDITH *continues.*] You may take my cloak now—but after this please go through the other door to my room. It's awkward when there are people here to have someone passing through. [LAURA *does not answer.* EDITH *lifts her voice.*] Do you understand, Laura? [LAURA *nods* "yes." EDITH *is a little annoyed as she continues, sharply.*] Look at me —please—when I speak to you—and answer me— [*The maid lifts her face—convulsed with weeping. Gently.*] Oh! I'm sorry. . . . You may go. [*There is a bare pause; the maid does not go.* EDITH *continues.*] Or is there something that you want to tell me? Perhaps I can help——

LAURA—No—it's— Someone telephoned— [*A sob checks her.*]

[*Suddenly* EDITH *is at the maid's side, her hands gripping both* LAURA's.]

EDITH—It's—not—Janet! [*There is no answer. Something falls from* GREENOUGH's *hand to the floor.* EDITH *is frantically shaking* LAURA *by the shoulders.*] Tell me—tell me—tell me——

LAURA—[*Convulsively.*] She's dead—the poor lamb—

[EDITH *slowly releases her and stares at nothing.* LAURA *weeps.*]

GREENOUGH—When—did you—hear this? You're sure ——?

LAURA—They're on the telephone now—the hospital—I meant to tell you first—I didn't want to tell her——

EDITH—[*Still staring at nothing and shivering slightly.*] Where's that scarf you brought a minute ago—Laura?

GREENOUGH—Put it around her— [*He touches* EDITH *on the shoulder as* LAURA *looks for the scarf.*] Edith—darling——

EDITH—[*With a long sigh.*] It must have happened very suddenly. . . . Or do you believe it, Walter? I can't get it through my head—that—it's so. I must go to her—I must go at once! [LAURA *hands* GREENOUGH *the scarf. He puts it about* EDITH *who shivers into it.*]

GREENOUGH—No, no; stay here. . . . Keep a good grip on yourself, darling.

EDITH—[*Suddenly.*] Someone must tell Julien! He's here, isn't he? Oh, poor Julien!

GREENOUGH—I'll see that he's told. [*He turns to* LAURA.] Stay here with her. . . . I'll go to the telephone, and then come back. [*He goes.*]

LAURA—Please sit down—Mrs. Fields—dear— [EDITH *sits down.*]

EDITH—[*Presently.*] You may go, Laura. [*But* LAURA *does not go.* EDITH *raises her voice.*] You may go. . . . I'd rather be alone. You might light the fire first. It's turning cold. [LAURA *looks in surprise at the brilliant sunlight pouring into the room. Then she kneels and lights the fire on the hearth.*]

LAURA—[*Pityingly as she goes.*] I don't like to leave you—but— [*She does not finish. Something stern in* EDITH's *attitude orders her away.*]

[*Left alone,* EDITH *moves toward the fire, shivering and warming her hands. Then, her eyes bright with pain, she lifts her head, whispering.*]

EDITH—[*To herself, brokenly.*] Mother's blessed comfort—Janet . . . darling——

[GREENOUGH *returns and comes and stands near her, looking down into the fire.*]

EDITH—Poor Julien! . . . [*There is a pause. Then she speaks suddenly.*] Walter—I gave you my word a minute ago.

GREENOUGH—[*Gravely.*] Not to go back to him. . . . I know.

EDITH—I can't promise that, now; you must give me my word back. He may need me. [GREENOUGH *does not answer.* EDITH *continues after a moment.*] Yes—I must be free to do as I think best, now.

GREENOUGH—[*Steadily.*] There's nothing I can say, of course— This isn't the time to say anything—about one's self. . . . It's the other man you want with you now. So —I give you your word back, Edith. And I—I'll get out. I'll send him to you now.

[*He goes.* EDITH *waits.* JULIEN *enters. His face is wet with tears. He goes toward her and she comes toward him. For an instant neither speaks.*]

JULIEN—Oh, Edith! [*He sobs on her shoulder.*]

EDITH—Poor, poor Julien! [*Her arms are about him.*]

JULIEN—What are we going to do—Edith? Death's so damnably final. She's gone. . . . And I can't bear it!

EDITH—I knew you'd feel like that. But you must bear it, Julien. . . . We'll have to bear it together. . . . Come here. . . . [*She makes him sit beside her. He huddles into her embrace.*]

JULIEN—I used to be so frightened—in the hospital. I kept thinking of Death—as a kidnapper. I used to hold on to her hand to make sure she was still there!

EDITH—I know. Put your head on my shoulder. You're my little boy again. And you need me again. And we have each other—just as we used to. . . .

JULIEN—[*Lifting his head.*] No, no. . . . That's not true. We haven't each other. The past is all gone—blown away like leaves in the wind. We can't ever get it back. And Janet is a leaf in the wind, too, now. [*He rises and walks about restlessly. She rises and stands near the fire, shivering again.*]

EDITH—But—you and I are still here, Julien. And everything's forgiven between us and set straight—because we need each other again, at least.

[JULIEN *is silent for a moment—then he comes and puts his arm about her as he realizes her meaning.*]

JULIEN—You're being very wonderful. You're all broken up now—and so am I. . . . But, Edith dear, I don't want you to think of doing—what you're thinking of doing. . . . Things are better—the way they are.

Heaven knows I'll think of you and Janet day after day
—and night after night—but we can't bring back the other
days. We'll bury them in the little grave they're making
for her.

[EDITH *moves away—groping for something. She finds
her long fur coat and puts it on. Then she sits down
—trembling—as if too weak to stand.*]

EDITH—It's turning very cold. . . .

JULIEN—[*Gently, but absorbed with his own thoughts*
Give him his chance. He'll make you a good husband.
I never did. . . . [*There is a pause. Then he continues.*]
To be honest, Edith, we'd find it impossible—without
Janet. . . . You're used to luxury now . . . and it suits
me to be alone. You mustn't think of it. [*He leans his
head on his hands, wearily.* EDITH *stares at him, as if
trying to understand something. He speaks again, rous-
ing himself, presently.*] Well—I'll go—I'm all in . . .
and I've got to be alone. Do people ever say good-bye?
Does anything ever really end, I wonder?

EDITH—[*Significantly.*] Sometimes, I think—things end.

JULIEN—I suppose so. . . . I've got to get out and walk
and fight this thing off—or it will get me. . . . [*He lays
his hand for a moment on her shoulder.*] Poor Edith—try
not to let it get you.

[*He goes. She laughs a little, and gets up and wanders
again to the fire. The maid enters, and busies herself
about the room, eager to be of some comfort or use, but
EDITH does not notice her. STEWART enters. Her back is
to him, and she does not notice him. He comes and stands
beside her, in front of the fire.*]

STEWART—Edith. . . . [*But he has to speak a second
time before she hears.*] Edith.

EDITH—[*There is a quality of great patience in her voice.*] Yes, Ned?

STEWART—I'm sorry; you know that. We all loved Janet.

EDITH—[*Simply.*] She was a good little thing; and getting very pretty.

STEWART—[*Repeating.*] I'm sorry.

EDITH—[*Coldly, very quietly.*] Why? [*But before he can speak, in his surprise, she continues in the same impersonal tone.*] This world is a very unsafe place. It's all shifting sands, Ned. Shifting sands and changing winds. It's just as well that Janet won't have to grow up. No. . . . I'm not sorry that the Kidnapper came and took her.

STEWART—But, Edith—this is a strange way to talk.

EDITH—[*Looking at him piercingly.*] You think so?

STEWART—[*Uncomfortably.*] Julien didn't go—did he?

EDITH—Yes.

STEWART—But Walter said——

EDITH—Walter was wrong. Julien didn't want me.

STEWART—But I thought . . . Walter thought . . . [*He hesitates; then he cannot refrain from asking, in great surprise and curiosity.*] What are you going to do now?

EDITH—[*Again she smiles.*] God knows.

THE CURTAIN FALLS

GREATNESS—A COMEDY

(THE TEXAS NIGHTINGALE)

GREATNESS—A COMEDY
(THE TEXAS NIGHTINGALE)

Produced at the Empire Theatre, New York, November 20, 1922, with the following cast:

BRASA CANAVA	Jobyna Howland
STEVEN TILLERTON	Cyril Keightley
RAYMOND TILLERTON	Percy Helton
SASCHA BLOCH	Georges Renavent
COUNT HOUDONYI-BLOCH	Paul Porcasi
INEZ	Beth Varden
WALTER PRESCOTT	Perce Benton
KITTY MULBERRY	Lizzie McCall

GREATNESS

THE FIRST ACT

A long narrow room, so lined with books in their cases that one might suspect a book-shop—one of those new Washington Square club-like places—if it were not for the signs everywhere of one habitual inhabitant. There is a fireplace in which a basket full of coal is almost ceasing to glow; there is a leaf-table with a student's lamp, and a lay-out of the pet supplies required by a rather eccentric writer. The ink is in a big pot; two dozen pens ready for use in their holders, stacks of papers, and neat blotters are at hand; also in a portfolio hundreds of neatly written sheets. There is a grand piano, upon which, at its curving point farthest from the keyboard, is a low glass bowl crowded with hyacinths, azure and white. There are deep chairs; doorways into two adjoining rooms, and one into the main hall (for this suite occupies a floor in an old house that has been made over into apartments). There is the sound of someone at the door.

Then a gentleman—one supposes him to be the writer, whose name is STEVEN TILLERTON—*lets himself in by a key. He is in evening dress, with an Inverness that was once rather smarter than it is now, and an opera hat, and cane. He carries his white gloves. A cigarette is in his mouth. Probably he's fifty—possibly more, possibly a little less. He goes directly to the piano—and plays the theme of the Ride of the Valkyries. Incidentally he is accompanied by another gentleman—his old friend,* WALTER PRESCOTT, *to whom he talks, but of whom he is not thinking very much just now.*

PRESCOTT—[*Feeling a little apologetic in the presence of* TILLERTON's *abstraction.*] I'm only going to stay a minute. It's after twelve——

TILLERTON—Take off your coat, anyway, won't you? And sit down. [*Without sitting, he continues to finger at the theme that still gallops through his head.*]

PRESCOTT—That sounds familiar.

TILLERTON—It should. You heard it tonight.

PRESCOTT—Oh, Die Valkyrie. Well, I'm tone-deaf. Still, I like to go to the opera every once in a while. There's something highly charged—electric—exciting, about the Metropolitan on a big night.

TILLERTON—I know. . . . Have a cigarette. [TILLERTON *stops playing, takes off his overcoat, and turns on the lights in the chandelier.*]

PRESCOTT—No, given up smoking. . . . Doctor's orders. [*He has taken up the evening paper. Seeing him absorbed in the headlines,* TILLERTON *is drawn back to the piano— and again touches the keys—playing the Ride. Prescott speaks presently, disapprovingly, suddenly.*] Do you always go when your wife sings?

[TILLERTON *arises, moves away from the piano, lights a cigarette, and finally decides to answer.*]

TILLERTON—You can hardly call *her that.* I had the honour of being only the second and most obscure of Madame Canava's four husbands, you know. . . . Yes, when she sings Brünnehilde, I'm usually there.

PRESCOTT—Expensive habit, isn't it?

TILLERTON—Very.

PRESCOTT—I should think you'd never want to hear her voice again. It's cost you too much. And when I say that I'm thinking of the money it cost you to take her to Paris and make a singer of her—and the *money* alone.

TILLERTON—Well, money was never better spent, was it?

PRESCOTT—[*Ignoring him.*] If there's anything I detest it's a sentimentalist. Have you heard anything more from the executors of your rich friend's estate?

TILLERTON—[*With a smile.*] A great deal more.

PRESCOTT—I hope you've explained that after she sang for him, he said he didn't want you to pay back the money he'd lent you to have her voice trained?

TILLERTON—[*After a pause.*] I explained that, naturally.

PRESCOTT—And that he told you he was going to tear up your notes for the eight thousand dollars you'd borrowed.

TILLERTON—[*Impatiently.*] But he didn't tear up the notes. They've found them. And there's nothing on earth to do but to pay them. There's nothing sentimental about that. It's very legal.

PRESCOTT—But they can't expect to come down on a man after twenty years and collect a sum like that—like that— [*He snaps his fingers to illustrate.*] The thing to do is to let them go ahead and sue you for it, if they want to. . . . Besides, if the money's got to be paid— Canava ought to pay it, not you.

TILLERTON—That can't even be discussed. I'll pay it, of course.

PRESCOTT—But you haven't got it.

TILLERTON—I've arranged for it nevertheless.

PRESCOTT—Eight thousand dollars isn't a mere trifle—

to a novelist whose novels have always refused to be best
sellers.

TILLERTON—Money's a dull subject. Let's talk of something else.

PRESCOTT—[*Suddenly, accusingly.*] Then you're going
to sell your books!

TILLERTON—You *are* curious.

PRESCOTT—[*Hotly.*] It's true, then? I heard it today
—that you were going to sell them—but I wouldn't believe
it. See here—let me manage this for you.

TILLERTON—[*Quietly.*] Hands off, my friend! This is
my own affair. Very much my own affair. . . . I'll be glad
to get rid of them. I'm a book-ridden man. I'm going
away somewhere—away from books. [*He continues in a
lighter tone.*] And maybe it's not too late to write something I haven't read before, after all.

PRESCOTT—And Brasa Canava gets three thousand dollars every time she sings! And since she's got the strength
of an ox and the soul of a cow, she'll go on pouring out
that golden flood of a voice for years and years and years.

TILLERTON—"To him that hath shall be given—" She
hath . . . that's all. That's *greatness.*

PRESCOTT—One sort of greatness, maybe.

TILLERTON—Even the great can have only their own
sort of greatness.

PRESCOTT—And it's often only that they're great
sponges. . . .

TILLERTON—Often, yes. Or great roses for whose blooming the trees have been pruned and stripped. But they
make the beauty of the world. And that's enough.

PRESCOTT—Having a voice has no more to do with true
greatness than the shape of her nose.

TILLERTON—[*Quietly.*] I know her better than you do. There's greatness there. Ludicrous greatness, if you like, the comedy of greatness rather than any of its thousands of tragedies; but great gifts, undeniably, and greath growth, and above all, great luck. Let's have some supper. That walk home has given me a bit of an appetite.

PRESCOTT—No, thanks. No late suppers for me. Doctor's orders. It's after twelve. I ought to be getting some sleep and so ought you. We're too old for late goings-on, nowadays.

TILLERTON—Yes. I suppose we are. And yet twenty years ago—twenty-five years ago—almost thirty years ago—we were the kings of the high-steppers. We were in the high-jumper class. Well . . . Tempus fugit.

PRESCOTT—Time flies? No. Time stands still. It's we who move. Time is the pole in the center of the merry-go-round. We're the children riding the lions and the tigers.

TILLERTON—Life doesn't seem to me such a holiday matter. And Time seems to me like a gray old cynic who always has his finger to his lip, hushing us to sleep—because he's too important to listen to anything we might happen to be saying . . . and yet—[*suddenly lifting a book from a table*]—a sick boy wrote a few poems . . . and he was more important than Time. . . . Time put to sleep the pompous men and the rich men and the fashionable men—and the pretty ladies, too, who looked down on the little Cockney poet, in his day—but Time can't put John Keats to sleep—ever.

PRESCOTT—No . . . and *that's* greatness!

TILLERTON—[*Not noticing the argument in the inflection which his friend has given to his words, but reading*

*instead the first lines that meet his eye as the book comes
open in his hand.*] "Much have I travelled in the realms
of gold"— [*He closes the book sharply, and continues,
speculatively*] . . . And yet, he must have been an odd,
lonely little chap—with a very stupid idea that he wasn't
worth his salt. . . . He was probably very apologetic for
being alive at all in such a practical world. [*He lays the
book down.*] By the way, there's a poem in the new
Bookman that I want you to read. It's on the table—
there. . . . [*The telephone rings.*] Pardon me. [*He
answers while* PRESCOTT *picks up the copy of the magazine and reads.*]

TILLERTON—Hello. . . . Yes? This is he. What—! [*His
voice changes and deepens.*] No; nothing you could ever
do would surprise me. . . . [*But surprise does affect his
voice and manner as he answers, presently.*] Certainly.
[*He hangs up the telephone and turns about suddenly elated
and speaks almost like a man a bit drunk as he goes and
slaps* PRESCOTT *on the shoulder.*] Well? Have you read
it? Isn't it fine?

PRESCOTT—Not bad.

TILLERTON—It's good enough to remember; and if I were
a magazine editor like you I think I'd not forget this chap's
name. What time is it by your watch? [TILLERTON *gets
out his own watch and compares it with a clock on mantel.*]

PRESCOTT—Twenty-eight minutes after twelve.

TILLERTON—You're ten minutes fast.

PRESCOTT—[*Defensively.*] I know it. I keep my watch
that way. What are you doing?

TILLERTON—[*Who has moved away and is bringing a
table over.*] Getting ready for some supper. [*Puts table
in place.*] You don't want any, you said.

PRESCOTT—[*Wavering a little bit.*] Well, if you've got anything that's easily digested——?

TILLERTON—[*Evidently anxious to get rid of him.*] Better stick to your resolution, if it's the doctor's orders. Wait a minute. [*He starts into the kitchen. As he opens the door, he sees a light inside.*] Evidently Kitty Mulberry is still here. The light's burning. [*He goes out for an instant and is heard calling, "Hello, Kitty," in a gay voice.*]

PRESCOTT—[*Following him to the door.*] If you've a cracker, just a little hard, thin, dry cracker of some sort, I think I could eat that.

TILLERTON—[*Calls back.*] All right. [PRESCOTT *takes up a cigarette and looks at it, then regretfully puts it down.* TILLERTON *returns, a small plate in his hand.*] Here you are.

PRESCOTT—Thanks. [*He takes the biscuit offered, and begins munching it solemnly.*]

TILLERTON—[*Suddenly.*] The remarkable part of it all was that she was a very good wife.

PRESCOTT—[*Not catching his drift.*] What?

TILLERTON—Yes, she was a very good wife.

PRESCOTT—Oh, you're talking about her.

TILLERTON—[*Still with the same elation. Going on, not heeding the interruption.*] She'd come home from the opera, even after her first big success, and wipe up the floor with our brand-new French servant because she wasn't neat enough in the kitchen—or had let us be overcharged for the chicken.

PRESCOTT—They say she is going to marry again.

TILLERTON—[*A little dampened.*] People always talk a great deal about the affairs of celebrities.

PRESCOTT—They say he's only twenty.

TILLERTON—What? Who?

PRESCOTT—Bloch. The Bulgarian violinist—whom she's going to marry.

TILLERTON—Sascha Bloch?

PRESCOTT—Yes.

[KITTY MULBERRY *enters.*]

KITTY—[*To* TILLERTON.] Would you like anything hot, sir? Or just what I have in the ice-box?

PRESCOTT—Hello, Kitty Mulberry. You don't keep union hours, do you? Why aren't you asleep?

KITTY—I'd have been a good three hours ago, sir, but the old man's been on a spree again and had the door locked agin me when I got home; and bein' as I had no money on me to go to a movie with, I came back here to wait for the likker to die on him. [*She turns to* TILLERTON.] I've some nice cold chicken, sir, if you'd like me to lay it out?

TILLERTON—Is there plenty?

KITTY—Yes, sir. If that friendly young woman who is always borrowing our stove don't come begging, sir. She's giving a party tonight and she's sure not to have enough to go around. But I hope you won't let her get anything away from you, sir.

TILLERTON—Find out what time it is by the kitchen clock, Kitty. [*He looks at his watch again.*]

KITTY—Yes, sir. [*She goes.*]

PRESCOTT—I know that young woman. She tries to write. She invites editors to her parties. She invited me to one tonight, and I replied I was going to speak at a banquet to the Mayor of Newark. [KITTY *enters.*]

KITTY—Eighteen minutes after twelve, the clock says, sir.

TILLERTON—It's slow. What time have you now, Walter?

PRESCOTT—[*Looking at his watch.*] Thirty-one minutes after. [*Then he pauses sharply.*] You're not catching a train or anything, are you?

TILLERTON—[*Not aware of his friend's facetiousness.*] It's about twenty-four minutes after. You're seven minutes fast, not ten. [*He hurries on as if to avoid some subject that he does not wish to discuss.*] Does that young woman really borrow our stove, Kitty?

KITTY—She takes it, sir. She comes tiptoeing to the kitchen door: "May I cook this on your stove?" she'll say. "You know I've only a kitchenette with one burner." And it's not that I begrudge the stove, sir, only there are so many things she hasn't got besides. Might I enquire of you gentlemen what the opry was about?

TILLERTON—About a great, golden-haired woman—a goddess named Brünnehilde.

KITTY—Then I wouldn't have liked it myself, sir. I like a tune as well as anybody, only I'm partial to a good, natural plot, and goddesses are a bit unnatural, to my way of thinking.

TILLERTON—So they are. That's their glory.

KITTY—I suppose, being as they're always in a furreign tongue, you might say that the opry is more or less the movie of the rich. But I'd better be minding my own business at this time of night, too. [*She goes.*]

PRESCOTT—[*Suddenly speaking soberly, apropros of nothing.*] You know, you would have been a great man, if it hadn't been for her.

TILLERTON—Nonsense.

PRESCOTT—No, it's not nonsense; it's the truth. You

had it in you. You'd have made the grade. But she drained you dry. She used you as long as she needed you and then she threw you away. That's what I've always had against her.

TILLERTON—[*Drily—not liking this turn of the conversation.*] Aren't you forgetting the facts? A divorce court decided that I deserted her.

PRESCOTT—Just a part of your delicacy. You cleared out because you knew you were in her way. You spoke of her luck just now. I can't help thinking that the greatest luck she ever had was in meeting you.

TILLERTON—Oh, someone would have drifted her way, and looked at her face—and heard her sing—and rescued her from those band concerts in those little raw prairie towns. . . . That was written in the stars of Hollyhock Jones, the Texas Nightingale.

PRESCOTT—I'd give a good deal to know what she thinks of it all when she looks back.

TILLERTON—She has no such weaknesses. She never looks back.

PRESCOTT—I wonder.

TILLERTON—[*More to himself than to his friend.*] But, of course, when it became clear that an incidental husband was no longer needed in that big career, I did get out. . . . She was a sort of museum piece, you know,—a little impractical for every-day use. . . . So they say she's to marry this Bulgarian chap, the violinist, do they?

PRESCOTT—Yes, that's what they say. . . . You never see her, do you?

TILLERTON—[*Drawing his finger along his neck.*] I have never set eyes on her, off the stage, since our last big scene, of which this scar is a delicate souvenir. But she's coming to see me tonight. However, she'll probably be much too formal to throw any more teacups.

PRESCOTT—[*A little alarmed.*] So that's who was telephoning! I'll go.

TILLERTON—Of course you will. She said she'd be here in ten minutes, and I've been watching the clock. I was just about to put you out.

PRESCOTT—Well, she's got a good voice. She knows how to sing. I'll say that much for her. Good night. [*Then he adds, grouchily.*] It's just like *her* coming here at this hour.

TILLERTON—[*Too pleased to understand the disapproval in his friend's voice.*] It *is* like her, isn't it? Good night, Walter. Good night. Good night.

PRESCOTT—[*Taking his departure a little awkwardly.*] Good night.

[*As he goes,* KITTY *enters from the kitchen, carrying a large tray.*]

KITTY—It's a good bit of supper, if I say it, as shouldn't. The chicken is cooked very pretty; and the asparagus just came in from the country this morning. There's some quince jelly; and a fine cheese. And now I'm going home, as it's on the table waiting.

TILLERTON—*Looking up, aware of what she is saying, now.*] That's right. . . . [*He looks at the supper, which she is setting out on the table.*] Yes, it looks very nice. . . . It was a shame to make you stay so late. I hope you're not very tired.

KITTY—I'm never tired. And never been tired since I was sixty. When I was younger I used to feel sorry for myself with all my complaints—but after you're sixty the work seems to come handier, somehow, and by that time you've got so used to it that the only thing you worry about is how long you can keep on giving satisfaction. Well, good night, sir.

TILLERTON—Good night, Kitty Mulberry. . . .

[KITTY *goes.* TILLERTON *moves about, a little restlessly. He places the chairs, just so; rearranges the light; stirs the fire; and at last goes to the piano and plays again, very badly, but with a ringing sound, the Ride of the Valkyries. There is a knock on the door which he doesn't hear; then another which he does; then another before he has time to reach the door; and a violent hand is heard on the door-knob, as, tripping himself over rugs and chairs in his haste, he delays an instant longer and calls out.*]

TILLERTON—Yes—I'm coming.

[*In another instant he has managed to get the door open, and* BRASA CANAVA, *like a magnificent thunder-cloud driving an invisible chariot, is whirled into the room by four great German police dogs, that strain, two by two, from the pair of chain leashes which she holds in each hand. She herself is frowning a little, and is a little annoyed—at this instant—in spite of the natural radiance flowing from her brilliant eyes and skin, her red hair, and her great height and grace.*]

CANAVA—[*Her first words are in the abruptly casual manner of a person taking up a conversation where it was interrupted a few moments ago.*] Why haven't you a bell?

TILLERTON—[*Abjectly—in bewilderment.*] But, my dear—— [*He pauses, staring at her helplessly.*]

CANAVA—[*Interrupting.*] Why haven't you a bell, I said? I had to knock three times! Made my hand sore.

TILLERTON—[*Staring at her still, a little lost.*] But how wonderful you look off the stage—how young!

CANAVA—[*Suddenly as sweet as honey.*] My Stevie looks won'erful, too. . . . A little thin, maybe.

TILLERTON—[*Swept along, but protesting a little.*] Now don't talk baby talk to me after all these years, Hollyhock!

CANAVA—[*In a voice of which she might speak of murder.*] Good heavens, man, don't call me Hollyhock! [*He laughs. She continues wryly.*] "Hollyhock Jones, the Texas Nightingale." I've not forgotten. I want to give my dogs a drink. Where's the kitchen?

TILLERTON—May I take them?

CANAVA—They may object. [*But he has taken the leashes from her hand. She pats their heads, speaking first to one and then the other.*] There—Tristan. . . . Ah, that booful Carmen! Their tongues are out. We walked down. They like you.

TILLERTON—You walked? After singing Brünnehilde? From the Metropolitan?

CANAVA—What's funny about that? . . .

TILLERTON—Please forgive me for being surprised at your energy. Come, Carmen—Tristan—and what——

CANAVA—[*Interrupting with the information he is about to ask for.*] Wotan and Tosca. I'm going to sing Tosca next year.

TILLERTON—But you've never sung Italian opera!

CANAVA—What does that matter? Why are you keeping those poor dogs waiting? Give them some water, and then come back.

TILLERTON—Of course—pardon me—take off your things, won't you?

[*He whistles the dogs out of the room, into the kitchen.*]

Left alone, MADAME CANAVA'S *first thought is to open both windows wide. Having done this, she takes off her hat, her furs, and her gloves; finds a cigarette; and then calls, loudly enough to awaken the neighbours, to* TILLERTON *in the kitchen.*]

CANAVA—Bring me a glass of water, too; but don't put any ice in it.   Where are the matches?

TILLERTON—[*Calling back.*] Just a moment— [*He returns with the water, and sees the cigarette which she is rolling between her fingers.*] Do you smoke? I thought most singers didn't dare.

CANAVA—[*Pausing one second to answer.*] They don't. . . . [*Then she drains the glass while he finds the matches before she continues, complacently.*] But nothing hurts my voice.   Now give me a light. . . . Do you think I can't sing Tosca?

TILLERTON—Of course; you can sing anything.   Only I heard you tonight, and after Brünnehilde I wonder why you bother.

CANAVA—You always come on my nights, I suppose?

TILLERTON—No, not always.

CANAVA—[*Judiciously.*] You should. . . . [*He lights her cigarette for her, and she continues in an irritable voice, as if arguing.*] I sang Carmen this year—with everybody saying I couldn't—and it wasn't worth while— and this, that, and the other. Ha! Don't I know them!

TILLERTON—[*In bewilderment.*] Know who——?

CANAVA—[*Calmly, but with eyes that alternately brood and gleam, as she smokes.*] My enemies—those damned cats around the opera-house—men cats as well as women cats! . . . The success-haters. . . . That's what I call them—the people who have never got what they want and turned sour on everybody who has. The world's full of them. . . . As soon as you've made good they begin to watch for you to fail: "Her voice isn't so good this year," they say—after an opening night, when you never sang better in your life. "Ah, a cold. . . ?" they say, if you ever do miss a performance. And the way they say it is a hint that what's really wrong is drink—drugs—an operation on your vocal cords—or an attempt at suicide! . . . For fifteen years my enemies have been trying to make out that I can't act. They've had to admit the voice. Good God—there's never been such a voice as mine!—although they've been watching me like hawks—listening for me not to take every note—lying—criticising—waiting —I know them!

TILLERTON—But—my dear—! [*He is a little appalled.*]

CANAVA—[*Continuing, but somewhat more calmly.*] So they say I can't act—I must stick to the great heroic rôles! That's why I thought I'd do Carmen for a change—and show them. And I showed them—didn't I? [*He does not answer. She goes on, half-angrily.*] Well? What did *you* think of my Carmen?

TILLERTON—I didn't see it. I didn't go. . . . You see, you're one of the goddesses to me—and I'd rather not see you do anything that you don't do better than anyone living.

CANAVA—[*In a deadly voice.*] Will you tell me *why* you think I can't do Carmen?

TILLERTON—She's not your type——

CANAVA—Why not? What do you know about it? Did you ever see a Spaniard in your life—who wasn't crazy about red hair? [*He laughs outright.*] Carmen must have been very much like me—blonde and tall. You ought to see—you *have* seen—the way those Spaniards follow me on the street—when I've been in Spain— Remember that time at Gibraltar——

TILLERTON—[*Smiling, but veering away from further discussion.*] You convince me, as always. Now come and have some supper. . . . I'll get out a certain bottle of champagne that I've been saving for a great occasion.

CANAVA—[*Deeply hurt.*] Do you mean to say you'd forgotten that I always drink milk? You know I never drank anything else!

TILLERTON—My dear! How was I to know that the world had let you go on drinking milk all these years! Forgive me.

CANAVA—[*Muttering.*] Think I'm a weather-cock?

TILLERTON—I ought to know better than that, oughtn't I?

CANAVA—You ought.

TILLERTON—Sit down—won't you? Here are chicken and asparagus—and—I'll get the milk. . . . Will you help yourself?

CANAVA—[*Sitting, her head suddenly in her hand, baby-ishly.*] No. . . . You wait on me. I want to be waited on.

TILLERTON—That's very charming of you. [*He serves her.*] Of course there's not much——

CANAVA—Aren't you going to have any?

TILLERTON—In just a minute—I'll be right back. [*He goes out.* CANAVA *tastes the food experimentally.* TIL-LERTON *returns with the milk.*] There— [*He fills her glass.*]

CANAVA—[*Judiciously.*] The chicken's cooked well—but it's been in cold storage. I'll give you my butcher's address. And I don't suppose you know where this asparagus came from?

TILLERTON—Isn't it right? I'm sorry.

CANAVA—Right? [*Indignantly.*] It's wonderful! Find out where you get it and let me know—please. . . . Did you notice what that conductor tried to do to me in the third act—tonight?

TILLERTON—I thought he took certain passages a little too fast——

CANAVA—Yes—and if he ever tries to hurry me again —this is good butter—if he ever tries to hurry me again he'll never conduct again when I'm singing. . . . Why did you leave me?

TILLERTON—Why did I—what?

CANAVA—That's one of the things I've always meant to find out—if I waited fifty years. But twenty's long enough. What made you leave me?

TILLERTON—[*Incredulously.*] You mean—why did I go away—twenty years ago——?

CANAVA—I asked you a direct question, didn't I? Why did you leave me? Can't you answer it? You're not eating anything—and the chicken's damned good—even if it has been in cold storage. I can always tell a cold-storage chicken the minute I roll my eye over it. I don't even have to taste it. [*She eats. He stares at her—a smile on his lips. Presently she lays her fork and knife down abruptly, with a clatter, and stares back at him with troubled eyes.*] You must have had some reason. What was it?

TILLERTON—The reason—whatever it was—has been forgotten.

CANAVA—Liar! There are some things nobody forgets.

And one is why you leave your wife or your husband. I
left my first husband because I didn't like him.

TILLERTON—Leslie Jones, you mean?

CANAVA—Yes, Leslie Jones. . . . I don't know why I
ever married an undertaker, anyway. I suppose it was
because he had an ear for music and I loved flowers, especially lilies. Always, after there was a funeral, he sent
me the flowers. Then, too, I liked him because he looked
as tenors ought to look—very romantic and sad. But he
was lazy and had no ambition and drank too much. So
I left him—not because he was lazy and drank and had
no ambition, though. I left him because I'd got to hate
him. Then, when you came along, of course, I was glad
I had had the sense to get free. You were just what I'd
always hoped for. Of course—[*she is suddenly humble
and compellingly sweet*]—I didn't know enough then to
really know how wonderful you are. I just knew you
were fine—like silk—and that everybody else I'd ever
known before seemed suddenly coarse and cheap—like the
commonest cotton. [*There is a pause. She has put out
her hand and touched his. Then she continues in a low
voice.*] I was always awfully afraid of you, Stevie. [*He
laughs aloud. She goes on wryly.*] You always laughed
at me, you know!

TILLERTON—But it was always very sympathetic laughter, Hollyhock.

CANAVA—Don't call me Hollyhock!

TILLERTON—Brasa—then. . . . You were a long time
letting me christen you "Brasa."

CANAVA—Yes. It took time for me to get used to your
ideas. I used to think that Hollyhock was a beautiful

name. Why did you leave me? That's what I want to know now.

TILLERTON—Is that why you came tonight?

CANAVA—[*Suddenly depressed.*] No. I came because I want your help. I'm at the end of my rope—about something. [*She hesitates and plunges again, half-angrily.*] You were in such a hurry to leave me that I don't suppose you stopped to consider what might happen after you'd gone?

TILLERTON—But I did consider. I considered everything. You had your first big contract to sing at Covent Garden the following season . . . and you'd made a great success in Paris. . . . I knew nothing could stop you—or happen to you——

CANAVA—I almost died—that's all.

TILLERTON—Died! You weren't ill?

CANAVA—[*After studying him a minute, in a matter-of-fact voice.*] I had a baby six months after you left me.

TILLERTON—What!

CANAVA—Don't tell me you never guessed——

TILLERTON—But of course not! Do you think I knew anything of the sort——

CANAVA—[*Shyly.*] I'd hinted——

TILLERTON—Good God!

CANAVA—I went around knocking wood. I didn't want to talk too much about it. [*Accusingly.*] You know I'm superstitious about such things!

TILLERTON—[*Again.*] Good God!

CANAVA—Well—don't you care what happened? Don't you want to know whether it was a boy or a girl?

TILLERTON—You damned crazy, funny, astonishing woman! . . . Tell me.

CANAVA—I'd like to know what's crazy or funny—or astonishing about having a baby, when you're married.

TILLERTON—It's not that; only you kept it such a secret —you've never let me know in all these years——

CANAVA—Why should I? I thought you didn't want anything to do with either of us. I wasn't going to bother you.

TILLERTON—[*Gently.*] And our child . . . we had a child. . . . Tell me, my dear. . . . Have I—a son?

CANAVA—[*Drily, grimly.*] You have. And so help me God—he's the damnedest poor excuse for a nineteen-year-old boy I've ever seen in my whole life.

TILLERTON—[*All at sea.*] You mean—he's—not turned out—well—? And he's nineteen. Yes—of course he'd be nineteen. Well—even if—as you say—he's not quite a model youngster—just the fact that he's alive at all—is great news—to me. Thank you—a thousand times——

CANAVA—[*Almost in tears.*] Stevie—I didn't know you'd feel like this. . . . You're making me want to cry . . . for having been such a fool—all these years. I wish I'd had better sense—only I thought—I thought you knew —and— [*She breaks off sharply—and dries her eyes violently—speaking abruptly.*] Just wait until you see him. Maybe you won't feel so sentimental then.

TILLERTON—But he's just a boy, isn't he? One doesn't expect perfection from boys, my dear——

CANAVA—Don't go on calling me "my dear." You used to call me "my dear" when you were angry.

TILLERTON—I seem to be having a hard time. Brasa— is rather professional, you know.

CANAVA—[*Petulantly.*] You can call me Ducky— can't you? You always used to.

TILLERTON—Of course. . . . By the way, what is our young man's name?

CANAVA—Raymond. . . . I got married a little later, you know——

TILLERTON—Yes—to Riboux; I know.

CANAVA—Riboux taught me everything I really know about music. You know, you never knew anything about *music*, Stevie. You knew the sort of things I ought to know—and you started me right—but it was just my voice that carried me along until I sang with Riboux.

TILLERTON—[*Haltingly.*] Of course. . . . It must have been a very wonderful thing for him to have had such a voice and mind as yours to teach.

CANAVA—He *was* wonderful—until I left him. He's never done anything since.

TILLERTON—None of us have—have we? Leslie Jones, the undertaker—who drank himself to death,—or Riboux, who has never conducted or composed any new work since your divorce—or Count Stowitstitsky—the sculptor—or I— [*He pauses a minute, regarding her curiously.*] I wonder why . . . ?

CANAVA—[*Firmly believing what she says.*] If *you* haven't gone on it's your own fault. You ought to have put a book before the public every year.

TILLERTON—[*Patiently.*] You were telling me about—our son——

CANAVA—You asked me what his name was, didn't you? He went by the name of Riboux—after I married him. . . . Everybody thought he was Riboux's son, instead of mine —if they bothered to think anything.

TILLERTON—That was rather natural, I suppose.

CANAVA—[*Drily.*] It was convenient; I didn't mean to tell him anything about you.

TILLERTON—That, too, was rather natural, I suppose—since you thought I'd deserted you and him. . . .

CANAVA—That reminds me. What made you leave me?

TILLERTON—I suppose now it was a great mistake—but you'd made a success—and seemed very much engrossed in your career—and in one or two persons who were the sort given to cultivating ladies with careers. . . .

CANAVA—You mean you were jealous of that Russian Grand Duke?

TILLERTON—Possibly that's the simplest way to put it. [*She is silent for a minute. Then she looks up, half smiling.*]

CANAVA—I got rid of him in short order—as soon as I found out what he was after.

TILLERTON—But didn't you know—from the beginning?

CANAVA—If I had—do you think I'd have let him hang around?

TILLERTON—But I told you very plainly that you couldn't accept diamonds from a man——

CANAVA—But it was such a beautiful necklace!

TILLERTON—Precisely.

CANAVA—And my first one. I have it yet.

TILLERTON—But do you mean that you kept it—and sent him away——

CANAVA—Of course I kept it! He gave it to me because he admired my voice. What's wrong about that? Every king and queen in Europe has given me something because they admired my voice. It's not the sort of voice they hear more than once in a lifetime—and they know it! But when I found it wasn't only my voice that inter-

ested the Duke I put him in his place. . . . After that—
whenever I met him—he doubled himself up with respect.
I dined with him—and his wife—in London several times,
my first season there. He was in love with me—but he
always behaved after I knocked him down that time.

TILLERTON—You really knocked him down—? [*He is
smiling.*]

CANAVA—Yes, I knocked him down—and threatened to
spank him. He was only about that tall, you know. [*She
indicates a distance well below her shoulder.*]

TILLERTON—And you'd not known what all his attentions
and gifts meant———?

CANAVA—Why should I? He knew I was married. I
thought he was just like lots of those rich foreigners,
crazy about music. . . . Besides, I couldn't understand
French—except what I happened to be singing—and I
didn't know what he was jabbering about half the time.
. . . I only knocked him down . . . but I suppose I'd have
killed him if I'd known he was the cause of your leaving
me. You're not eating, and you're not drinking. What's
the matter?

TILLERTON—Tell me more about—Raymond. . . . He
must make up to me for a great deal . . . now.

CANAVA—[*Without enthusiasm.*] You'd better see him
for yourself.

TILLERTON—What is he like—whom does he look
like?

CANAVA—A jockey. . . . [*Then she adds as she shakes
her head sadly.*] I don't know what to do with the boy.
. . . That's why I'm here to tell you that you'll have to
help me get some sense into his head.

TILLERTON—[*Slowly.*]   Of course, it's rather awkward
—until I see him.   But what does he like to do—best?

CANAVA—Spend money.

TILLERTON—Most boys have a tendency of that sort—
and I'm sure you've been very generous with him.   I wish
I could be. . . . Has he—has he any talent, of any sort?

CANAVA—[*Drily.*]   He says he's a poet.

TILLERTON—[*A little appalled.*]   A poet? Well, is he?

CANAVA—Yes—but what of it?

TILLERTON—[*Reflects an instant.*]   If he's really a real
poet——

CANAVA—[*Repeating.*]   Yes—what of it?

TILLERTON—It's very wonderful—and also, in certain
ways, very unfortunate.

CANAVA—[*With great energy.*]   That's exactly what I
think.   [*She pushes her plate away.*]   No more. . . . I
want a cigarette now.

TILLERTON—Match?

CANAVA—I always roll mine first. . . . You know a poet
is a damned nuisance to have around.   Now you can give
me a light.

TILLERTON—So the boy's a poet . . . and a nuisance.
Why is he such a nuisance?

CANAVA—He's unhealthy, in the first place.

TILLERTON—He can't help that.

CANAVA—Nonsense. . . . He'd be healthy if he'd do
what I tell him—but he won't take enough exercise and
he won't eat the right food—and he won't keep regular
hours.   He's finicky, and nervous, and lazy, and silly.
Besides that he's uppish.   He's uppish with me.   He
criticises me.   Makes fun of me.   And he tries to keep
me from doing things I want to do. . . . He talks like a

Bolshevist. . . . Says he believes in the brotherhood of man and he doesn't believe anybody ought to have any private property. Then he goes out and sends me flowers. Beautiful flowers—everything that's out of season—only I pay for them, myself, at the end of the month. He's got your mania for books, too. Only regular books don't suit him. He's got to have first editions. He's always in debt—and never tells me until somebody is going to sue him. He makes fun of the stage settings at the Metropolitan and designs costumes for me I'd be arrested for wearing. And he sulks if I don't take his advice about everything I do—from buying a hat to singing Carmen.

TILLERTON—[*Half smiling, half serious.*] No wonder you find our poet perplexing.

CANAVA—[*Grimly.*] And now he's gone and found a tart he wants to marry because she has a beautiful soul and a sad story.

TILLERTON—Good heavens!

CANAVA—And—believe it or not—the boy's ashamed of his own mother for being a virtuous woman!

TILLERTON—That doesn't seem very likely, Ducky.

CANAVA—[*With heat, almost in tears.*] Oh, yes. He's told me. He says it's very bourgeoise to be always getting married—that it's not necessary for the artiste to *marry.* . . . I suppose he'd make a tart of me, too,—if I'd listen to him. But no man that walks this earth—has ever been able to do that—and I'm not going to lose my character now just because I've a son who's a poet. You've got to help me manage him, Stevie. You've got to try and make a man of him— [*There is a knock at the door.*]

TILLERTON—Pardon me a moment— [*He opens the door. A very young man in a dinner-jacket, without a hat,*

*is there.   The only thing that mars his form is a white
kitchen pail which swings from one hand.*]

THE YOUNG MAN—[*With a polite drawl and quite an air.*]
Pardon me—but the young woman who lives on the next
floor—I think her name is Stanley or Standish—asked me
if I'd ask you if she could borrow some yellow rat cheese
or some eggs or anything you might happen to have? She's
giving a party and there's not enough spaghetti to go
round.   She didn't expect all of us, you see.   [*He is in
the room by this time.*]

CANAVA—[*Turning about abruptly, and speaking
grimly.*]   Are you in the habit of going to parties where
you're not expected,—given by strange young women
whose names you're not sure of?

THE YOUNG MAN—[*Calmly.*]   Of course, Ducky.   Everyone is, these days.   You never know where you're going
to be taken on to next.

TILLERTON—[*With a frown and a smile.*]   And is this
—the poet?

THE YOUNG MAN—[*Whose name is* RAYMOND, *of course.*]
Ah—my mother's told you I'm something of a poet, evidently. . . . .   I didn't know you were in the habit of these
tête-à-tête suppers, Ducky,—with—[*he studies* TILLERTON
impertinently]—strange young men. . . .

CANAVA—[*Rising—very sadly and addressing* TILLER-
TON.]   Well—?   [*She makes a helpless gesture.*]   You've
seen him.   What do *you* think of him?

RAYMOND—You might introduce us, Ducky.

CANAVA—[*Ironically.*]   He's   your   father.   You've
heard me speak of him.   [*There is a slight pause.* RAY-
MOND *gets his bearing first.*]

RAYMOND—[*Calmly.*]   Ah, yes—you were one of mother's husbands, I believe. The second, wasn't it? I've heard her mention you.

TILLERTON—[*Huskily—emotion beating at his heart in spite of the casualness of the situation.*] But it happens that I never heard of you—until tonight. . . . Don't you think we might shake hands?

RAYMOND—If you like—only don't get sentimental, old man. And how about those eggs? Anything that can be cooked over one burner or in a chafing-dish will do.

CANAVA—Don't mind him, Stevie. He's deeply touched. I know him. He likes to act like this—as if he didn't care. But he'll write a beautiful poem about it, tonight, or tomorrow. See if he doesn't. [*Suddenly motherhood overcomes her and her arms are about* RAYMOND, *as she talks to him in the language usually reserved for babies.*] Who's the mos' won'erful thing in the world? Muvver's little boy is the mos' won'erful person in the world . . . and he writes the most boo'ful poems—he's a smarty——

RAYMOND—[*Bearing her shower of kisses patiently.*] There, there, Ducky—let's not embarrass Mr. Tillerton——

CANAVA—Call him "Father." . . . He's my little boy's real father.

TILLERTON—Yes—I hope you can condescend to such informalities, my—my son. I'm going to call you Raymond, you know.

RAYMOND—Certainly—only these things are always a little awkward. It usually takes a little time for me to get used to the idea of addressing strange men as "father." . . . It's happened before, you know.

TILLERTON—At least, let's hope it will never happen again.

RAYMOND—[*Suddenly struck by an idea.*] I say—could

you give me a little of your time? I want your help about something. I need it.

TILLERTON—Of course. I hope we are going to be together a great deal.

CANAVA—[*Suspiciously.*] Go get those eggs, Stevie..

TILLERTON—Yes—I'll see what I can find. . . . Pardon me. [*He goes.*]

CANAVA—[*Violently, to* RAYMOND, *as the door closes on* TILLERTON.] Look here! What are you up to? What do you want your father's help about?

RAYMOND—What did you hunt him up for? [*They glare at each other an instant.*]

CANAVA—[*Accusingly.*] You're going to try to make him help you keep me from marrying Sascha!

RAYMOND—Precisely. Weren't you trying to get him to help you keep me from marrying Inez?

CANAVA—I certainly was. You're under age. He's your father—and the girl's a tart.

RAYMOND—And Sascha Bloch is only a year or two older than I am——

CANAVA—*He's* been famous since he was ten.

RAYMOND—He's just one of those musical freaks——

CANAVA—I'm of age—and I'll marry whom I please. . . . He's one of the greatest artists in the world. And his father's always lied about his age, anyway. He's twenty-six—instead of twenty-one. And I'm only a few years older. I'm a young woman. And I'm lonely——

RAYMOND—Oh, mother— [*This time there is a real cry of distress in his voice.*] If only you wouldn't go on making yourself ridiculous!

CANAVA—[*After a pause, half-gently.*] Will you give up this tart?

RAYMOND—She's not—that. She's an exquisite thing. I'm the only person who understands her. She needs me. I—I can't desert her——

CANAVA—[*Abruptly.*] She's thirty and a tart; and we'll see whether you give her up or not! And we'll see whether you're going to interfere in my affairs or not. . . . A boy who can't even earn carfare——

RAYMOND—If you ever torture me about not being able to make money, again, I'll shoot myself. I swear it!

CANAVA—[*Half muttering—tears in her eyes.*] You're always going to shoot yourself.

RAYMOND—Yes . . . the strange thing is that I've never done it yet. I'd like to know why anyone wants to stay in "this world that is no better than a sty." . . . Shakespeare knew what he was about when he called it that . . . *sty!* [*He rises and goes over to the window.*] May I put this down? . . . It's cold in here.

CANAVA—Do anything you like.

[*She sits again brooding in her chair at the table—her head between her hands. Presently she rolls a cigarette.* RAYMOND *sees the magazine open on the table and picks it up and stares at it.* TILLERTON *returns.*]

TILLERTON—Here's everything I could find—five eggs —some bacon—and some cheese—though it's Roquefort——

RAYMOND—Thanks I'll take it up. Miss Whateverher-name-is will be no end grateful. . . . By the way— somebody's been reading a poem of mine. [*He indicates the magazine.*]

TILLERTON—You're not "John Grey"?

RAYMOND—Yes. I usually sign my things like that.

TILLERTON—[*Looking again at the poem—and then lay-*

ing his hand on the boy's shoulder and speaking with emotion.] I wish you'd signed it Raymond Tillerton. I'm very proud of you, my son.

RAYMOND—[*His eyes full of sudden tears.*] Thanks— father. . . . [*He touches the open pages of the magazine.*] Beauty's all that matters, anyway—isn't it?

TILLERTON—It matters most—to people like us. It's the great illusion. [*There is a pause.*]

RAYMOND—Could you lunch with me tomorrow, sir? At the Ritz—at one?

TILLERTON—I'll be there.

RAYMOND—You write novels, don't you?

TILLERTON—Not very successful ones.

RAYMOND—I despise success anyway. . . . [CANAVA *grants, in derision.* RAYMOND *turns to her and continues, placatingly.*] When you get ready to go home, Ducky, I'll take you—if you'll call me. [*But she is still proud and hurt.*]

CANAVA—[*Huskily.*] I'll walk!

RAYMOND—Alone?

CANAVA—I brought the dogs.

RAYMOND—Well, you've more energy than I have —which is nothing new. . . . See you tomorrow. . . . [*He lingers, as he opens the door, for one more remark.*] We're all of us a bit odd, I expect. [*Then he is gone.* TILLERTON *comes over and touches* CANAVA *on the shoulder, tenderly.*]

TILLERTON—You and I have got to respect that very young, young man, Ducky.

[CANAVA *jerks away from his touch and goes to the windows, throwing both open as far as they will go, with a monosyllable of explanation.*]

canava—Hot! [*Then she turns and surveys the room a little scornfully as if she were seeing it for the first time. She comments in a perfectly matter-of-fact tone.*] You're rather shabby here, Stevie. You need new curtains and a new carpet. . . . Of course what you really need is a good housekeeper. [*She goes about, finding dust on everything she touches—straightens a picture on the wall—and continuing impatiently as she pushes chairs out of her way.*] One thing I like about the Metropolitan Opera House is that I always feel I have plenty of room there. [*Again she paces about—looking for something.*] Who ate the matches? [*He is quick with a candle for her cigarette. She drapes herself affectionately about his shoulder. Then after an instant she speaks, half-angrily, half-tearfully.*] Find that damned poem and read it to me, Stevie!

THE CURTAIN FALLS

NOTE: When this play was produced by the Charles Frohman, Inc., it was considered impractical to bring on the dogs, at Madame Canava's entrance; consequently the following changes in the text were made in reference to this episode.

tillerton—Good night, Kitty Mulberry. . . . [*She goes.* tillerton *moves about a little restlessly. He places the chairs just so; rearranges the light; stirs the fire; and at last goes to the piano and plays again, awkwardly, but with a ringing sound, the Ride of the Valkyries. There is a knock on the door. Then another. Then another.*] Yes—I'm coming— [*But he has paused to place some primroses on the supper-table, and again the knock is repeated, and a violent hand laid on the doorknob.*] Yes, yes—right away! I'm coming.

[*He gets the door opened, and* BRASA CANAVA, *like a magnificent thunder-cloud, enters. She is in dark street clothes, overhung with splendid furs. She is frowning and annoyed in spite of the natural radiance flowing from her brilliant eyes and skin, her red hair, and her height and grace.*]

CANAVA—[*Her first word is shy, then she continues instantly in the abruptly casual manner of a person taking up a conversation where it was interrupted a moment or two before.*] Hello. Why haven't you a bell?

TILLERTON—[*Abjectly—in bewilderment.*] But, my dear——

CANAVA—[*Interrupting.*] I had to knock three times. Made my hand sore.

TILLERTON—I am sorry.

CANAVA—[*Again interrupting.*] Are you alone?

TILLERTON—Yes.

CANAVA—Then shut the door, give me a drink of water, and I'll stay a while.

TILLERTON—[*Closing the door, but a little lost as he stares at her.*] But, my dear, how wonderful you look off the stage—how young!

CANAVA—[*Melting suddenly.*] My Stevie looks won-'erful, too. . . . A little thin, maybe.

TILLERTON—[*Swept along, but protesting a little.*] Now don't talk baby-talk to me after all these years, Hollyhock!

CANAVA—Good God, man, don't call me Hollyhock! [*He laughs. She continues wryly, in a voice in which she might speak of murder.*] "Hollyhock Jones, the Texas Nightingale." I've not forgotten. Where's that glass of water? My tongue's out. I walked.

TILLERTON—You walked? After singing Brünnehilde? From the Metropolitan?

CANAVA—What's funny about that? . . . Yes, I walked; and I've just made up my mind to sing Tosca next year.

TILLERTON—But you've never sung Italian opera, have you?

CANAVA—What does that matter? Get me that glass of water and then we'll talk.

TILLERTON—Just a moment. [*He goes into the kitchen.*]

CANAVA—[*Calling loudly.*] Steve! Don't put any ice in it. Have you any matches?

TILLERTON—[*Calling.*] I'll find them. [*He returns with the water after she has rolled a cigarette, finds the matches, and offers her the water. She drinks while he is speaking.*] Do you smoke? I thought most singers didn't dare.

THE SECOND ACT

The basement kitchen in MADAME CANAVA'S *town house.*
A beautiful kitchen, shining and white—and present-
ing something of the same aspect of scientific efficiency
as an operating-room in a hospital. At the back there
is a door that opens from the hall. Steps can be seen
outside, leading to the back hall upstairs. There is a
door at one side into the servants' sitting-room, and at
the other there is a magnificent coal stove, with a glow
inside, side by side with an electric stove. There is a
long table—that has the look of Elizabeth's rural Eng-
land; and a few straight chairs set here and there.
There are a few red geraniums blooming on the sill
of each neat white-curtained window on either side of
the stove. There are white-globed incandescent lamps
in wall brackets and a cluster in the ceiling.
The room is in darkness except for the glow from the
stove and the moonlight through the windows. Steps
are heard on the uncarpeted steps outside, however,
and RAYMOND'S *voice.*

RAYMOND—Wait a minute; I'll turn on the light so that
you can see. Don't fall. . . . [*Almost instantly there is*
a blaze in the hall outside. RAYMOND *in the doorway calls*
back.] Coming, sir?

TILLERTON'S VOICE—I'm coming. [RAYMOND *switches on*
the kitchen lights, full tilt. TILLERTON *arrives immediately*
after him, a little bewildered, his hands full of typewritten,

234

badly damaged manuscripts. TILLERTON *wears street clothes,* RAYMOND *a dinner-jacket.*]

RAYMOND—[*Quick on the trigger.*] Put the poems there on that table. . . . I've got a great idea. . . . That's why I really got you down here . . . to explain . . . and to talk to you alone. [*He comes close to him.*] What do you think of Inez?

TILLERTON—She's only been in the room five minutes—and during most of that time I've been trying to think where I've seen her before.

RAYMOND—[*Impatiently.*] On the stage somewhere, probably. . . . She's been in half a dozen musical comedies, in roof shows, and in dreadful bedroom farces and things. There's no secret about that—but does it matter?

TILLERTON—[*Quietly.*] Probably not.

[*There is a pause.* RAYMOND *is sitting on the table. He stares at his father in great disappointment as* TILLERTON *does not say more but gives all his attention to the manuscripts in his hand—as if trying to arrange the pages properly.*]

RAYMOND—[*Presently, sulkily.*] I suppose you *would* be on mother's side.

TILLERTON—[*Looking up.*] Why? [RAYMOND *does not answer.* TILLERTON *indicates the poems, however, with a charming smile.*] These matter a great deal, however. . . . Thank you for showing them to me.

RAYMOND—[*Despondently.*] I wouldn't care if you put them in that stove and burned every one.

TILLERTON—That's not a bad idea. . . . They mean more to me, naturally, than to anyone else in the world—but an early book of poems has proved a very embarrassing skeleton in the closet of many a man of letters.

RAYMOND—Are they as bad as all that?

TILLERTON—You may think so some day. . . . [*He reads one, silently, tenderly.*]

RAYMOND—I was talking about Inez——

TILLERTON—I know. . . . But these are so much more important. . . . "Beauty is all that matters"—isn't that what you said to me the other night?

RAYMOND—*She is Beauty.*

TILLERTON—[*Paying attention to the papers.*] Think so? Tastes differ, of course. . . . Well, shall we burn these—or edit them very carefully for a book?

RAYMOND—[*Emotion catching hold of him now.*] A book! Father! [*He pauses sharply and then continues gravely.*] You know—I never thought I had it in me—really. . . . I mean, to be any good, really. I knew I was better than nearly everybody else—but that didn't mean much. They're most of them—eighteenth rate.

TILLERTON—I know. But if you're adrift on the eternal seas of Art, my boy, you'll only make port by watching your star and your compass. You can't steer by the course of other barks . . . And now don't you think we'd better go back upstairs?

RAYMOND—[*With sudden energy.*] Oh, no. You don't know my plan yet.

TILLERTON—What is it?

RAYMOND—A cooking party. . . . Did you know mother could cook?

TILLERTON—For three years she cooked for me about three times a day.

RAYMOND—[*A little amazed at the idea.*] Oh, was it ever really as bad as that? I mean, didn't you have any sort of servant—for three years? . . . She's said so—but it never seemed quite possible.

TILLERTON—For three years we didn't have any sort of servant. We might have had—only we'd borrowed money to live on so your mother could study, and it didn't seem quite honest to her to spend any of it on a cook—until the time came when her voice began to pay.

RAYMOND—[*Shuddering, his face in his hands.*] It's a strange thing she should have *me* for a son! It must be a tragedy to her. I really ought to shoot myself, you know——

TILLERTON—Do you think she'd like that?

RAYMOND—No; she'd hate my doing that more than she hates any of the other things about me. . . . She—she's really fond of me; besides, she needs me. She doesn't know she needs me—but she does. She'd let herself get very ridiculous if I didn't keep her on the right track. At that, sometimes she puts one over on me and gives silly interviews; and puts on too much make-up—off the stage, I mean; and gets her hair the wrong colour—when it's touched up; and buys the wrong kind of evening dresses. You know, I really dress her, father. . . . And I've kept her from marrying a number of times since she divorced Stowitstitsky. And I tried to keep her from singing Carmen. I was sure she couldn't do it, even the papers were making fun of her for trying. . . . But it was all right. . . . She was wonderful. . . . She put it over——

TILLERTON—[*Smiling quietly.*] I'd never worry about her if I were you. It's been her destiny to float upstream.

RAYMOND—So far . . . I'll admit. But she's awfully hard to manage. That's why I'm glad you're here. She —she respects you. . . . And we've got to keep her from marrying Sascha Bloch, you see. I couldn't bear that. . . .

TILLERTON—[*A little shaken.*] Your mother's affairs —aren't exactly my affairs any more. . . . We're off the track again—very far off the track again. . . . You were saying something about a cooking party. . . .

RAYMOND—[*Listlessly.*] Yes. . . . I was plotting to defraud her that way. [*He laughs curiously, bitterly, and continues.*] She loves to cook. It—it always gets her into a good humour. And I've got to get her into a good humour tonight so that I can get some money from her. A lot. I've brought Inez here to meet her—and that will make her hate me, to begin with, although I promised to be civil to Sascha if she'd let me bring Inez just once——

TILLERTON—[*Quietly.*] Is he coming tonight?

RAYMOND—Yes, she's bringing him home with her, after his concert.

TILLERTON—[*With a movement as if to go.*] You didn't tell me that.

RAYMOND—I know it. And it wasn't fair of me. I knew you'd not come if he did. But I can't be direct like mother. . . . I'm always a little tricky. . . . Please don't go—I've got to get five thousand dollars from her tonight—unless you'd lend it to me until she's in a better humour.

TILLERTON—You've never earned any money, have you?

RAYMOND—No—but I can't be tortured about that. One of my poems might be as beautiful as a cathedral—and I couldn't get more than fifty cents a line for it—! Fifty cents a line! Ten dollars for an immortal lyric, maybe! It's not fair to remind me I can't earn money!

TILLERTON—I understand all that. [*He pauses as if thinking how to say what he'd like to say.*]

RAYMOND—Then you don't want to lend it to me?

TILLERTON—Are you very much ashamed of me for not having it?

RAYMOND—Oh! [*He is terribly embarrassed.*]

TILLERTON—I suppose—if it's anything you can't talk about—I could raise that sum, somehow——

RAYMOND—[*In a low tone, but with sudden resolution.*] No. . . . I'll tell her. . . . She'll pay it—if I handle her right. Never mind. Don't worry. [*He changes the subject suddenly.*] I'll get some comfortable chairs from the servants' sitting-room—and call Inez and Mr. Prescott. [*He bounds to the doorway and calls upstairs.*] Inez! Inez!

INEZ—[*In a thin voice, calling from upstairs.*] Oo-hoo——

RAYMOND—Come on down— Bring Mr. Prescott— Follow the light.

INEZ'S VOICE—All rightie. [RAYMOND *comes back into the room, before going to the other door.*]

RAYMOND—I'll turn on the light in the other room and get the chairs— [*He starts out, and then turns back wistfully, speaking guardedly, as steps and the same light voice are heard from the hallway.*] Do try to understand Inez, father. . . . There's something more than just her wonderful beauty— Oh, I forgot—you don't see even her beauty —do you? But it's there. . . .

[*Without waiting for an answer he goes into the next room, stubborn pride in his manner and voice. His own thoughts transfix* TILLERTON *for the moment. A young woman,* INEZ DALTON, *enters, followed rather patiently by* WALTER PRESCOTT. *She is in a blue serge dress, and wears a hat and fur scarf. She carries long soiled white gloves and a beaded bag. Her age is anywhere between twenty-*

*five and thirty-five. She is rather effectively tricked out,
but only a shade more than the most commonplace pretti-
ness, of the slightly mature "chicken" type, distinguishes
her from thousands of other women of her type, just as
shallow, just as vain, just as cheap.*]

INEZ—[*As if continuing an argument, to both men.*] You
know, really, I ought to be dressed—[*She regards herself
with a downward look.*] Raymond didn't tell me we were
coming to his house after dinner. . . . I don't mind not
having on an evening dress—though I suppose Madame
Canava will have one on—but I'm sure I never looked
worse. . . . This dress is a thousand years old. I'd never
wear it because it's so unbecoming. What did Raymond
want us all to come to the kitchen for? Where is he?

PRESCOTT—But isn't it an enchanting kitchen? [*He
stares about. She looks at him as though he might be
making fun of her.*]

INEZ—Enchanting? [*Cautiously, glancing around.*] I
suppose everything's the best. . . . The stove certainly
looks expensive—only it seems silly to spend so much money
on a *stove,* doesn't it? [RAYMOND *enters, shoving a big
chintz-covered chair in front of him.*]

RAYMOND—Hello— [*He shoves the chair toward his
father.*] Take this, will you, and settle Inez in it? I'll
get some more— [*He disappears.*]

TILLERTON—[*Placing the chair.*] Suppose I put it
here——?

INEZ—But are we going to *stay* in the kitchen?

TILLERTON—It's Raymond's idea to have a cooking
party——

PRESCOTT—Supper here? That'll be ever so jolly.

INEZ—But who's going to cook? I don't know a thing about cooking.

TILLERTON—I'll let him spring his own surprises. [RAYMOND *enters with another chair.*]

RAYMOND—These things are heavier than they look——

INEZ—[*Facetiously.*] Never worked so hard in your life, did you, Raymond?

TILLERTON—[*Helping* RAYMOND.] I'll take this— [*He relieves* RAYMOND *of the chair.*]

RAYMOND—Thanks. [*He goes out.*]

INEZ—Well—since we're to have a party here— I don't know whether to take off my hat or not. I suppose my hair is dreadfully mussed. And there's not a mirror—is there?

TILLERTON—There's probably one in the next room.

INEZ—Where Raymond's moving all the furniture from?

TILLERTON—Yes——

[*Again* RAYMOND *enters.*]

RAYMOND—[*Coming toward the group with a light rocking-chair.*] This one isn't so heavy.

INEZ—Is there a mirror in there—so I can do my hair?

RAYMOND—Yes, of course—though it looks lovely— [*She has taken off her hat, and her hair is rather becomingly loose.*] Why you're always doing something to it is a mystery to me. [*He looks at her in frank, almost stupid adoration.*]

INEZ—[*Jumping up—with a rather foolish laugh.*] Silly! Everybody doesn't feel like you about—about such things, maybe. I'm sure I'm a sight. [*She turns to the others, self-consciously.*] Excuse me. I won't take very long. . . . Oh, where's my bag? I've got a comb in it— [*she makes a joke as she digs for her bag*]—as well as other little necessities—"what every woman knows!"

[*Pleased with her archness, she follows* RAYMOND *into the next room.* WALTER *and* TILLERTON, *sitting comfortably in the heavy chairs, glance at each other for a long instant. Then* TILLERTON *slowly, reluctantly, grimly smiles.*]

TILLERTON—And two weeks ago I didn't know anything about a father's feelings!

PRESCOTT—The blind young idiot——!

TILLERTON—No, I'd say—the four-eyed idiot!

PRESCOTT—Meaning that his imagination is the same as an extra pair of eyes, I suppose?

TILLERTON—Something like that.

PRESCOTT—Well, seeing what is not there and not seeing what is comes to the same thing as blindness.

TILLERTON—Not exactly always.

PRESCOTT—Well, about.

TILLERTON—Yes, about. [*A pause comes between them. Suddenly.*] I don't think Raymond's mother needs to worry. I don't believe Miss Inez Dalton has any such honourable intentions as matrimony.

PRESCOTT—But hasn't she promised to marry him?

TILLERTON—She's made him think something of the sort. . . . But she knows there's nothing in it for her. So she's going to break his heart instead. . . . I almost wish she weren't. Lots of men marry women with tissue-paper souls, and never find out the difference.

PRESCOTT—You mean to say that you'd approve of such a match?

TILLERTON—Of course I wouldn't approve—but since when has love been a thing for middle age to approve? In a case like this—when a boy has lost his heart to the wrong woman, apparently—we can only stand by and pray

that Fate is a better matchmaker than ourselves. . . . No,
she likes to have him about, because he tells her she is
beautiful—and believes it when he says it. . . . His mother
needn't worry. . . . There's much more occasion for *his*
worrying about her. *She takes* what *she* wants—and it
seems that she really wants her musical prodigy. . . . She's
talked to me about him—the Texas Nightingale hasn't a
glimmering of what it is to be self-conscious, you know. . . .
I can't tell you, Walter, how strangely interested I am in
her affairs—and Raymond's . . . and how amused . . .
and how agitated! The pair of them make me feel very old
indeed. . . . And very humiliated by the realization of
how long I've been standing stock-still, living my life without energy or imagination for many years. And I wonder
if peace is enough for any man . . . ?

[*But he speculates no further.* PRESCOTT *finds a cigarette, and lights it in silence. Then he remembers and
offers his case to* TILLERTON.]

PRESCOTT—I beg your pardon, old man. . . .

TILLERTON—Thanks, Walter. . . .

[*But there is a sense of sympathy given and taken in the
act, and their few words regarding it. There is another
bare pause.* RAYMOND *opens the door from the other room.*]

RAYMOND—[*In the doorway. Plaintively.*] I wish you'd
both come and help me persuade Inez that she doesn't
have to wear her hat. It hurts her head, but she says she
looks better with it on.

PRESCOTT—[*A little impatiently.*] Then how can anything we might say prevail against her own opinion?

RAYMOND—She says she'll let you decide.

TILLERTON—[*Rising.*] This is a matter of moment,
Walter. . . . We mustn't evade our responsibility. [*Rather*

absently he goes about switching off lights. WALTER *goes into the next room.*]

RAYMOND—[*Holding the door open for his father, who is about to follow* PRESCOTT.] Why are you turning out those lights?

TILLERTON—[*Realises suddenly that he has left only the center light burning.*] Oh! [*He laughs.*] Habit. . . . The habit of a man who has been at the mercy of an economical female like Kitty Mulberry for many years. . . . [*He regards his work half-whimsically.*] However, it will do no harm to leave them off—and by doing so we'll possibly save your mother—a fourth of a cent a minute. . . . Can you understand things like that? I never could. . . .

[*But* RAYMOND *hasn't waited to return to* INEZ—*and* TILLERTON *follows him as he realises that he has been addressing the air. For an instant the stage is empty; then* TILLERTON *returns, with* RAYMOND *at his side.*]

RAYMOND—That's what I told her——

TILLERTON—[*Seriously, as he goes and slumps into a big chair.*] You were perfectly right. It's all nonsense —her keeping on a hat, if it hurts her head!

RAYMOND—[*With deep appreciation, following him, and speaking in a low voice.*] The nicest thing Ducky ever did for me was to pick out for my father the most perfect gentleman it's ever been my good luck to meet.

TILLERTON—[*Somewhat awkwardly, embarrassed, too, but very pleased.*] Oh—you'd have felt the same—anybody would—about any other man who had happened to have the luck to have you for a son.

RAYMOND—[*Flatly.*] You're wrong. I'm very critical. As you'd have found out, all right, if you'd turned out not quite the right sort. The Texas undertaker. . . . Or poor

old Riboux, or crazy Stowitstitsky. . . . It was funny about
Riboux— He was a great man. Do you know why he
fizzled out?

TILLERTON—No. And I've wondered.

RAYMOND—[*Sagely.*] It was all Ducky and her con-
science. He'd always been very fond of women, you know.
A sort of Don Juan who liked to teach and liked to be
looked up to. A lot of women kept up his morale as a
great man. . . . Then he met Ducky. And he very soon
realised that she'd have no goings-on. So he gave up the
others. And then one day he realised that he bored her . . .
He was getting old—and domestic—and by that time she
didn't need him any longer. She'd learned everything he
had to teach her, and she was going on, and he'd stopped.
So he got out—he was very sensitive.

TILLERTON—And Stowitstitsky. . . . You called him
"crazy." I shouldn't be curious, I suppose . . . ?

RAYMOND—[*Enjoying gossiping with his father immensely.*] Oh, Stowitstitsky wasn't really crazy—he was
just morbid, and Ducky hasn't much patience with that
sort of thing. She thought *he* didn't take enough exercise.
He was young and very good-looking—and she likes that.
She's like a school-girl about good-looking men. It's a
weakness with her. That was why she married the undertaker, she told me once. She liked to look at him.

TILLERTON—I know. But it's a very honourable weakness—one that springs from a love of all beauty.

RAYMOND—However, I don't believe that was why she
married Stowitstitsky——

TILLERTON—[*Involuntarily.*] Then—? [*But he checks
himself and says no more.*]

RAYMOND—I think it was because—the very first time

she met him—he insulted her by asking her to pose for him as Diana—in the altogether, you know.

TILLERTON—[*Inscrutably.*]   Oh!

RAYMOND—It made her furious, but it pleased her. He told her it would be the most beautiful new thing in the world. . . . So she married him. He did do his Diana; then he stopped. He seemed content. He said he would never do anything to touch it again. Ducky tried to make him go on working. But he wouldn't. So of course she left him. You can see how she would. She had decided he was lazy—and anybody who is lazy gets on her nerves.

TILLERTON—[*Quietly.*]   You must have been a very precocious boy.

RAYMOND—[*Also quietly.*]   Oh, God, I was!

[*Each is quiet for an instant. Then the door is flung open, as* CANAVA's *voice shouts.*]

CANAVA—Don't move!

[*There in the brighter light of the hall, she stands in full view—her arm extended straight from the shoulder, her hand holding a gleaming pistol. She too gleams. Her evening coat is like snow and ice and silver wires. The gown beneath has the same scintillating whiteness, but there is a diamond wreath on her red, roughly curling hair. Both* RAYMOND *and* TILLERTON *have leapt to their feet.*]

RAYMOND—Ducky!

TILLERTON—Hollyhock!

CANAVA—[*Sternly.*]   Don't—call—me—Hollyhock!

TILLERTON—I mean—Ducky. . . .

[*She pays no attention to his meek apology, however, as she enters, closes the door behind her, and advances to the table, glaring at* RAYMOND.]

CANAVA—So it's you! I thought so. Who turned off

these lights? [*She has thrown her revolver on the table and is going about turning on the lights that* TILLERTON *has turned off.*]

TILLERTON—I did. [*But she interrupts him.*]

CANAVA—Nobody's going to get me to cook. I know his tricks, Stevie. He wants something. But we're going to have supper upstairs. Sascha's coming. Oh, God, Stevie! [*As she speaks she suddenly goes limp and drops into a chair, covering her face with her hands and shaking with sobs.*]

TILLERTON—[*Connecting her mood, somehow, with the revolver, which he picks up.*] Ducky! Did something frighten you? Whose is this?

CANAVA—[*Sobbing.*] Mine. . . . I always keep one handy— [*She looks up, confidentially explaining.*] I like to be armed when I hear things. I thought it might be burglars I heard down here when I let myself in a minute ago.

TILLERTON—Oh, that was what was worrying you.

CANAVA—[*Furiously, with a big sob.*] Good God, no!

TILLERTON—[*As she bends her head, weeping again.*] But, Ducky——?

RAYMOND—[*Feeling that his father is worrying unnecessarily.*] I don't think it's anything very much.

CANAVA—[*Lifting her head to glare at* RAYMOND.] What do you know about it! [*Then she confides in* TILLERTON.] It's Sascha—Stevie——

TILLERTON—[*A little amazed.*] Yes——?

CANAVA—[*Still confidentially.*] He—he played so beautifully!

TILLERTON—Oh!

RAYMOND—I thought that was it.

CANAVA—[*Weak one instant, and valiant the next.*] It broke my heart. I'm not over it yet—! God! It was wonderful! Is my nose red? [*She is powdering her nose.*]

TILLERTON—Not—not now.

CANAVA—I'm exhausted. I nearly died at that concert. I had to put black on my eyes five or six times. I'm not going to cook, I said. [*She rises.*]

RAYMOND—[*Limply.*] Oh, Ducky . . .

CANAVA—[*Listening, suspiciously.*] Who's in that room, there?

RAYMOND—You said I could bring Inez here to meet you——

CANAVA—[*Firmly.*] I said you could bring her to meet me *if* you'd be civil to Sascha.

RAYMOND—[*Impatiently.*] I'm going to be civil. I promised I would. But I wanted father to see her, too, and got him here——

CANAVA—[*To* TILLERTON.] He has some idiotic notion that one look at her drives away anyone's common sense— [*The door-bell rings. Her head goes up.*] Ah, that's Sascha. And the Count, too, I suppose. [*There is a kind of wrathful pleasantry in her observation. Then her eyes fall on* RAYMOND, *as she speaks to* TILLERTON.] Go up and see, Stevie.

RAYMOND—I'll go. Don't send father. He doesn't like Sascha.

CANAVA—[*To* TILLERTON.] Run upstairs, Stevie, and if there's not a maid about open the door, will you, and bring Sascha down here.

[TILLERTON *looks a little hesitant.*]

RAYMOND—I'll go—if you can't wait for a servant to open the door. Don't send father. *He doesn't like Sascha.*

CANAVA—He doesn't have to like him to open the door for him, does he? Besides I want to say something to you before you see Sascha— Run on, Stevie—and tell him to come down— [*A bell rings again.*] Sascha's like me—very impatient. [*Evidently from her tone she approves of impatience.*]

TILLERTON—[*Reciting her orders.*] Tell him to come down. . . . And the Count?

CANAVA—Let him wait. No one asked him to come, anyway.

RAYMOND—[*Uneasily, as the door closes upon his father.*] You'll remember your promise to be civil to Inez, won't you, Ducky?

CANAVA—[*Calmly.*] *I* promised to let you bring her here, and take a look at her, if you would be civil to Sascha; but I didn't promise to be civil to *her*——

RAYMOND—Oh!

CANAVA—[*Triumphantly.*] And if you want me to be you've got to promise something else.

RAYMOND—[*Baffled.*] Of course I didn't expect you to insult her, once you got her here——

CANAVA—*I* didn't get her here; you got her here. . . . Well?

RAYMOND—What do you want me to promise?

CANAVA—To go with me to Carnegie Hall Tuesday afternoon to hear Sascha play. Do you hear? And talk to him tonight. I want you two to like each other.

RAYMOND—I don't want to hear him play.

CANAVA—But you've got to hear him play!

RAYMOND—I can't. I've taken an oath not to go to any of his concerts. And I don't want to like him. He's made you ridiculous.

CANAVA—[*Furious.*]   Nobody in this world could make me ridiculous!

RAYMOND—[*Muttering.*]   Then you've made yourself ridiculous.

CANAVA—What did you say?

RAYMOND—Nothing.

CANAVA—I ask you again: will you talk to him tonight, and make him like you, or not?   [*He is silent.*]   You heard what I said a minute ago.

RAYMOND—[*Weakening.*]   I can't have her insulted. Yes—damn it—I'll talk.

CANAVA—You promise?

RAYMOND—Yes.   If you promise to be civil and make her love you tonight.

CANAVA—I'll be civil—but that's all. And I don't want her to love me.   And I'm not going to cook.   I know you. . . . Go and get her.

RAYMOND—[*Wistfully.*]   Do be as civil as you can— please, mother; she's awfully afraid of you.   Everybody always is, you know.

[CANAVA *makes some sound that might be taken for a grunt of derision.* TILLERTON *appears again in the doorway from the hall.*]

TILLERTON—He's coming——

[*A young man dashes past him, and almost hurls himself at the outstretched hands of* MADAME CANAVA, *which he seizes impetuously in both of his.*]

CANAVA—Sascha!

SASCHA—[*At the same instant, crying out.*]   Brasa! [*He is a very radiant, very young man; but in height and vitality the two seem, oddly enough, very well matched. He is dark and extraordinary-looking—unquestionably a per-*

sonality, although in MADAME CANAVA'S *presence he has only the vague value, at first, of an appurtenance. His accent indicates his foreign birth; but it is the accent of a cosmopolite who speaks half a dozen different languages comfortably and even thinks in any of them.* TILLERTON *finds himself, awkwardly enough, arrested and interested.*]

SASCHA—[*Impetuously to* CANAVA.] But why did you not wait?

CANAVA—[*With bluntness and yet—somehow—with coquetry.*] I never wait for anyone.

SASCHA—But I fought quickly to be free of my admirers —and you had gone. Did I not play well? Was that your reason?

CANAVA—If you want to know why I didn't wait—ask him— [*She indicates* TILLERTON, *and then remembers details.*] Oh, I don't think you know each other. . . . This is Sascha, Stevie. . . . He's Steven Tillerton—my son's father. Used to be my husband.

SASCHA—[*Bowing as if to an audience; delightfully impersonal.*] How do you do?

[TILLERTON *manages a very stiff bow.*]

CANAVA—[*Rushing ahead with her evidence.*] He saw me when I came in. He can tell you.

SASCHA—[*With a sudden thought.*] But perhaps you did not like my own concerto—that I played tonight for the first time? It is not easy to grasp.

CANAVA—[*Frigidly, then bluntly.*] Oh! Isn't it? I cried until I was sick over it!

SASCHA—[*In delight.*] Really? [*He kisses both her hands, with sudden radiance.*]

CANAVA—[*Still angry in spite of his penitence, almost exploding at him.*] It's the most beautiful thing I ever heard in my life! That's how difficult it was for me to grasp.

SASCHA—My darling!

CANAVA—I wasn't fit to be seen afterward. I almost stood up in the box and told you to stop because I couldn't bear any more. [*Almost weeping now.*] I—I had to be alone— Don't start me again——

SASCHA—I understand. It is like that for me always when you sing. My heart is left vulnerable and bleeding. I must hide away with it.

CANAVA—[*To* TILLERTON, *as she winds her arm about* SASCHA's *neck, deeply content with his words, and almost lapsing into baby talk.*] Ah—he's the most wonderful person in the world, Stevie. [*But she adds, as if explanation were unnecessary.*] But you've heard him play?

TILLERTON—Often.

CANAVA—[*Insistently, stroking* SASCHA's *cheek as if he were a kitten.*] And isn't he the mos' won'erful person in the world?

TILLERTON—In his own way—quite.

CANAVA—[*Leaning her face against* SASCHA's, *and announcing babyishly.*] Makes his Ducky cry. 'Cause his music is so boo'ful. Boo'ful things are always awful sad. . . . Sad. [*A flash of memory makes her suddenly alert as she turns to* TILLERTON *energetically.*] I remember I thought you were crazy the first time I ever heard you say that! I thought beautiful things were just pretty-pretty then. . . . I didn't know what on earth you were talking about. [*She turns back to* SASCHA, *intimately.*] I thought he was making fun of me when he showed me a Botticelli and told me it was beautiful. I stood there and nearly laughed myself to death. Those long-legged, sheep-faced women do look funny when you see them the first time. Then— [*She reverts to her mood of reverie and baby talk.*] They begin to get boo'ful. They get more boo'ful every time you see them. Now I think they're almost as boo'ful as my Sascha's music. Maybe not quite so sad. . . . [*But she argues this out with herself.*] They're saddest when they're dancing. Anything dancing is awful sad. [*She shakes her head as she meditates profoundly in baby talk.*] Everything dances gotta stop some day—Botticelli's stopped—but his sheep-faced women—they go on. My Sascha's gotta stop, but his boo'ful new concerto— that'll go on dancing—long, long time—long as there's anybody to play violin. . . . But I don't s'pose anybody'll ever play it like he played it tonight again. . . . ever. [*Again she pats his cheek, her spirit rising.*] He's my smarty. . . . Is he awful hungry?

SASCHA—[*Deep in her mood.*] Yes, Ducky; awful, awful hungry.

[*A little, odd-looking man has come bubbling into the room with the aid of a monocle.*]

THE LITTLE MAN—[*With an immediate stare at* TILLERTON, *offering his hand.*] Bon soir, monsieur. We have met before, I presume? I meet everyone; but faces I do not always place at the moment; pardon me.

TILLERTON—[*Obviously at sea.*] Ah, I see. But I don't believe we have met before.

THE LITTLE MAN—[*Indicates* SASCHA.] No? I am the papa.

CANAVA—Of course you haven't met. Count Alexander Houdonyi-Bloch, Mr. Steven Tillerton. The Count is Sascha's father, Stevie. Mr. Tillerton is my son Raymond's father, Count.

THE COUNT—[*Bent on being agreeable.*] Ah, then we
have much in common. Will you smoke a cigarette, monsieur? The tobacco is excellent. They are sent to my son
by the governor of one of the finest tobacco provinces in
Turkey. You will perceive the Houdonyi-Bloch insignia,
which is on each one, as a compliment. Turkey is a very
interesting country. The governing classes have a great
admiration for music. On Sascha's last visit to Constanti-
nople——

SASCHA—[*Frankly, a little contemptuously.*] My father
will talk too much, monsieur, if you will listen. Do not
let him bore you. [*The* COUNT *shrugs hopelessly.*]

THE COUNT—[*To* TILLERTON.] Ah—these sons. . . .
But you, too, know something of their manners—and when
they are artists— [TILLERTON *is lighting the cigarette
that the* COUNT *has pressed upon him.*]

CANAVA—[*Judiciously.*] Sascha's manners are much
better than Raymond's.

TILLERTON—[*To the* COUNT, *a little proudly.*] My son
—our son—happens to be a poet.

THE COUNT—[*Sympathetically but not really interested.*]
Ah, yes; that I have heard from Madame Canava. The
poetry does not pay, she tells me. It is unfortunate.

TILLERTON—[*Proudly still.*] One cannot deny the fact
that there's no more money in being a poet than there is
in dying for one's country.

THE COUNT—[*Still agreeably, and without bothering to
understand.*] Ah, yes; monsieur is romantic; his son no
doubt is like him.

CANAVA—[*Bluntly.*] Count, he means it's a fine thing
to be a poet, and he's glad Raymond is one, whether there's
any money in it or not; don't you, Stevie?

TILLERTON—[*A little wearily, but somehow amused.*] Exactly.

THE COUNT—With music I am glad of saying it is very different. Sascha has made himself very rich.

SASCHA—But everybody knows that, my father. Why do you brag?

TILLERTON—He is very fortunate, in that respect, at least.

THE COUNT—[*Complacently.*] It is true. And I have both his arms and each finger insured for sums aggregating half a million dollars, in American money, so that if an accident should happen— [*He shrugs.*] One never knows. . . . Also he is fortunate that he is to marry Madame Canava. In their first concert tour together there will be a fortune. They can get ten—twenty-five—fifty dollars a seat everywhere!

CANAVA—Rot!

SASCHA—My poor father is always greedy. [*The* COUNT *bubbles on, not noticing their interruption.*]

THE COUNT—And when he has her to take care of him I can retire to my large estates in Europe and live the life of a gentleman which suits me well. . . . She will keep him out of trouble for me. We fathers like to be left in peace after a while, eh? Is it not so, monsieur?

TILLERTON—[*Uneasily.*] Is—is this marriage to take place soon?

THE COUNT—That is for madame to say. . . . It will be pleasant if, when the opera closes, we sail all together, that the honeymoon may be in the castle of Sascha's great ancestors in Bulgaria.

CANAVA—[*As if realising it for the first time.*] I've

never been married to a Bulgarian—or even engaged to one.

THE COUNT—In our country the Houdonyi-Blochs are like kings.

CANAVA—[*Practically.*] That doesn't mean as much as it used to—though I will say that if I'd been married to the Czar he'd never have lost his throne. [*Suddenly she rises.*] Sascha, take your father upstairs to the dining-room and tell the maid to give him a bottle of brandy. Stevie, tell Raymond we'll have supper at once.

[TILLERTON *is glad to disappear into the next room.*]

THE COUNT—Alas! That we could stay.

CANAVA—Stay? Of course you can stay.

THE COUNT—No; it is not possible. It is for that reason that I came myself—to take Sascha away at once.

SASCHA—I am not going, my father.

CANAVA—Of course he's not going!

THE COUNT—[*Imperturbably.*] To the dentist at ten tomorrow morning he has an engagement. A tooth must be taken out or in his arm there may be difficulty. Five great doctors have decided it. I have consulted the best. Tomorrow at ten I must take him. It is important that I remember. I do not dare to address myself to your delicious brandy or the matter might go from my head.

CANAVA—[*Overflowing with tenderness.*] Oh—poor little smarty! He has to go and have tooth pulled!

SASCHA—But it is nonsense. I have no pain from it. It is these doctors. My father has me looked at by them often—even when I am so strong and well—and they must find something wrong for their money.

THE COUNT—Yes; with my race-horses and Sascha it is

the same. One must find out troubles before they come, or some day there will be sickness and great losses.

CANAVA—Your father's perfectly right. You'd better go and have your tooth pulled.

SASCHA—But I'm hungry——!

CANAVA—[*Sagely.*] Better not eat anything. Have some hot milk after you're in bed. Good night, Count.

SASCHA—What you tell me I do . . .

THE COUNT—Good night, madame. I will wait upstairs, Sascha. [*He goes.*]

SASCHA—[*With his arms about* CANAVA.] I do not like to leave you, Ducky.

CANAVA—[*Caressingly.*] But he's got to go home like a good little boy and be put to bed early—— Oh, God, Sascha—that was a magnificent thing you played tonight! I wonder if those people in that audience knew what *they* were hearing?

SASCHA—[*With sudden despondency and doubt.*] And what, I wonder, did they hear? I don't know.

CANAVA—[*With thrilling conviction.*] I know!

SASCHA—[*Clinging to her.*] Without you I am nothing. . . . I am sure of nothing. . . . I need you so much.

CANAVA—[*Caressing him with her usual patter of baby talk.*] My little smarty. . . . Nobody ever lived who played like my angel. . . . And that's not all— [*Serious and inspiring now, almost sombre.*] You're one of the great composers, Sascha . . . already.

SASCHA—[*Relaxing, and staring at her.*] If people had wings instead of arms yours would be the biggest and the whitest in all the world.

CANAVA—[*Literal and a little silly again.*] But my

smarty couldn't play his fiddle if people had wings instead
of arms.

SASCHA—[*Not paying any attention to her, busy with
his own thoughts.*] Maybe you *have* wings, as it is—big
white wings that carry you farther than anybody can follow—even I . . .

CANAVA—[*Shaking her head, then changing the subject.*]
No. . . . You must go, now. Your father's waiting. He's
a damned leech, Sascha.

SASCHA—I know. [*He speaks like an old man suddenly.*]
But most people who live on people like us are leeches.
And he's more useful than most. He really does all the
tiresome things for me—and I let him alone and obey him
most of the time because he's usually right—and it's easier
for us both that way. I try to save his self-respect for
him by letting him pretend I'm half a child and half a fool.
. . . Besides, he's really and truly fond of me. At least,
so I believe.

CANAVA—[*Drawing his face against her own and patting
it approvingly.*] Nobody fools my Sascha. . . . But I
wish he hadn't been so damned clever about making everybody think you're five years younger than you are! [*She
pushes him away and frowns.*]

SASCHA—Now—now—now. . . . Let's not start all that
argument over again, Ducky.

CANAVA—But it makes me seem an extra five years older
than you.

SASCHA—What's five years? . . . Or fifteen years? . . .
Or five hundred years? . . . As long as you live you'll love
my music—and as long as I live I'll love your wings.

CANAVA—[*Angrily.*] You don't say anything about *my*

music. A voice, to you, is just an accident. Nothing to be really respected——

SASCHA—[*Flatly.*] I won't quarrel with you. We've not got time. . . . Good night, Ducky. . . . When I leave you I always feel as if I'm going away limping. . . . It's such a wrench.

CANAVA—[*Still sulky and cross, but gradually melting.*] Good night. . . . Don't forget your hot milk. . . . I suppose we'll be happy together about three years. I've never been happy with any man longer than that—and if the truth were told I don't believe many women ever have—not what *I* call happy.

SASCHA—We'll be happy—we'll have a kind of happiness always.

CANAVA—[*Drily.*] No. I don't want to throw cold water, but if that's what you're looking for—and can't get on without—you might as well cut your throat right now. . . . It doesn't happen in this world, my boy.

SASCHA—I don't believe you. My love will last.

CANAVA—Oh, no. But I don't expect it to.

SASCHA—Don't you think anything ever lasts?

CANAVA—[*Quietly.*] Maybe what you feel for your work . . . or your child . . . and that's enough. Whoever is responsible for this world and the human beings in it probably didn't intend anything more. [*Her mood changes as* RAYMOND *comes to mind.*] You've got to learn to get on with Raymond. But—we'll talk about that some other time. [*She doesn't finish her sentence, but adds half-angrily.*] Good night. . . .

SASCHA—[*Reluctantly.*] There's always so much to say —isn't there? But . . . Good night. [*He lifts her hands, kisses each one, sighs, turns—and drags himself*

*away from her. She turns about so that her eyes follow
him. At the door he pauses, and announces very simply.*]
You're so beautiful. . . . You look like your voice, tonight.
[*Then he goes.*]

[CANAVA *is dreamy for an instant—standing staring at
the door through which he has gone. Then she goes suddenly and flings open the door into the next room.*]

CANAVA—What in the name of God are you all doing
in there? Where's that— [*But she checks herself, sub-
stituting, as* RAYMOND *appears in the doorway,* TILLERTON
following.] Well,—where is she?

RAYMOND—[*Wearily.*] Gone.

CANAVA—Gone! Gone where?

TILLERTON—She persuaded Mr. Prescott to take her
home—and they slipped out by the servants' entrance.

CANAVA—Why?

RAYMOND—She really is afraid of you, mother. [CANAVA
grunts. He continues.] And when she heard Sascha
Bloch was here, too—it was too much. She wanted to
wait, to meet you both when she was looking better.

CANAVA—Oh, she did, did she? Well—nobody wanted
to take a photograph of her.

RAYMOND—I don't know why she felt like that. She
looked perfectly beautiful tonight. . . . She always does.
She doesn't need clothes.

CANAVA—What did you think of her, Stevie?

TILLERTON—I didn't have much opportunity to judge.

RAYMOND—[*Miserably.*] I'm afraid he didn't understand her. . . . She's very self-conscious with strangers.

CANAVA—H'm. . . . [*She goes over and jerks on the keys
of the electric stove.*]

TILLERTON—Your friends haven't gone, too, have they?

CANAVA—[*Getting an apron out of a drawer.*]   Yes.
Sascha had to have a tooth pulled tomorrow.

TILLERTON—Even greatness doesn't escape the dentist's
chair, it seems.   [*He smiles.*]

CANAVA—What's funny about that?

TILLERTON—It only seems a bit ironical.

RAYMOND—What are you going to cook, Ducky?

CANAVA—I don't know yet. . . . I'll see.

RAYMOND—Did you ever taste mother's waffles, father?

CANAVA—*Did* he?   You remember my waffles, Stevie?

TILLERTON—No one who has ever tasted them once
could forget them.

CANAVA—I'll make a soufflé!   A soufflé is one of the
hardest things in the world to make.   I've never had a
cook yet whose soufflés could touch mine.   Raymond, go up
and tell Greta she can go to bed—if she's anywhere about
—and bring the sweet butter out of the ice-box in the
pantry, and find something for your father to drink.

RAYMOND—Right-o—   [*He goes.*]

CANAVA—[*Coming to the table.*]   Got a cigarette?   [*He
gives her one, and offers her a match.   She refuses, impatiently.*]   Can't you ever learn?   I always roll mine first.

TILLERTON—I *am* stupid.

CANAVA—[*Denying that.*]   No!   [*More casually.*]   I've
got to wait for that electric stove to get hot.   Takes time.
. . . Now you can give me a light.   [*He holds a match.
She puffs.   Then she speaks abruptly.*]   What do you
think of Sascha?

TILLERTON—He—he's a great musician.

CANAVA—[*Drily.*]   Everybody knows that.

TILLERTON—He—he seems—very nice——

CANAVA—[*Puffing at her cigarette, thoughtfully.*] You mean he seems very young.

TILLERTON—All the world knows that, too, doesn't it? He's young, of course.

CANAVA—He's not so young as they think. Does he seem very much younger than me?

TILLERTON—My dear—I *know* your age!

CANAVA—[*Accusingly.*] You think I oughtn't to marry him?

TILLERTON—I don't say that. . . . I'm afraid Raymond feels very strongly about it, however.

CANAVA—Raymond's got nothing to do with it. What is that tart like?

TILLERTON—Like millions of other women whose lovers and husbands think them beautiful.

CANAVA—I want to marry Sascha.

TILLERTON—If you do—I suppose that you will.

CANAVA—It's a mistake for a woman to think her life's over at forty.

TILLERTON—That's true enough.

CANAVA—[*With a sudden thought, frowning.*] Are you in love with anybody, Stevie?

TILLERTON—No.

CANAVA—[*Half-threateningly.*] You've never been married since you left me, have you?

TILLERTON—No.

CANAVA—[*Vainly.*] You never cared for anybody else, did you?

TILLERTON—No.

CANAVA—We didn't have a kitchen like this one, did we?

TILLERTON—No.

CANAVA—Remember when I made my début in Faust?

TILLERTON—I'll never forget it, Ducky.

CANAVA—And remember I said I was going to sing Wagner?

TILLERTON—Yes.

CANAVA—Well, I did—didn't I?

TILLERTON—Better than anyone in the world.

CANAVA—Remember that Russian Grand Duke who gave me the diamond necklace?

TILLERTON—We spoke of him the other day.

CANAVA—Something funny happened this week—about him. Remember I told you I dined with him and his wife, in London, now and then?

TILLERTON—Yes.

CANAVA—The first time I ever met her I noticed that she had a necklace exactly like mine. You know you said the way it was put together was different from anything you'd ever seen before.

TILLERTON—I remember something of the sort.

CANAVA—Well, the Grand Duchess said there were only two in the whole world like it, and both had once belonged to the Duke's family. . . . Naturally, I didn't tell her he'd given the other to me. . . . Two days ago I saw hers at a jeweler's, and bought it. . . . Now I've got both.

TILLERTON—[Quietly.] It might amuse the Duke to know that.

CANAVA—What would he find amusing about it?

TILLERTON—The irony of it. Now that Fortune has turned on him, he has had to sell the necklace that he gave his wife—when she was a bride, perhaps. . . . So her jewels find their way to join those with which he once tried to buy you. . . .

CANAVA—And which made you leave me. [A pause

falls. She tries to probe his silence.] What are you thinking about—smiling like that?

TILLERTON—[*With a start.*] Was I smiling? I was only thinking—a slang phrase came into my head, somehow—that the world is very much your oyster, Hollyhock.

CANAVA—Don't call me Hollyhock.

[*He takes her hand between his, and pats it lightly.*]

TILLERTON—And that's just as it ought to be, Ducky. You've the capacity for a very big oyster—and life has served it up to you in fine style.

CANAVA—[*Touched, and as always a little petulant when moved to tenderness.*] I want my Stevie to have a big oyster, too. . . . Anyway, he can have a boo'ful soufflé! [*She becomes suddenly energetic, and moves away, getting out plates, pans, and glasses from the shelves, and making her preparation with the quick, sure touch of one who knows what she is about. She indicates the plates.*] Put these on the table, and— [RAYMOND *enters, aimlessly, empty-handed, his eyes seeing nothing.*] Well—didn't you bring anything?

RAYMOND—[*Startled.*] Oh—no . . . I forgot.

CANAVA—What did you go for?

RAYMOND—To tell Greta she could go to bed—and I forgot the rest.

CANAVA—What's the matter with you?

[*He flings himself down at the table, his face in his hands.*]

RAYMOND—[*Desperately.*] Everything! [CANAVA *and* TILLERTON *stare at him for an instant. Then at each other. Again, with sombre passion.*] I've just been thinking. . . . Everything! [*There is a sob in his words.*]

TILLERTON—[*Touching his shoulder.*]   Tell me—if you can—my son.

RAYMOND—[*His eyes filling with tears.*]   Don't—father —don't—or I'll cry like a baby——

CANAVA—Yes—don't start him, Steve.

RAYMOND—Oh, God! [*It is too late. He is sobbing, indeed, his head in his arms—like a child.*]

CANAVA—[*Undisturbed, but impatient.*]   Maybe I ought to take *you* to the dentist. Something may be wrong with your teeth. . . . He's not healthy, Stevie. I told you that. He gets these spells now and then. Usually it's about money. But sometimes it's just pure hellishness. If he'd take more exercise—and get up at eight o'clock every morning, like I do—and not eat things that upset him— he's always had a weak stomach——

RAYMOND—[*Wildly.*]   If you go on talking like that, I'll shoot myself!

CANAVA—[*Muttering.*]   Oh—take poison for a change.

RAYMOND—[*Passionately.*]   I warn you!

TILLERTON—[*Intervening, gently.*]   What's the matter, my son?

RAYMOND—[*Brokenly, lifting his face.*]   I—I don't know. I'm so miserable—all the time. Everything hurts. There's nothing ever right. Even love. . . . Oh, father— [*He does not finish. Again his head goes down into the curve of his arms—but he's no longer shaken by sobs.*]

CANAVA—[*With a significant look at* TILLERTON.]   Go upstairs, Stevie, and bring down anything you can find in the pantry that you want to eat or drink.

TILLERTON—[*Reluctantly, with a sigh.*]   Very well. . . . But——

[*But at a sign from* CANAVA *he goes.* CANAVA *finds an-*

other cigarette in the box TILLERTON *has left on the table, and rolls and lights it. Then she goes over and slaps* RAYMOND *rather smartly on the back. He is unresponsive. She sits on the table and tries to draw his hands away from his face.*]

CANAVA—Look up here. [RAYMOND *is obdurate, and stares down, bracing his head with his hands.* CANAVA *manages, however, to get one hand under his chin. Her tone is absolutely matter-of-fact.*] I want to know what's the matter? Money?

RAYMOND—[*Mastering his voice.*] Money — Inez — Sascha Bloch—life—everything.

[*There is a pause.* CANAVA *considers.*]

CANAVA—[*In a very businesslike tone.*] How much do you need? [*He is silent. She gets a new idea.*] Has that tart been trying to get money from you?

RAYMOND—If ever you speak of her like that again I'll never speak to you again as long as I live. [*There is an obdurate silence on the part of both of them.*]

CANAVA—[*Suddenly taking her apron off and sweeping majestically to the stove, turning off the current.*] I won't cook!

RAYMOND—[*Presently, sulkily, but making a move toward peace.*] Please cook.

CANAVA—[*Firmly.*] No.

[*There the matter ends for a moment. Presently* RAYMOND *begins again, tearfully.*]

RAYMOND—I don't know what you see in him. . . . He's just a musical prodigy who can't talk about anything. . . . You can pay three dollars and get the best he can give you at any concert. You don't have to *marry* him—but—but— if you're so crazy about him you—in God's name, why

don't you go—just go somewhere with him—and not let
anybody know— Don't let me know. Just go—but be
decent about it—don't marry him—before all the world.

CANAVA—I don't like such talk. And you know it. If
you were a man you'd shoot anyone who talked to your
mother like that.

RAYMOND—[*Wearily.*] Let's not bother to pretend.
You know I haven't your primitive Texas sense of honour.

CANAVA—No— Nobody would ever accuse you of having anything very primitive about you. And they'd probably run you out of Texas if you ever went there.

RAYMOND—[*Passionately.*] Oh, yes! Make fun of me,
if you want to! You can. You're not little and weak and
thin-skinned. Nothing ever hurts you. You've never had
to go through hell! You just happened. You're just a
lucky shot. You're just one of life's mysteries. You—
[*He has grown rather interested in what he is saying, but
pauses sharply as if hardly daring to say what comes next.*]

CANAVA—[*Patiently, perfectly seriously—as she thinks
it over, rolling a cigarette.*] Go on. Most of what you've
said is perfectly true. And thank God it is. For, believe
me, my boy, you don't come as far as I've come from a
Texas prairie without having the wind at your back.

RAYMOND—[*A slow, reluctant smile on his lips.*]
You're wonderful, Ducky. . . . I'm sorry, though, you had
to have me for a son. . . .

CANAVA—[*Angrily.*] If I'm not sorry, why should
you be?

RAYMOND—I'm only sorry for you. You'd be so proud
of a son more like yourself.

CANAVA—[*Melting, and suddenly getting him into her*

arms.] I don't want any son but my funny little poet. . . . I like my Raymond. . . .

RAYMOND—[*Presently, his face against her shoulder.*] Ducky——

CANAVA—Yes, angel?

RAYMOND—[*Faintly.*] You asked me if I needed any money. . . .

CANAVA—[*A little cautiously.*] Well?

RAYMOND—I do.

CANAVA—How much?

RAYMOND—A lot.

CANAVA—How much?

RAYMOND—Five thousand dollars.

CANAVA—[*Almost hurling him out of her arms.*] Five thousand dollars! What for?

RAYMOND—It's to be a surprise—for you.

CANAVA—It would be all the surprise I want if you weren't always in debt.

RAYMOND—I—I'm going to be sued—unless you pay.

CANAVA—Very well—let them sue this time.

RAYMOND—Father would have given it to me if he'd had it. . . . He said he'd manage somehow to get it—if I had to have it.

CANAVA—I don't want you to ask your father for money. He hasn't anything—and never did have. . . . What do you want it for?

RAYMOND—[*He changes his mind, however, about telling, and makes a clean breast of it.*] I—I've had my portrait painted—for you.

CANAVA—Your portrait—? [*She takes it in at last.*] For me?

RAYMOND—For you, of course—*and Posterity.* . . .

[CANAVA *stares at him with a helpless smile.* RAYMOND *continues evenly.*] I've always thought there might be something in me—you know, that might make Posterity care to know what I looked like— And I don't take good photographs. . . .

CANAVA—But——

RAYMOND—The man who painted it wants five thousand for it. It's been finished four months—and he—he keeps calling up— [*He halts, adding lamely.*] He—he wants his money.

CANAVA—[*Drily.*] Naturally.

RAYMOND—[*Discouraged.*] He's rather beastly.

CANAVA—Perhaps he *needs* it.

RAYMOND—I never thought of that.

CANAVA—[*At last.*] I never knew anybody—not even your father—with less sense about money than you have.

RAYMOND—[*Passionately, on the defensive.*] And how much sense would you have about it if you were singing in a tone-deaf world?

CANAVA—The world doesn't appreciate poetry, I suppose —you mean? Well, perhaps that's why every poet that ever lived has had to be carried around on somebody's hip. . . . Is this damned portrait any good?

RAYMOND—Pierce says so.

CANAVA—Did Pierce do it?

RAYMOND—Yes.

CANAVA—He's a fakir. . . . Why in the name of God didn't you tell me if you wanted your portrait painted?

RAYMOND—I didn't want to bother you. . . . You were getting ready to sing Carmen . . . and I . . . I had been having premonitions of an accident of some sort. I thought I was going to die suddenly—and you'd be glad—after I was dead—that you had the portrait. If I should die— you would be glad—wouldn't you?

CANAVA—Oh! Angel! Don't talk like that. I can't bear it! [*Her arms are about him again.*] My poor little boy! Don't talk like that. . . . [*Suddenly practical.*] Have you been having pains anywhere?

RAYMOND—Not lately. . . .

CANAVA—Then it's all right . . . and if the portrait isn't as boo'ful as my baby we'll get one as is. . . . [*She pushes him away once more and goes to the door, calling.*] Stevie. . . . Come on down. . . .

RAYMOND—Ducky. . . . Please cook something.

CANAVA—[*As* TILLERTON *enters, empty-handed.*] Well —didn't you find anything, either?

TILLERTON—[*Startled as he realises it.*] Oh—I—I forgot—too——

CANAVA—What was the matter with *you*?

TILLERTON—I suppose I was—just thinking—like Raymond.

CANAVA—[*Practically.*] Put the plates on the table, you two. I'll get the eggs. [*She opens a door in the wall, showing a huge refrigerator, which she points out proudly.*] You see this, Stevie? It's a back door to the big refrigerator. The cook doesn't have to go into the hall.

TILLERTON—I see.

CANAVA—[*Upon closer examination of its contents.*] You know, I've got to get rid of this cook. She leaves everything to the kitchen-maid—this refrigerator hasn't been cleaned properly this week. . . . I've only kept her because good cooks usually complain about my singing. The last one told me she could stand everything but noise. [*She has found the eggs and slams the door shut. Then she turns to* RAYMOND.] Go up and get that butter out of the other ice-box, Raymond. . . . Give me that bowl, Stevie.

RAYMOND—[*Suddenly wistful.*] How happy we all are now! . . . I wish tonight could last. [*His eyes go from his father to his mother significantly.*]

CANAVA—[*Pausing, sharply, getting his idea and speaking with grave abruptness, a kitchen spoon lifted in her hand.*] Don't you suppose I wish that, too, my boy? [*Her manner changes quickly.*] Now go—and see if you can remember what you're going for, this time.

RAYMOND—Butter—and—something to drink. . . . All right. [*He goes.*]

CANAVA—[*As she busies herself with breaking eggs, then presently finds* TILLERTON'S *eyes on her.*] You can say what you like, but a kitchen is one of the damnedest most romantic spots in the whole world. . . . It could almost get me tonight—if I'd let it. . . . The kitchen and Raymond and remembering . . . and everything. . . . You know . . . ?

TILLERTON—[*Almost with a cry.*] Don't I know! [*Something dreamy and sad comes over* CANAVA, *and she goes to* TILLERTON *and lays her hands on both his shoulders, looking straight into his eyes, her lips quivering, shivering a little—and the half-silly, half-tender baby talk on her lips.*]

CANAVA—But it's cold, Stevie. . . . It's all cold. . . . It's awful, awful sad . . . sad. . . . But— [*Vehemently, with tragic triumphant common sense.*] But it's *life!*

[*They stare at each other, uivering smiles on their lips —as——*

THE CURTAIN FALLS

THE THIRD ACT

STEVEN TILLERTON's *apartment, a week later. The after-noon of an early spring day is on the wane. There is something very wrong about the room—the bookcases are empty!*

STEVEN TILLERTON, *without a coat, is very dustily engaged with a large box of old manuscripts. The box is on the floor. Two waste-paper baskets receive most of the papers he is throwing away. A few, however, go into the drawer of a desk which stands open. He works, assorting them, quickly, decisively.*

WALTER PRESCOTT, *smoking a cigarette, stands near the fire, watching. For a moment neither speaks.*

TILLERTON—[*Suddenly.*]   Don't wait for me any longer, Walter.

PRESCOTT—But you've almost cleaned that box out——

TILLERTON—But there's another like it—and I want to do a neat job.   I want to finish them both . . . so don't wait.

PRESCOTT—[*Not moving.*]   You'll come back from a walk all the fresher for these damned morbid goings-on.

TILLERTON—[*Gaily.*]   Ha!   If you think these are morbid goings-on, you're all wrong. . . .

PRESCOTT—If you don't call it morbid—throwing away all the manuscripts you've been working on for years, I do.   [*Another bundle of papers is tossed into the basket.*

272

PRESCOTT *glances at it with concern as he continues.*]
What was that, now—that you just threw away?

TILLERTON—[*Gravely, but smiling.*] That? . . . Another unfinished novel. [PRESCOTT *makes a move to take
it out of the basket.* TILLERTON *checks him by a quick, imperative gesture.*] No, please! Any rescue work is absolutely forbidden. [*He adds in a low voice.*] I know
what's what. I really do. . . . I'm not throwing away
any masterpieces, my friend. [*He finds a few more pages,
and a smile, rather wry, comes over his face.*] I used to
think there was something in this, though. . . .

PRESCOTT—What is it?

TILLERTON—Another unfinished novel. . . . [*He looks
up, smiling keenly.*] But it was begun before the other—
ten years before, in fact. . . . This, and Texas—and the
Texas Nightingale were all mixed up in that exciting Mex-
ico era. . . . I was still rather young then—for a young
man who was going to be thirty some day. . . . [*He flings
the pages away, and then laughs and adds as he sees* PRES-
COTT's *long face.*] · I told you I wasn't throwing away any
masterpieces. . . . All this old paper that's going up in
smoke in a few minutes is only—old paper. Anyway, of
what use to any man are the dead dreams of great things
that he's never done?

PRESCOTT—[*Turning away from the subject, moodily, as
he turns away from the fire and faces the empty bookcases.*] I wish to God you hadn't gone and sold your
books. This room looks like— [*He doesn't finish.*]

TILLERTON—[*Taking up his words and the empty box at
the same time, and moving toward the kitchen.*] Yes,
those empty cases aren't very pretty, are they? Well,

we'll tear them out some day—and paint the walls and hang up some pictures.

PRESCOTT—[*Suddenly.*] What has Madame Canava had to say about your selling your books?

TILLERTON—[*Stopping short.*] She hasn't been here since they were taken away the other day. But it won't be anything very serious. She doesn't believe in reading too much. She has an idea that an energetic person hasn't time for a few thousand books. [*He is smiling, as he continues gravely.*] And I think that she's quite right.

PRESCOTT—I hope to God she gets the truth of this transaction out of you, at any rate.

TILLERTON—She never will—and she's very clever at getting the truth out of people, too.

PRESCOTT—But what would *she* have done, under the circumstances?

TILLERTON—[*Pondering a moment.*] She wouldn't have paid that money back; and she wouldn't have let me pay it. She'd have spent ten times the sum to prove what the facts were; and incidentally she would damn me with her mightiest damns for having been worm-like and over-delicate. And she'd be right. . . . The Texas Nightingale has a stern, uncomfortable sense of justice—and I don't want to quarrel with her, because she's been very—[*he pauses, looking for the right word; then he finds it, flushing and halting a bit, as he speaks*]—very—*sympathetic*—since she discovered that I didn't know Raymond was on the way when I deserted. . . . Wait a minute, will you, while I get rid of this box? Kitty Mulberry can have it for kindling-wood now. [*He starts out, but decides to take the waste-paper baskets, too—glancing down at their contents, and managing to collect both with his free hand.*]

And she can start a good many fires in her old-fashioned kitchen stove with these, too.

PRESCOTT—[*Calling after him.*] I wish you'd come for that walk . . . and finish this job when you get back.

TILLERTON—[*From the next room.*] No. I'm going to the opera tonight. That means dinner early. . . . It's Brünnehilde, you know—and it's after four now. [*Then he continues, reverting to the subject of the loan, as if it had not been interrupted.*] Then, besides, it gives me a flattering sense of importance to feel for the first time that those few thousands which went into the making of that great voice were my personal contributions, after all.

PRESCOTT—[*Drily.*] I suppose *you* would get a certain satisfaction out of feeling that way. Well, I'm sorry you won't come for that walk, but—[TILLERTON *has brought another box from somewhere, and is already bending over it.* PRESCOTT *shrugs*]—if you must burn your bridges— I suppose you must.

TILLERTON—[*Quietly.*] But they weren't bridges, Walter. That's what I've tried to tell you. They never led to anything. . . . And never would have.

PRESCOTT—[*Soberly.*] That's something you can't be so sure about. I'm off. . . .

TILLERTON—Good-bye.

[PRESCOTT *goes.* TILLERTON *continues to sort out papers —reading a few lines now and then.* KITTY MULBERRY *comes in carrying a big scrap-book and a newspaper; she watches him silently for an instant.*]

KITTY—[*Suddenly.*] You oughtn't to be smoking, sir, while you're doing a job like that. It's dangerous, I'd say.

TILLERTON—Never mind, I'll be careful, Kitty.

KITTY—Yes, sir. But the lady who used to be your wife wouldn't have it, sir. [TILLERTON *smiles but does not answer, and she continues.*] What I come in to say, sir, was to ask if you've finished with the morning papers, sir?

TILLERTON—Oh, yes. You needn't keep them.

KITTY—Then you must have noticed this article, sir, about the lady who used to be your wife going to get married again . . . ?

TILLERTON—[*A little sternly.*] What about it?

KITTY—[*Awkwardly.*] Nothing, sir. Only I was glancing at the paper myself, sir, a little while ago, and my eye fell on the lady's photograph. Pardon me for thinking it might be of interest to you, sir.

TILLERTON—[*Gently.*] You were right, Kitty Mulberry. Madame Canava's affairs are of interest to all the world—and in all the world there's no one more concerned about what happens to her than I.

KITTY—[*Sympathetically.*] Yes, sir; so I thought. . . . Do you think she'll be happy this time, sir—with him so young, and her own son so set against it?

TILLERTON—You mustn't worry about that. Things have a way of happening right for her.

KITTY—[*Still depressed.*] Yes, sir. . . . Well, I'll get back and fly at my cake again. I've been having foolish ideas, I expect. . . . She always seemed so fond of you.

TILLERTON—[*Quickly.*] That's all right. She is, I think.

KITTY—And she's had a pleasant way—once you got used to it—of making herself very free around here, sir.

TILLERTON—That's all right, too. She—she's used to making herself very free—wherever she happens to be.

KITTY—Yes, sir. . . . I've cut out the article to put in

the scrap-book I keep about you, sir. [*He busies himself with his papers. She continues presently.*] There'll be a great many more later, maybe.

TILLERTON—Oh, yes.

KITTY—They'll fill up very nice, I must say. I haven't had much to put in about you, these last few years. Items have been getting very scarce. [*She doesn't see the look on his face as his head goes up, and her tone is a little more lively as she continues.*] But there will be your son's beautiful poems to add to it, now and then, as time goes on. I've already pasted in two.

TILLERTON—[*Looking far off with something like elation.*] Oh, yes—there'll be my son's beautiful poems to add to it as time goes on. . . .

KITTY—But, of course, literary mentions and poems, and such, don't show up like a wedding with a lady in it, and photographs, and such. [*Philosophy comes to her aid.*] And one can take it as a great honour to have had a lady like that in our scrap-book at all.

TILLERTON—[*Gaily, suddenly, his voice a little strangled.*] You're right, Kitty Mulberry; that's the way to take it! That it's been a great honour to have the lady in our scrap-book at all.

[*She looks at his face. And suddenly she has the sense to say nothing, but goes—leaving the conversation at an awkward stop. There is, almost immediately, a quick knocking at the door. TILLERTON opens it himself. RAYMOND, as glum as rainy darkness, enters with a barely audible word. He is to be followed, as TILLERTON sees with great surprise, by several other persons.*]

TILLERTON—[*At the door, in amazement.*] Oh—hello.

RAYMOND—Hello. [*He is instantly slumping into silence and a chair.*]

[INEZ *comes next. She is sulking and ill at ease, and almost as inexpressive as* RAYMOND.]

INEZ—Hello.

[*Now* SASCHA, *as if he were at a funeral, enters, hostility and embarrassment in his stiff demeanour.*]

SASCHA—[*Jerking into a bow, almost gulping down his own words, uttered like a formula.*] How—do—you—do?

[*He finds an isolated spot behind the piano, near the empty bookcases, where, however, half a dozen volumes lean together in a loneliness that emphasises their isolation. One by one, he takes them down and stares through them. . . . It gives him something to do. His pompous father enters next, strangely without his grand manner. His salutation is entirely in pantomime—a wave of the hand back toward one ear—that might on the proper occasion be a blithe and taking gesture. Now, however, it is a mere inadequacy. He takes a firm position well forward in the room, beside a table, on which he plays a tune with his gloved fingers. There is a pause.* TILLERTON *remains, his hand on the door, wondering what in the world has brought these four silent, annoyed people here.*]

TILLERTON—[*Trying to get his bearings, and looking from one to the other, finally addressing* RAYMOND's *averted head, in particular.*] This—this is an unexpected pleasure.

[*There is, for the instant, no answer. Then suddenly the* COUNT *wheels about, speaking with great excitement.*]

COUNT—May I suggest, monsieur, that you close that door instantly? [TILLERTON *closes the door.*]

TILLERTON—Certainly. I didn't realise. . . .

INEZ—[*From the window, briefly, crossly.*]   There's no one coming. [*No one answers her.*]

TILLERTON—[*Still perplexed.*]   Is someone coming——?

COUNT—[*With his hand to his brow, desperately.*]   Mon Dieu! Your American reporters—! One knows never when they may not come. They are scoundrels. Never are they gentlemen to artists.

SASCHA—[*Suddenly turning about, pointedly.*]   You do not think that, my father, when we arrive on the ship and you make them listen to your large talk for pleasant pieces in their papers about me. [*He turns his back, and takes down another book.*]

TILLERTON—[*A little sharply.*]   Raymond—! [RAYMOND *lifts his head. Continuing.*]   Suppose that you explain?

RAYMOND—[*Gloomily.*]   There's nothing to explain.

COUNT—[*Quickly, bombastically.*]   There is much!

INEZ—[*Icily, turning around.*]   I should say there is!
[*Then, as she turns back to stare out the window, she exclaims.*]   Here are two fellows coming now! [*There is an alert pause. Then she speaks again.*]   No—they've gone on by. [*Everyone breathes more easily.*]

TILLERTON—Something must have happened.

RAYMOND—[*Passionately.*]   Ducky never gives anything a *chance* to happen!

COUNT—[*Furiously to* TILLERTON.]   It was your son, monsieur, who did not give us a chance to arrange for our marriage license——

RAYMOND—*She* prevented Inez and me from getting ours —and I'll never forgive her if— [*He breaks off. The pause grows.*]

TILLERTON—[*Patiently, impatiently.*]   Then there was
some sort of scene at the marriage license bureau?

COUNT—[*With intense sarcasm.*]   Ah, that at least becomes clear to you, monsieur?   Your son and this charming young woman—   [*He pauses, looking at* INEZ.]

TILLERTON—[*Interrupting.*]   But I thought Madame
Canava was singing tonight?

RAYMOND—[*Turning back, scornfully.*]   Do you think
that would keep Ducky from mixing in when someone was
getting a marriage license for her!   [*After an instant's
pause he continues, vehemently.*]   She *always* goes along
on such occasions.   She's afraid it won't be legal enough
unless she attends to everything herself.   [*His voice is a
barely audible mutter of disgust as he continues.*]   And
she's got to have it good and legal—even if she always lies
about her age.

SASCHA—[*Slamming a book shut and turning about.*]
It was necessary, it seems, for you to lie about your age.

RAYMOND—[*Angrily.*]   At any rate, I wasn't lying about
being five years younger.

INEZ—[*Turning again from the window to take* RAY-
MOND'S *part.*]   I think it's so nice when people are the
same age.   That's why Raymond said he was twenty-two
—the same as I am.   [*She turns back, sure that this shaft
has hit* SASCHA.]

COUNT—[*To* INEZ, *gallantly.*]   Ah, but you are so
young, my child!   That makes the difference.   If Madame
Canava could be twenty-two I would permit Sascha to be
twenty-two also as a compliment to her.

RAYMOND—Oh, would you?   When he's only twenty-
five!

COUNT—[*Exasperated.*]   But a famous musical prodigy
cannot be thirty-five—the lowest age it seems plausible to

give for Madame—so about the matter we cannot quarrel.

TILLERTON—[*As everyone glowers at everyone else.*] But why—? [*However, he decides not to be rude enough to ask them why they have come, and changes his question.*] Where is Madame Canava now?

ALL FOUR—[*Answering at once.*] She— [*Each one pauses with hostile courtesy for the others.*]

RAYMOND—[*At last, as everyone else has dropped the matter.*] She's coming here—so we can have it out. She stayed behind to tell the reporters there wasn't any row at all. They knew something was up.

COUNT—[*Elaborately.*] It is at her suggestion that we intrude upon you, monsieur.

RAYMOND—[*Bitterly.*] "Suggestion"! Her orders, you mean.

TILLERTON—I see.

RAYMOND—She wanted you in it. Besides, she thought we might have the reporters on our trail if we went home.

INEZ—[*Sagely.*] Well, all we can do, now that we're here, is to wait. [*A pause follows.* INEZ *leaves her post beside the window and sits down.*]

COUNT—[*Suddenly getting out his cigarette-case, and going over to* INEZ.] Will you have a cigarette, mademoiselle?

INEZ—Thanks, no. I never indulge.

COUNT—[*Trying* TILLERTON.] A cigarette, monsieur?

TILLERTON—Thanks, no. But go ahead.

[*The* COUNT *goes ahead and smokes. A pause follows. Then* MADAME CANAVA *is pounding loudly at the door. Immediately there is excitement. Everyone stands.*]

SASCHA—There she is!

INEZ—[*At the same time.*] She's here.

RAYMOND—That's Ducky!

count—[*Also in the chorus, expectantly.*]   Ah!

[tillerton *is at the door which* madame canava *is attacking violently. She flings it wide the instant he has released the latch—almost knocking him over—and storms into the room, taking everyone there into her glance.*]

canava—[*To all of them.*]   Well?   You're here, are you?   [*Then she turns to* tillerton.]   Let's have some tea, Stevie.   I need it.   [*With great violence she adds.*] I'm *exhausted!*   [*Then she grips her throat hurriedly, feeling it and patting it with her hand, as she speaks in a worried whisper.*]   Don't let me talk.   I've got to save my voice.

tillerton—I know.   You're singing tonight.   Suppose you take off your coat and sit down.   [*He is assisting her to take off her coat, and places a chair for her.*]

canava—[*Muttering.*]   Glad to see somebody has some consideration.   [*She drops into the chair and then looks up at* tillerton, *and speaks confidentially, as if she were doing him a great favour.*]   I want to relax.

tillerton—[*Gently.*]   That's right.   I'll see about the tea.   [*He goes.*]

canava—[*Vehemently, to the others.*]   Don't talk to me, anybody, until I've had my tea.

[*Then, ignoring everyone, she deliberately closes her eyes and rests her head against the back of her chair. The others stand about rather foolishly, looking at one another and pretending a dignity that no one feels.* tillerton *returns with a cup of tea in his hand. At the same moment* raymond, *out of nervous restlessness, perhaps, begins to pick out the Toreador air from Carmen on the piano. The sound arouses* canava *instantly.*]

canava—[*Furiously, shouting.*]   Will you stop that

noise? Why in the name of heaven I can't get a moment's peace——!

TILLERTON—[*Warning her gently.*] Ducky — your voice!

[*She remembers, and again her hand goes to her throat as she glares across the room at* RAYMOND, *who is now sitting dejectedly on the piano-bench.*]

CANAVA—[*To* TILLERTON *in a mighty whisper.*] I know. But he's trying to annoy me.

RAYMOND—[*To the floor.*] Sorry. . . .

TILLERTON—[*To* CANAVA.] Here's your tea. Kitty Mulberry had it ready. [*To the others.*] She'll bring more in a moment, but— [*To* CANAVA.] I poured this cup for you without waiting for the tray to be ready.

CANAVA—[*Taking the cup and sipping the tea cautiously, then almost throwing it on the small table beside her.*] Thanks. . . . Hot! [*She begins to exercise her voice with extreme care—listening anxiously to the queer tones that come through her closed lips.*] M—mn—mn—mn—mum—m— [*Again she pats her throat, this time with relief and affection, as she comments.*] Not bad. . . . What do you think I caught Raymond doing this afternoon, Stevie?

RAYMOND—[*Sullenly.*] He knows.

CANAVA—And if I hadn't happened along, accidentally——

RAYMOND—You came to get a marriage license yourself.

CANAVA—[*Sarcastically.*] Oh, I did, did I?

RAYMOND—And I don't see how you can call a thing like that accidental.

CANAVA—Don't you? I do. I might have gone there any other day. But if I hadn't gone today—and if it hadn't

been Monday, and my lucky day—and the fourth besides
—four is my lucky number—you know that, Stevie—he'd
have had his license by this time—and a wife too, I suppose, for me to support. [*She cannot help glaring at*
INEZ.] And then there would have been a family, perhaps. [*She gets an inspired suspicion as she stares again
at* INEZ, *and then at* RAYMOND.] Good heavens—perhaps
there's going to be one anyway— [*She halts an instant,
in midair, as it were, to ponder on this.* INEZ *is first to take
in her meaning.*]

INEZ—[*Greatly agitated—scarcely able to believe what
she's thought she's heard.*] Oh, gracious! [*But* MADAME
CANAVA *has turned quickly, decisively, first to the* COUNT,
then to SASCHA.]

CANAVA—Count, suppose you two leave us alone a moment? [*Both* SASCHA *and his father stir, ready to obey.
She continues swiftly.*] You can go outside and walk up
and down, or go into the bedroom and sit on the bed—or
into the kitchen and have your tea there while you're waiting—I don't care which.

COUNT—[*Rather put out.*] I will wait outside. Come,
my son.

SASCHA—[*Listlessly.*] I will go to the kitchen, my
father.

CANAVA—[*Instantly.*] Show Sascha where the kitchen
is, Stevie. . . . [*With sarcasm.*] I suppose you know
where the sidewalk is, Count?

COUNT—[*Stiffly.*] Yes, madame. Au revoir, madame.
[*He manages to retreat from the room.*]

CANAVA—[*Calling to* TILLERTON, *who has gone with*
SASCHA *into the kitchen.*] Tell Kitty Mulberry to give
Sascha some cake—if she has any—with his tea. [*Then she*

continues in a loud, alarmed whisper to herself.] I've got to save my voice! [*But she turns instantly to* INEZ, *and asks bluntly, loudly.*] Well—is there? [*But* INEZ *is stupidly dumb.* CANAVA *drives ahead, however.*] Go ahead. You'd better be perfectly frank with me. I want to know the facts.

INEZ—[*Again in an appalled tone.*] Oh, gracious!

CANAVA—Because if there is—while I have no intention of becoming a grandmother at my age——

RAYMOND—[*Interrupting sternly.*] Mother — you're outrageous!

CANAVA—[*Coolly.*] Well—you've always had ideas that I considered outrageous; and if you've persuaded this young woman to practise what you've preached—to me—about free love, and that sort of thing—why shouldn't something of the sort happen? It would be perfectly natural, and it might explain why you were in such a hurry about a marriage license.

INEZ—[*Again, involuntarily.*] Oh, gracious!

[KITTY MULBERRY *chooses this moment in which to hesitate in the doorway with the tea-tray she has been getting ready.*]

KITTY—Did I understand rightly or not that you wanted tea served, madame?

CANAVA—[*Impatiently, since tea isn't the important issue just now.*] Yes, put it down. . . .

[KITTY *quickly deposits it on a small tea-table which she places at* MADAME'S *right hand.*]

KITTY—Is there anything more, madame?

CANAVA—[*Suddenly gentle with the old woman.*] Not now. [KITTY *goes, having received one of the smiles that has helped to make* CANAVA *famous. . . .* TILLERTON *re-*

turns. CANAVA *does not smile, however, as she turns suddenly and addresses* INEZ.] Sit over there. [INEZ *takes the chair indicated.* CANAVA *turns to* RAYMOND.] Sit down—why don't you?

RAYMOND—I don't want to sit down.

CANAVA—You want some tea, don't you?

RAYMOND—No, thanks.

CANAVA—Oh! Sulking again.

RAYMOND—I'm not sulking.

CANAVA—Of course you're sulking. [*She speaks to* TILLERTON, *confidentially.*] He always drinks tea, except when he sulks. If there's anything I can't bear it's a person who sulks. . . . [TILLERTON *is sitting at her left, just a little distance away;* INEZ *at her right—close to the tea-table, on the other side.* CANAVA *addresses her again, pouring a cup while she talks.* RAYMOND *lurks in the distance beside the piano, on which he drums with the tips of his fingers—taking care, however, to make no sound.* To INEZ.] You'll have tea, I suppose?—Miss—Miss Whatever your name is—Walton—isn't it?

RAYMOND—Her name is Dalton—not Walton.

INEZ—[*Afraid to refuse, and bent on being as amiable as possible.*] Yes, thank you, if there's plenty.

CANAVA—[*To* INEZ, *ignoring* RAYMOND.] Don't worry. There's plenty. Nobody's had any yet. . . . How do you like it—strong or weak?

INEZ—[*Politely.*] It doesn't matter. [*Involuntarily,* MADAME CANAVA's *soul snorts in derision of such indecision. At that faint but belittling sound* RAYMOND *rallies to the support of his beloved.*]

RAYMOND—She likes it weak.

CANAVA—[*Pouring hot water into the cup.*]   Hm. . . .
[*Again to* INEZ.]   Lemon or cream?

INEZ—Oh—either.

RAYMOND—[*Quickly.*]   She takes lemon.   [*This settles that.*]

CANAVA—Hm. . . . [*Firmly, holding a lump of sugar for* INEZ's *direction.*]   One or two?

INEZ—Whichever's most convenient.   [CANAVA *drops the sugar and the sugar-tongs and sets the cup down desperately, on* INEZ's *side of the table.*]

RAYMOND—She takes two.   She hates to be any trouble.

CANAVA—Let her take them herself.   Then she'll be sure she's no trouble.

INEZ—Oh—I don't think I want any tea at all—if it's just the same to you.   [*But* CANAVA *has already turned to* TILLERTON.]

CANAVA—You want tea, don't you, Stevie?

TILLERTON—Not now, thanks.   [*There is the slightest pause.   He speaks again, uneasily.*]   The Count is walking up and down, you know—waiting . . . ?

RAYMOND—[*Coming closer, with sudden energy, exploding.*]   I don't know why Inez and I are here, anyway!

CANAVA—Don't you?   I do.   You know you tried to sneak away and get married, I suppose.   And I want to know why you were in such a hurry.   That's what I'm trying to find out now.

INEZ—[*Uneasy at the speculation in* CANAVA's *eyes and tone.*]   I'm sure I don't know what sort of a person you think I am, but—there never was anything wrong between us, was there, Raymond?

RAYMOND—[*Loftily.*]   I won't even discuss such things.

CANAVA—[*Drivingly.*]   Then why were you going to marry him?

INEZ—[*Weakly.*]   I—I—just to oblige him.

[CANAVA *grunts. The conversation halts for an instant.* INEZ *blandly gets out a little mirror from her bag and critically inspects herself.*]

TILLERTON—[*Taking a hand and explaining graciously to* INEZ.]   You see, my—Madame Canava feels that it's not a very sensible thing for you two to do.   Our son isn't self-supporting, you know, and any money that he has he receives from her, so naturally she expects him to consider her wishes—naturally——

[*He stumbles a bit.*]

INEZ—[*Interrupting sharply.*]   He's got his allowance, hasn't he?

CANAVA—[*Unable to keep still.*]   And where do you suppose that comes from!   Heaven?

RAYMOND—[*To his mother.*]   I can't stand this!   If you've anything more to say, say it to me alone.   Inez isn't to blame.

CANAVA—[*Calmly.*]   Very well; she'd better go into the bedroom, then—or outside with the Count.

INEZ—[*Always willing to oblige.*]   I guess I'd better go home.   [*She gets out her powder-puff and refers to her mirror again by way of starting.*]

RAYMOND—No, not yet!   Come in here—   [*He indicates the bedroom.*   INEZ *hesitates.*]

INEZ—I'll go outside, if it's all the same to you.   I—I—I think I'd rather walk around with the Count—he seemed so nice and friendly.

RAYMOND—I'll take you down.

INEZ—All rightie.   [*To the others, as she turns back,*

rather prettily, from the door RAYMOND *is holding open.*]
Bye-bye. See you later. [*Their silence means nothing to her as she goes—and the door closes upon her and* RAYMOND.]

CANAVA—Oh, my God! [*She bursts into heroic laughter; then she continues, half in anger, half in hilarity.*] And I've been hearing how beautiful she was for six months—! I thought I was going to see the sort of face that all the poets in the world ever dreamed of. Maybe I have! Maybe that's the sort of face that got Dante's goat. Maybe Helen of Troy was a little washed-out blonde who didn't know whether she liked lemon or cream in her tea! You can't believe a damned thing a poet says!

TILLERTON—They have a very difficult time with facts— of course—poets,—and lovers. [*He is still smiling—a smile in which concern mingles with humour.*]

CANAVA—[*Suddenly serious.*] Don't smile! I won't have any such nonsense out of him—! I won't have it! You've got to get some sense into his head.

TILLERTON—[*Gravely.*] That may be very difficult, Ducky. And we can't watch him every moment.

CANAVA—[*Weakly—her hand at her throat, her voice sinking to an alarmed whisper.*] I can't sing tonight!

[RAYMOND *enters. He comes, and stands between them —for an instant stern and manly and strangely touching.*]

RAYMOND—Have you thought of anything to do about it?

TILLERTON—What I am going to do is to ask you to wait. You can do that, can't you?

RAYMOND—I could wait a thousand years—if I had to. Only—why?

CANAVA—[*Quietly, after a pause.*] I'll give up Sascha. You give her up.

RAYMOND—Oh, mother! [*Hope is in his voice for a minute. Then he shakes his head.*] No—I can't trade her off, like that . . .

CANAVA—[*Still quietly.*] You're making a great mistake, my boy. You can't marry that girl. Don't you realise that she's a fool?

RAYMOND—[*Also quietly.*] You frighten her. You do most people, you know. But she's not a fool. She's only shy—shy and beautiful—and mysterious. . . . [*He turns his back and goes over to the window. There is silence. CANAVA is grave and intense. She turns to look at him, and suddenly lifts the back of her hand to her wet eyes.*]

TILLERTON—[*Gently.*] Ducky—dear——

CANAVA—[*Helplessly, in a low voice.*] He means it, Stevie. There's no use talking to him. It's love—just— [*but she gets angry as she whispers*]—just plain simple bull-headed calf-love. And he's as stubborn as a mule about it. [*Defeat is in her face and voice as she lays one hand on* TILLERTON's *shoulder and the other over her heart.*] I don't like to feel like this, Stevie. I don't like not having my own way.

TILLERTON—[*Quietly.*] You will have your own way—about Sascha Bloch, at any rate.

CANAVA—[*Suddenly, as her eyes focus on the door through which* SASCHA *has gone.*] Go into the other room, both of you.

RAYMOND—[*From the window, turning about a little.*] What did you say, Ducky?

CANAVA—I said for both of you to go into the other room. I want to talk to Sascha. . . . [*He doesn't move. She continues angrily.*] There's a window in there you can look out of—if you can't keep your eyes off her.

RAYMOND—[*Turning half-apologetically, a little stupidly, as if drawing his thoughts away from* INEZ *with some difficulty.*] Oh . . . I see. You want to talk to him alone.

TILLERTON—[*Tactfully, to* RAYMOND.] And I'd really like to talk to you alone—my son. There are certain things I feel I ought to say to you——

CANAVA—[*Drily.*] Yes—maybe you have some influence over him, even if his mother hasn't.

RAYMOND—[*Desperately.*] Ducky—I can't stop loving Inez just because you want me to. You don't understand her. And anyway—how could you respect me if I did?

[*She grunts; then in a sudden panic, with her hand on her throat, she begins to try her voice to see if it is all there.*]

CANAVA—M—mn—mng—ghm—[*etc. As they stare at her, she explains.*] I thought I couldn't sing tonight—but—but it's all right.

RAYMOND—For God's sake, Ducky, don't look like that! —as if you thought I'd tried to kill your voice, even!

CANAVA—[*Bitterly.*] What do you care how I look?

RAYMOND—[*Half-angrily.*] You know I'd rather be dead than—than hurt you.

CANAVA—Then why do you do it?

RAYMOND—I've got to—if you're going to be hurt because I love Inez. I can't help loving her. No one can ever help loving anyone.

CANAVA—[*Drily.*] No; but that's no reason why you should lose your senses—and go on like this when you're too young to know what you want to do.

RAYMOND—That's not true. You know I'm not really young. Haven't I always been more like a father to you, Ducky, than a son?

CANAVA—Come here. [RAYMOND *comes slowly. Looking into his eyes, she hovers over him a minute and drapes her arms about his shoulders and begins to talk baby talk with quivering lips.*] Muvver's little boy! Does he feel awful, awful old?

RAYMOND—[*Huskily.*] Yes. Awful, awful old, Ducky . . . except, sometimes, with her—when I feel almost like a boy. . . . [*Then he tries to draw away, crying out sharply.*] Don't! Or I——

CANAVA—[*Sagely, gravely, to* TILLERTON *as she still holds* RAYMOND *close.*] He's right. That's the way with love, Stevie. It makes you feel as young as a jonquil one day and as old as the stars the next. Doesn't it?

[*But, instead of answering,* TILLERTON *goes quickly into the bedroom, leaving the door open. Now she is melting over* RAYMOND *again, caressing him by playing her hands about his head and face and planting a kiss now and then on his hair.*]

CANAVA—And muvver's won'erful lil' boy—he always feels awful old, anyway. That's 'cause he's so smart. He gets old sad thoughts in his head all the time; that's why he writes such boo'ful poems. And now my poor little smarty's heart aches 'cause he thinks he's in love—and that makes his mother's heart ache, too. Maybe she's jealous. . . . She didn't think he'd go round getting in love so soon.

RAYMOND—[*Pulling away, interrupting.*] Please . . . Don't! I can bear everything in the world—except your tenderness, Ducky. It's awful when I'm wrong—and you're nice to me—only I don't think I *am* wrong this time. She —she's so terribly *important!*

CANAVA—[*Suddenly, quietly.*] Marry the damned fool if you want to!

RAYMOND—Ducky . . . ?

CANAVA—Only for God's sake keep her away from me until she gets more sense. I might forget myself and choke her to death. You know how much I love fools! [*But RAYMOND seizes on the note of gentleness in her voice, and ignores the harshness of her words.*]

RAYMOND—You mean—you'll really let us get married!

CANAVA—Yes.

RAYMOND—Oh! [*She moves away from him and sits down heavily. He follows and stands beside her. There is a pause. Then he touches her hair, suddenly noticing it.*] They got it pretty red this time, didn't they? It's better one shade lighter.

CANAVA—[*Sombrely.*] It's going to get as grey as it wants to—one of these days.

RAYMOND—No. It's going to stay bright—up to the very last minute.

CANAVA—[*Sternly—with a sudden thought.*] Remember —when I die—I want you to see that there's black on my eyelashes! I don't want them to look red!

RAYMOND—I've promised that a hundred times. Let's —let's not be morbid, Ducky.

CANAVA—I'm never morbid. . . . I don't know how I can stand her around, but— [*Again she has her arms about him.*] When muvver's little boy gets over being in love —we can always get a divorce for him——

RAYMOND—[*Sternly.*] Ducky! Don't say such things——

CANAVA—[*Angrily.*] Am I trying to make you happy —or am I not?

RAYMOND—[*Nodding, miserably.*] Yes—only . . . [*He*

can't find the right words, for an instant. Then he continues hopefully.] You'll love Inez when you really get to know her. [CANAVA *grunts.*]

CANAVA—Hm. . . .

[RAYMOND *can't think of anything more to say at the instant, so he lifts her hand and kisses it.*]

RAYMOND—[*In a low voice.*] So . . . thanks a thousand times. . . . I'll tell father. . . . Then I'll go down and bring her up. [*He goes into the next room. But he turns suddenly, a frown banishing the light in his face, as he indicates by a nod of his head the room where* SASCHA *is waiting. A little uncertainly.*] Of course you've still got *him*. . . I'm glad I went to that concert. His music sort of explains. . . . And I suppose you've as much right to try to be happy, in your way, as anybody. . . . Of course dignity means such a lot to me.

CANAVA—[*With supreme sarcasm, annoyed at his attempt at generosity.*] Well, well! Do tell! [*Then, seriously, quickly, sternly, as he goes toward the bedroom.*] Shut that door, and don't come back until I call you. [*He looks as if he might answer, but she is already on her way to find her handkerchief which is in her muff, and to open the kitchen door—so he obeys, meekly enough. As the door closes behind* RAYMOND *she calls out to* SASCHA.] Sascha! come in here. Bring your tea if you haven't finished. [*He comes, bringing a cup of tea—and a large piece of cake, which he is eating. She frowns at him.*] How many cups does that make?

SASCHA—Four.

CANAVA—It's too much. How's the cake?

SASCHA—[*Gravely, his mouth full.*] Very excellent.

CANAVA—It ought to be good. I told her how to make it.

[*There is a bare pause.*]   We're going to say good-bye, right now, Sascha.

[SASCHA *looks up to find her eyes tender and intent upon him, although she has spoken almost flatly.*]

SASCHA—[*After a pause.*]   I knew all the time this was soon to come.   [*He speaks very gravely, and with perfect composure, although there is distress in his voice.*]

CANAVA—[*Also gravely, and with equal composure.*] Yes, I knew it all along, too.

SASCHA—All good things are like dreams.   And it was never quite real—that you should love me.

CANAVA—You're a very wonderful person, Sascha.   The most wonderful I've ever known—except Raymond.

SASCHA—[*Impersonally.*]   About poetry I know nothing and I care nothing; but always I think you value your son too much.   However, you are a mother.   So that is as it should be. . . .

CANAVA—Give me a bite of that cake. . . .   [*She helps herself from his piece—and eats thoughtfully, commenting.*]   Not bad. . . . Mine is better, though. . . . You've got all the good years ahead of you, darling.

SASCHA—No.   The best of all is ending now.   It was one year ago, tomorrow, I played for you alone—that night.

CANAVA—[*Unhappily.*]   Don't talk about that. . . . You'll marry someone else . . . before another year is out.

SASCHA—That is impossible.   I am very tired of my poor father's company.   But for a long time I will tolerate him because he will talk of you, and go into bad tempers because I was not clever enough to make this good match.   I shall listen, very much amused but with a great ache at my heart.

CANAVA—[*Unhappily.*]   That's all right to say, but some simpleton will get hold of you, sooner or later—like the one Raymond's picked out!

SASCHA—[*With a shrug.*] Will it matter? [*She grunts angrily, broodingly. There is a little pause. He catches at her hands—and presses them across his closed eyes, speaking more to himself than to her.*] It was too much! It was not good to need another so much! I have known that, and sometimes I have had the sense to be afraid of your hands over my eyes—shutting out everything. [*He kisses each of her hands, and again presses each one against his closed eyes, with a sigh.*] But love is such a wonderful darkness!

CANAVA—[*Unhappily.*] You've got to work . . .

SASCHA—[*Dropping her hands and straightening up.*] Oh, yes. I will work. Though I do not know, now, how —or why. . . . Good-bye. . . . You will hear from me, sometimes—in music that I might have had no need to make—if you had not taken your strong hands from over my eyes—and left me staring at an empty world. [*He turns about, finds his coat and hat, and goes to the door, rather awkwardly. But he turns back with a sudden thought, and a charming smile.*] You have found me much more philosophical, Ducky, than I shall find my poor greedy father when I tell him we have not got you, after all.

[*He goes quickly. There have been signs of tears in her eyes—and for an instant she blinks them away. Then* RAYMOND *opens the door from the bedroom.*]

RAYMOND—Ducky—may we come in now?

CANAVA—[*Violently, in a weepy voice.*] No. Wait a minute! [*She quickly applies her eyebrow stick, lip-rouge, and powder. Then she announces.*] All right.

[RAYMOND *enters.* TILLERTON *follows.*]

RAYMOND—I've told father. . . .

CANAVA—[*Without enthusiasm.*] Have you?

RAYMOND—And now I'm going to tell her. . . . I'll bring her up—so you'll get to know her better right away——

CANAVA—[*Putting out her hand wearily, as if to ward off his enthusiasm.*] Not—not now, my boy. Take her home. I'm singing tonight, you know——

RAYMOND—But couldn't you just say something to her —now—just a word to make her feel you're glad?

CANAVA—[*Angrily, loudly.*] No. I've got to save my voice. You know that.

RAYMOND—Yes, I know—but——

TILLERTON—[*To* RAYMOND, *tactfully.*] Tomorrow will do. There'll be plenty of time tomorrow.

CANAVA—Yes, the world isn't going to end tonight—although it might as well as not—for all I'd care.

RAYMOND—[*Protesting.*] Ducky——!

CANAVA—Go on down. Don't keep her waiting. I'll see her tomorrow—and the next day, and the next, and the next, I suppose! [*Suddenly she claps a hand on* TILLERTON's *shoulder, and another on* RAYMOND's, *and begins to laugh. Then, as both stare at her, she breaks into explanation hilariously.*] Everything in the world always has to happen on the days when I'm singing! Last Friday two of the dogs almost died; and the Tuesday before all the pipes burst and I had to move to a hotel! And the Saturday before that— [*She begins her exercises.*] Mm—mng—gmn—oh-ho—ho! Oh-ho! [*Her voice, husky at first, rises into the cry of the Valkyries, and for an instant floats magnificently through the room. Then she speaks again, judiciously.*] Sounds pretty good, eh?

TILLERTON—Oh, you'll be all right.

RAYMOND—[*Who has been thinking—àpropos of his own*

meditations.] We *are* a bit odd—I suppose—the three of us.

CANAVA—[*With instant solemnity.*] Yes; I wonder how in the name of God the three of us ever happened. . . .

RAYMOND—[*Uncomfortably as she stares with tender derision first at him, then at* TILLERTON.] Well, I'll go. . . . See you later. . . . And I'll give her your love. [*He turns and gets out quickly to avoid further sentimentalities.*]

CANAVA—[*As the door closes, shaking her head.*] Oh, God, Stevie! We're letting that fool of a boy make a terrible mistake. And I know it and you know it—just as well as we know we're standing here. But what can we do about it?

TILLERTON—I'm sorry. Terribly sorry. But there's nothing to do about it, I suppose, except to pray for a lovers' quarrel.

CANAVA—[*With bitter humour.*] Oh, no—that won't happen. He never quarrels with anybody except his mother! But never mind. Perhaps I can knock some sense into her head. She may have just enough intelligence to learn to answer the telephone—in time—and put the flowers into fresh water every morning—and take the dogs out.

TILLERTON—[*Trying to be gay.*] Yes, she may develop unsuspected virtues as the daughter-in-law of a prima donna. She may even learn to autograph the photographs.

CANAVA—[*With her usual sarcasm.*] She'd have to know how to write to do that. . . . No other woman in this world could go through what I've gone through today and sing Brünnehilde the same night. . . . Not one of them!

TILLERTON—That's true—probably.

CANAVA—[*Suddenly very energetic.*] I've got to go.

I've got to have my dinner right away, and save my voice. [*She falters.*]   At least, I ought to—but . . . What time is it?

TILLERTON—Just five.   [*A silence falls between them.*]

CANAVA—I ought to have dined two hours ago.   [*She moves about restlessly.*]   Give me a cigarette. . . .   [*He does so.*]

TILLERTON—[*Producing a match.*]   Now; have you rolled it?

CANAVA—Yes. . . . Thanks. . . . [*She accepts the light. Then she rests one hand on his shoulder, and her eyes seem to survey a whole lifetime in the look she gives him.*] Stevie . . . ?

TILLERTON—Yes, my dear . . . ?

CANAVA—[*Her eyes are bright and there is a look of pain shining from them as she hesitates and then takes him into her confidence with an outburst, half melancholy, half ludicrous in baby talk.*]   Ducky's got awful far-away, unhappy thoughts, Stevie.   She's been awful, awful successful; and she's gone all the way up a great big, long hill; but at the top of the great big, long hill she's looked round and found she's all alone—all alone.   Everybody's left her all alone.   And now that she's getting old she's 'fraid it's going to be awful lonely going back down that big, long hill she sees the road going down.

TILLERTON—Not for you!   Oh, not for you!

CANAVA—[*Energetically, her dreaming, sad, silly mood dying.*]   Why do you say that—that way?   What's to keep me from being lonely?   That's what I'd like to know.

TILLERTON—Your work—   [*She grunts in derision.*]

CANAVA—What else?

TILLERTON—There's the whole world at your feet——

CANAVA—If you think it's going to stay there—until I'm ninety—you're wrong.

TILLERTON—[*Hesitantly.*] And Sascha Bloch. . . . Only this afternoon you went to get your license to marry Sascha Bloch.

CANAVA—Who said I went to get a license to marry him?

TILLERTON—Didn't you? Didn't you go with him to the marriage license bureau?

CANAVA—[*Angrily.*] Yes, but do you know why I went there with him?

TILLERTON—I should think the answer is obvious.

CANAVA—I went to stop the Count from getting the license, or trying to. And I went the minute Sascha came and told me that that was what his father was up to this afternoon.

TILLERTON—Oh. . . . The Count must be a very enterprising man—not to consult the prospective bride.

CANAVA—Damned enterprising. I did promise Sascha I'd marry him—but that was two months ago—before I'd met you again. . . . [*He is speechless. She begins, a little shyly, about something else—trying to make her voice casual.*] They've named a new oil-town in Texas after me, Stevie. They want me to be there to raise a flag, at a big celebration—as soon as my season ends at the Metropolitan. It would be sort of fun—for you and me—to go back—to Texas together—wouldn't it? Then to Paris, together, again?

TILLERTON—I'm afraid you're talking gracious nonsense, my dear.

CANAVA—[*After a pause, abruptly.*] You mean you don't want to marry me again?

TILLERTON—Why should you marry me again?

CANAVA—If I want to marry you, why shouldn't I? [*There is a pause. Presently she turns, abruptly.*] What have you done with your books?

TILLERTON—I sold them.

CANAVA—[*Angrily.*] Sold your books! Why? Why couldn't you have kept them for Raymond?

TILLERTON—I wish I could have. . . . But I happened to need the money. I'm a very unsuccessful sort of person, you know.

CANAVA—[*Her arm about his shoulder again.*] No! He's the mos' won'erful thing in the world! But he needs his Ducky to take care of him—make him work!

TILLERTON—[*Helplessly.*] Oh—but the Texas Nightingale has become the Bird of Paradise of the whole world, and what is a humble citizen like me to do with a Bird of Paradise, anyway?

CANAVA—Don't wanta be Bird of Paradise. Wanta be wren—just my Stevie's little brown wren.

TILLERTON—You're sure . . . ?

CANAVA—[*Vehemently.*] Of course I am sure! [*Her hand goes around her throat and her voice is again a loud whisper.*] I've got to save my voice. Mustn't talk. . . . [*But she adds with her usual energy.*] Well? Are we going to get married again, or are we not?

TILLERTON—[*Gently, smiling.*] Not today, at any rate. . . . My pride lies a little too low for that. My pride is in the dust of the years; and the idea of becoming a bridegroom all of a sudden again is a little bit alarming. . . . You must forgive my humility.

CANAVA—You mean that? [*He nods "yes." Then her manner instantly changes. She is baffled and hurt, but sud-*

denly winged with dignity. The pause between them grows. She goes over and gropes for her cloak.]

TILLERTON—You're going now? [*She nods "yes." He helps her, a little awkwardly, with her cloak. Presently he speaks.*] We must keep on being the greatest friends. We've Raymond, you know.

[*She agrees with a nod. Then, all ready to go, she suddenly moves toward the fire. He follows her.*]

CANAVA—[*After an instant, rather formally.*] Good-bye, Stevie. . . . Let me hear from you—sometime, after I go away. . . . I'll be going somewhere soon, of course; only not—not to Paris.

TILLERTON—Thanks. I'll keep in close touch with you, always—now that I've found you again. [*She puts out her hand. He takes it and holds it.*]

CANAVA—[*Huskily.*] There's always been something in me that's belonged to you, Stevie. Those three years were the best of all.

TILLERTON—[*Also huskily.*] Thanks. . . . They were my best, too—the rich years of a lean life. My heart's gone on feeding from them ever since. . . .

CANAVA—Then it's a damned shame— [*She doesn't finish; but presently she begins again in a low, quiet voice.*] I said it was all cold, the other night. It seemed that way then. And I suppose it is—compared with what it was when we were young. But— [*She breaks off, and then resumes impersonally, shivering a little.*] Human beings are lonely and restless things, aren't they?

TILLERTON—[*In a low voice.*] Oh, yes.

CANAVA—[*Suddenly bitter and humorous again, picking up her gloves, decisively.*] And damned fools—all of them. Even me. However— [*She pauses, and laughs—bracing*

*herself, unconsciously, as if against the burden of many
lonely twilights; and her silence and the lift of her chin
say that she is ready for whatever they have to offer.*]

TILLERTON—[*Suddenly repeating.*]   Oh, yes—damned
fools—all of them. Even me. So I'll tell you a secret I've
not been able to keep from myself. You go your way, and
I'll go mine—a little while longer. Then one fine day I'll
come a-wooing . . . in a tall, shiny hat, with an elegant cane,
and a gardenia in my buttonhole . . . and if there's no
Sascha . . . and if——

CANAVA—[*Quickly, happily, angrily, half laughing, half
crying.*] I'd like to know how in hell I'm going to sing
tonight—! [*Her hands go to her throat, as if to allay some
tumult there; then suddenly a frail butterfly of tone strug-
gles from her lips—but there is no nonsense about* CANAVA
as she exclaims critically.] Ah—pretty good—in spite
of Raymond, and you—and all that I've been through!
Where's my bag? [*She has swathed herself in her fur coat,
and now she lifts the collar about the precious throat as she
snatches up her gloves and bag, in the manner of one who
is in a great and important hurry.*] I can't stand here talking all day. I've got to go and get a little rest and quiet
—if I'm to sing tonight. You'll be there, of course?

TILLERTON—Oh, yes, of course. [*She does take time,
however, to linger hectically a moment longer, gathering
him close to her with a wide sweep of her arm.*]

CANAVA—You'll come around for me afterward, of
course?

TILLERTON—Oh, yes, of course.

CANAVA—Sort of like it used to be in Paris—when I first
began—isn't it?

TILLERTON—Yes——

CANAVA—And Stevie——

TILLERTON—Yes—Ducky——

CANAVA—[*Very businesslike.*] Do you think Sieglinde is a better rôle than Brünnehilde?

TILLERTON—Not for you——

CANAVA—I could sing either!

TILLERTON—I know it.

CANAVA—I'll sing her some day—and show them. She's got all that first act, you know. Kiss me. . . . Kiss me! [*She races to the door—and, looking around at a very dazed, happy man, shouts out in a voice to wake many dead.*] See you later!

As she slams the door shut—

THE CURTAIN FALLS